Pure and Applied Sociological Theory

• • •

Problems and Issues

Calvin J. Larson

University of Massachusetts at Boston

Harcourt Brace Jovanovich College Publishers

Fort Worth Philadelphia San Diego New York Orlando Austin San Antonio
Toronto Montreal London Sydney Tokyo

For E.M., E.J., and A.A.

Editor in Chief	Ted Buchholz
Acquisitions Editor	Chris Klein
Project Editor	Laura Hanna
Production Manager	Monty Shaw
Book Designer	Diana Jean Parks

Address for Editorial Correspondence
Harcourt Brace Jovanovich College Publishers, 301 Commerce Street, Suite 3700, Fort Worth, TX 76102

Address for Orders
Harcourt Brace Jovanovich College Publishers, 6277 Sea Harbor Drive, Orlando, FL 32887
1-800-782-4479, or 1-800-433-0001 (in Florida)

Printed in the United States of America

Library of Congress Catalogue Number: 91-78389

ISBN: 0-03-055348-2

3 4 5 6 7 8 9 0 1 2 016 9 8 7 6 5 4 3 2 1

CONTENTS

• • •

CHAPTER 1

Pure and Applied Sociology: An Historical Overview . . . *1*

*Pre-World War I Views and Premises, Ward's Dynamic
Sociology, Fairchild's Interpretation; The Period After
World War I and Before The Great Depression; Between
the Depression and World War II; From World War II to
The Present, The World War II Period, The Period from
1945 to 1960, From the 1960s to the Present; Summary
and Conclusion.*

CHAPTER 2

Pure Sociological Theory *23*

*Theory or Fact: Which comes First?; The Elements of
Basic Sociological Theory; Frames of Reference and Conceptual Schemes, Structural Perspectives and Conceptual
Schemes, Symbolic Interactionist Perspectives and Conceptual Schemes; Recent Developments; Section Summary; From Hunches to Axioms, Axiomatic or Logical-
Deductive Theory; Summary and Conclusion.*

CHAPTER 3

Applied Sociological Theory *49*

*Applied versus Pure Sociology; Are Pure and Applied
Sociological Theory One and The Same?; Types of Applied
Sociological Theory, Social Engineering, Clinical Sociology; Applied Sociological Theory: Desired Qualities; Summary and Conclusion.*

Foreword

Nearly forty years ago, I was teaching "Principles of Sociology" to a class of undergraduates at a good little liberal arts college in Pennsylvania. We were nearly three-fourths of the way through the course of study and the brighter students were pressing me to explain why there seemed to be so very few principles to learn. The textbook and I leaned on one another in fashioning a reply that was as old as Lester Ward and the nineteenth century: sociology is a very young scientific discipline, I explained. Unlike physics and chemistry, it has not enjoyed centuries of academic exploration and refinement; it has yet to fully mature, I said.

It was late afternoon and verging on wintertime. The ablest, most curious and earnest student in the class, a physics major, rose from his desk and stalked toward the back of the room. He stood there in the waning light, frowning at my account. "You've had time enough to come to a principle or two," he said. "Time's up!" With that, he pulled the light switch and banged the door behind him, leaving us baffled and uneasy in the shadowy room.

Calvin Larson's text reminded me of that little epiphany on the one hand and illuminated my imagination on the question on the other. As he shows us, we've been searching for Auguste Comte's hypothetical laws of society for generations now, with very limited success. Generally, we've given up the aspiration, just as few if any among us have Comte's pioneering confidence that such laws, if discovered, will be inherent parts of nature. Our sociology, Larson demonstrates, continues to be short on theory summatively and even shorter on theory capable of guiding and shaping the occasions when we call on the practitioners in our field to utilize knowledge for betterment of the human condition. He also demonstrates that, historically, we have tried to stop copping the plea that we are low on laws because we have yet to reach scientific adulthood. He points a firm and convincing direction out to his readers, and it is not that of toddling along toward a distant landscape dotted with principles planted like so many burning bushes aflame with scientific knowledge.

Larson shows us the flaw in the Victorian agenda for sociology, a crack running across the rock of Comte's and Ward's grand agenda. They were innocent and marvelously arrogant in their shared conviction that patient observation, systematic study, and the rising power of scientific analysis would gradually equip sociologists with a general, theory-based knowledge capable of being applied ultimately to the elimination of ignorance, war, pestilence, and famine. It did not matter whether they anticipated that interventions would be successful or misguided; it mattered that sociology would culminate in a usable science, whether of evolutionary social engineering or of intellectual prediction. This grand yet gradualistic plan, Larson shows us, lacked a workable set of connections between the pure and increasingly academic domain and the applied realms of policy and practice.

Calvin Larson has done sociology and its students a valuable service. Without digressing into social, political, or economic trends and without exploring the corners of the sociology of knowledge, he has charted an elegantly concise and historically informed pathway through several of the original questions of the field. He shows us, for example, how to deal with Lynd's question: "Knowledge for What?" He takes us to the persistent if academically neglected underworlds of the applied and shows us how social theory in our century became detached from groundlines that once linked it to earthly social reality. And he demonstrates that some American sociologists ever since Lester Ward have labored to draw on social theory in the course of their contributions to social policy and practice, uncommon as this effort may have become over two generations.

I think this book can help students of sociology in at least three fundamental respects. First, it can teach them with clarity and examples the necessity for drawing consciously and explicitly on social theory in the process of applying social scientific knowledge to policy and practice. It shows how short the intellectual distance we can travel in utilizing our technologies of inquiry is if we presume to travel in ignorance of theory. Second, this book shows us the vital connections between ethics, social theory, and the conduct of sociology. These connections arise, Larson makes plain, out of far more than the fact that applied research and development impose burdens on respondents. And, third, this book challenges those of us who use sociology to intervene in society to discard the discouragement of neglect among the academics and to concentrate on ways of contributing in the course of our empirical and practical labors to the improvement of theory. Taken in combination, this forthright historical overview of the separate sides of sociology shows us by implication that we must learn to reunite the pure with the applied or we shall be exiled by absorption into more robust and systematic realms of meaning in the social sciences.

Robert A. Dentler
University of Massachusetts at Boston

Preface

Those instrumental in initiating sociology in Europe and the United States envisioned a discipline with an applied or practical mission. They prescribed the application of the scientific method to the study of society in order to amass the kind of knowledge they thought essential to the construction of progressive public policy and effectively guided social amelioration. To accomplish the goal, the discipline was divided into two branches. One (pure sociology) was assigned the task of examining social processes toward the end of isolating societal laws. The other (applied sociology) was to commence only when pure sociology had accomplished its goal. Its task was to develop strategies and programs to improve the human condition based on the evidence of scientifically determined social laws. At some distant point, then, pure and applied sociology would become simultaneous endeavors. Nothing was said about how the two were to relate when this point was reached. Regardless, and as one might expect, sociology has not developed in the precise manner suggested by its initiators. Pure, or basic sociology, and applied, or as some would have it, practical sociology have long existed side by side. Some practice both and others specialize in one or the other.

Two realities have deflected the course of sociology as envisioned by the founders. The most apparent is the difficulty of reconciling scientific social planning with the democratic process. It is not apparent that sociologists, or any other group of experts, no matter what the basis of their expertise, should have administrative control over social affairs related decision making. And, of course, social planning requires agreed upon goals, something that all citizens have the right to influence. The second is that application of the scientific method has not led to the identification of what most behavioral and social scientists are willing to accept as lawlike findings. In consequence, there is growing willingness to question the validity of the principle of the unity of science and to consider alternative aims.

It is increasingly being argued, for example, that behavioral and social phenomena require analysis from a theoretical slant, by methods that reflect their uniqueness rather than comparability to all other natural phenomena. Many of those who take this view advocate achieving "a level of understanding" of their subjects in place of seeking to identify laws or the precise combination of variables presumed to determine individual acts, the course of social processes, and social regularities of any sort.

The unsettled state of affairs is reflected in the fact that contemporary practitioners of basic and practical sociology lack an acknowledged division of labor and common goal. Those who pursue basic work seek general knowledge of society with no necessary practical aim in mind, and those engaged in applied work seek to advise and assist clients with practical needs of no necessary general knowledge import. The consequence is a discipline marked by considerable topical variety but little apparent coherence of purpose.

Some believe that clarity of purpose is to be achieved by developing and applying ever more rigorous research methods. Others believe the dominating influence of this position is at the heart of the problem. A major aim of this work is to put the present situation in historical perspective through the ideas of those who have influenced thinking about disciplinary means and ends, the interrelation of pure and applied sociology, and the relationship between theory and method. The working assumption is that theoretical integration of pure and applied sociology is prerequisite to a more vital, unified, and practically effective discipline.

This point of view must be regarded as somewhat controversial because there is much to indicate the existence of a general atheoretical if not anti-theoretical mood in contemporary sociology. Theory construction and testing have been restricted primarily because of the implicit assumption that until the measurement problem is resolved (the ability to accurately measure and quantify social facts), theoretical interpretation is likely to be more misleading and fictional than precise and factual. Those who advocate theoretical reinvigoration have largely confined their work to matters of pure or basic sociology. While applied sociologists have shown some interest in making their work more theoretical, their intent has been to make better use of theory to enhance the quality of their work rather than to forge a link with pure sociology toward the end of general knowledge growth. Theoretical integration of the work of pure and applied sociologists is possible but not without clarification of the problems and issues involved and the advantages to be obtained.

On a personal note, I must acknowledge indebtedness to Professor Robert A. Dentler for assistance and guidance throughout the writing of this book. I must also thank Harcourt Brace Jovanovich's Chris Klein for his patience and encouragement, Linda Wiley for the competent manner in which she administered manuscript reviews, and Laura Hanna for being so thoughtful in overseeing the work's production. Lastly, homage must be paid to several anonymous reviewers for their comments and criticism.

Boston, Massachusetts

Introduction

A major recent trend in sociology is the widespread proliferation of courses and programs (at both the undergraduate and graduate levels) in applied sociology. While the 1960s concern with making academic sociology more practically relevant has something to do with this fact, the greatest impetus behind the trend has been the need to devise a means of countering the loss of majors during a period of rising conservatism and a switch in student interest from the liberal arts to occupational preparation in areas such as business and law. Along with growing competition for well paying and satisfying jobs, declining employment opportunities for sociologists in the academic job market (Freeman and Rossi, 1984; Lyson and Squires, 1984) has spurred academic departments to complement basic and traditional education with practical training—including the provision of diverse internship opportunities and job placement.

Student interest in a more applied curriculum has been matched by growing involvement of social scientists in applied employment. The past Executive Officer of the American Sociological Association, William V. D'Antonio, reported (1) a doubling in Association membership of sociologists employed in business and industry between 1976 and 1983, and (2) a tripling in the number of applied area positions advertised in the Association's Employment Bulletin between 1982 and 1988. Despite the extensive and undoubtedly expanding involvement of sociologists in applied endeavors, surprisingly little attention has been given to the problem of integrating pure and applied sociology.

Although early American sociologists proposed a working division of labor between the discipline's pure and applied branches, they, nonetheless, conceived of them as interrelated activities. The goal of pure sociology (Ward, 1883; Small, 1897) was to uncover the laws of social order and change preliminary to the construction of policies and plans to ameliorate the human condition. But the goal has not been realized. As Alvin Gouldner noted, "There are in present day sociology few validated laws or broad generalizations; nonetheless . . . there is a great acceleration of applied social science" (1965: 6-7). The separate rather than interrelated development of pure and applied sociology has led to expressions indicative of a gap, if not a schism between their respective devotees.

In his 1984 presidential address to the Southern Sociological Society, Joseph Fichter warned of a developing schism that could lead to the separation of applied sociologists from the parent discipline just as years previously another schism led to the departure of social workers. He supported his claim by reference to the following words contained in a letter written to the Southern Sociological Society's membership Chairperson:

> What does the SSS have to offer the sociologist who works in a for-profit setting?
> Very little. My position is that if we are going to solicit for-profit sociologists we
> ought to be offering them more than the opportunity for maintaining profes-
> sional and social contacts. (1984: 582-583)

"Perhaps," observed Fichter, "we all have to convince ourselves that we are sociologists first and educators second. . . . If we are serious about our profession, and if we really want to contribute to a better society, we have no choice except to promote the perspective of noncampus applied sociology" (1984: 582–583).

Although many sociologists would not agree with Fichter's position, it is, nevertheless, one with deep roots in American sociology. For example, to Lester Ward (1841–1913, generally regarded as the initiator of American sociology and the first president of what is now called the American Sociological Association) "the true test of a science is the application of its principles to some useful purpose" (1898: 263).

Unfortunately, Ward and his contemporaries did not go much beyond providing a general outline of a one-sided view of the relationship between pure and applied sociology. Because they did not not seriously entertain the likelihood that the two could be simultaneous endeavors, they did not consider the possible bearing of applied theory and experience on the development of pure sociology. Neither did they much appreciate the complex ethical and moral questions involved in the application of acquired social knowledge. The details of their theoretical visions were left to what was conceived of as an overriding and inherently progressive cosmic evolutionary pattern.

While much of their thinking has not withstood the passage of time, the views of the first American sociologists on the nature of pure and applied sociology have not been radically revised. Doubtless most early and contemporary sociologists would find little to quibble with in the Oxford English Dictionary definition of pure science as concerned with "the simply theoretical part of a subject, apart from its practical application," and applied science as something "practical, as distinguished from abstract or theoretical." Contemporary sociologists may differ from their predecessors in regarding pure and applied work as simultaneous and mutually influencing but they continue to regard the one as essentially theoretical and the other as essentially atheoretical. Writing in 1983, for example, Robert Merton, one noted for concern with interrelating theory and research and pure and applied research, cites with approval the following observation by philosopher Alfred North Whitehead:

> Science is a river with two sources, the practical source and the theoretical source. The practical source is the desire to direct our actions to achieve predetermined ends. . . . The theoretical source is the desire to understand. (1983: 45–46)

Also in 1983, in a paper devoted to assessing "the role of theory in applied sociology," Jean Giles-Sims and Barry Tuchfeld write that "when a specific piece of research is designed by a sociologist to test a theoretical idea, it is referred to as basic research," and "when empirical research is conducted to test the outcomes of specific programs of a client, it is called applied research" (1983: 37).

A working assumption of the present work is that it is time to question certain presumed differences between pure and applied sociology. The aim is not primarily to dramatize the practical element in pure sociology but to challenge continued acceptance of an essentially atheoretical applied sociology. Whether the goal is general knowledge growth or the development of effective social policy to treat major social problems, theory building, it is contended, is the common link and basic prerequisite. Subjects of central concern include the nature and variety of pure and applied social theory, and related topics such as the influence on theory selection and application of ethical and moral considerations and restrictions in basic and applied research, and the role of theory in the social policy recommendations of applied social scientists.

The book is intended primarily for advanced undergraduates and beginning graduate students, especially those opting for applied concentrations. Theory has an important role to play in applied endeavors, and this work is an effort to identify and interrelate relevant topics and concerns in support of this little examined thesis.

Chapter 1 focuses on the basic context of the entire work, that is, the nature of and difference between pure and applied sociology. The positions and premises of sociologists past and present are detailed and critically examined. Of particular interest is the extent to which the presumed aims and purposes of the discipline's two branches have been both differentiated and interrelated. The purpose is to present a historical overview of the nature and status of pure and applied sociology in American sociology.

The chief concern of Chapter 2 is pure sociological theory—its essential elements and purposes. The discussion focuses on basic and classical viewpoints rather than the range of major contemporary perspectives, primarily because it cannot be assumed that most of those likely to read this book will have a great deal of prior knowledge of sociological theory. Thus, the initial subject is a debate that has long concerned social scientists: the proper relationship between induction and deduction, theory and fact. Discussed are the positions of those who would emphasize theory-guided research and those who would emphasize the reverse. The bulk of the chapter is devoted to examination of the basic elements of theory building—frames of reference, conceptual schemes, hunches, hypotheses. Central to the discussion are some of the more basic structural and symbolic interactionist perspectives. Recent developments such as semiotics and Anthony Gidden's structuration theory are touched upon to demonstrate contemporary interest in developing a theoretical orientation combining the insights of both objective (or structural) and subjective (or individual) perspectives. The last section examines axiomatic theory, its structure, uses, and current status in sociology.

Chapter 3 examines the underdeveloped subject of applied sociological theory. Undoubtedly, many would question the relevance of the subject, because there is a tendency to regard applied work as essentially atheoretical. And even among those who believe that theory is an integral part of applied sociology there is disagreement over its nature, uses, and aims. Because this situation is largely a consequence of unresolved differences of opinion on the nature and purposes of the discipline's two branches, initial pages examine various views of the difference between pure and applied sociology and the bearing of theory in applied work. Central portions discuss the role of theory in different types of applied sociology—social engineering and clinical sociology, for example. Latter sections examine opinions concerning desired qualities in applied sociological theory and questions involving the interrelationship of pure and applied sociological theory and disciplinary goals, such as knowledge accumulation.

Philosophical problems and issues involving the goals and means of the human sciences are the subject of the fourth chapter. The two science debate, natural versus social science, that arose among German scholars is the initial topic of concern. Highlighted are the views of Wilhelm Dilthey and Max Weber. This is followed by an examination of positivism, its unified view of science and basic principles. Detailed next is the anti-positivism movement, particularly the growing sense that "the covering law" model is inappropriate for social science. Latter sections explore alternatives to positivism, the hermeneutic perspective most of all. Highlighted are the views of Roy D'Andrade, Roy Bhaskar, Hans G. Gadamer, Ernest Gellner, Jürgen Habermas, and Richard Shweder.

Chapter 5 examines ethical and moral dilemmas involved in applied research and their effect on the structure and content of applied sociological theory. The first topic dealt with is issues surrounding the problem of scientific objectivity and value-neutrality—the aims and rules of science on the one hand and the commitments and biases of individual investigators on the other. Integral to the discussion are problems and issues involving matters such as informed consent, subject privacy, deceptive practices, and research fraud. Concluding sections discuss the influence of moral and ethical factors on the character of applied sociological theory. Marxian theory is a case in point.

Chapter 6 explores the bearing of sociological theory (pure and applied) on social policy. Primary consideration is given to the experiences of sociologists in national social policy relevant endeavors. Of initial interest is the so-called Coleman report, *Equality of Educational Opportunity* (1966). The report was based on a study commissioned by the federal government to determine the quality of educational resources available to students of different ethnic and racial origins. The study's results are summarized and the views of its defenders and critics examined. Of key concern are its theoretical underpinnings and the connections between its theoretical orientation and its social policy implications.

The second topic discussed is the reactions of sociologists to participation in Presidential Commissions. A common theme is primary reliance on their discipline's methodological rather than theoretical sophistication. A second is the tendency to base policy recommendations on implicit ideological predilection rather than explicit theoretical orientation.

The last part of Chapter 6 focuses on the War on Poverty program of the Johnson administration. Of primary interest is the structural sociological theory upon which the program was based and the critical response it provoked from important conservative social policy writers such as George Gilder and Charles Murray.

The last chapter summarizes and elaborates upon such important topics as the major philosophies of science and their bearing on pure and applied sociological theory, the role of ethical and moral considerations in social research and theory formation, and the importance of interrelated pure and applied sociology. Of particular interest is the growing sense of aimlessness in social science resulting from increasing doubt of achieving the goal of identifying societal laws. Concluding paragraphs discuss this problem in relation to the primacy given to methodology and the depressed status of theory in sociology. The proposed route to a solution is renewed interest in theory building and integration of problems studied, theory, and methods.

REFERENCES

Fichter, J.H. 1984. "Sociology for Our Times." *Social Forces* 62: 573–584.

Freeman, H.E., and P.H. Rossi. 1984. "Furthering the Applied Side of Sociology." *American Sociological Review* 49: 571–580.

Giles-Sims, J., and B.S. Tuchfeld. 1983. "Role of Theory in Applied Sociology." In H.E. Freeman, R.R. Dynes, P.H. Rossi, and W.F. Whyte, eds., *Applied Sociology*. San Francisco: Jossey-Bass Publishers, 32–50.

Gouldner, A.W. 1965. "Explorations in Applied Social Science." In A.W. Gouldner and S.M. Miller, eds., *Applied Sociology: Opportunities & Problems*. New York: Free Press.

Lyson, T.A., and G.D. Squires. 1984. "The Promise and Perils of Applied Sociology: A Survey of Nonacademic Employers." *Sociological Inquiry* 54: 1–15.

Merton, R.K. 1983. "Social Problems and Sociological Theory." In A. Rosenblatt and T.F. Gieryn, eds., *Social Research and The Practicing Professions*. Cambridge, MA: Abt Books, 43–99.

Rossi, P.H., and H.E. Freeman. 1985. *Evaluation: A Systematic Approach*. Beverly Hills: SAGE Publications, 3d ed.

Small, A.W. 1897. "Points of Agreement Among Sociologists." *American Journal of Sociology* XII: 633–649.

Ward, L.F. 1883. *Dynamic Sociology*. New York: D. Appleton and Company.

Whitehead, A.N. 1961. *The Interpretation of Science: Selected Essays*. New York: Bobbs-Merrill Company, Inc.

CHAPTER 1

● ● ●

Pure and Applied Sociology: An Historical Overview

However useful it has been or may be to divide sociology into pure and applied branches, the distinction is misleading. Pure sociology suggests the study of society without any particular motivating purpose or problematic concern. But, wherever sociology arose, the acknowledged antecedent was a major socially disrupting event or process—in France, for example, the 1789 revolution, and in western Europe generally and America, rapid industrialization and urbanization. To some degree, sociologists have always sought practical applications and outlets for their theories, methods, and humanistic concerns.

As mainstream sociology developed, however, formal interest in practical or applied matters became secondary to "pure" pursuits, such as establishing the discipline as a respectable scholarly and scientific endeavor. Applied sociology generally became something sociologists did individually and informally. The nature and extent of such involvement are an integral part of the unwritten history of sociology. One obtains a sense of the concerns and activities of the practically inclined primarily by means of the occasional autobiographical reflection.[1]

Current interest in applied sociology is a consequence of several factors. Among the most important of these is a decline in the number of sociology majors stemming from the general demand for a more practically relevant undergraduate curriculum. Another is a decrease in the demand for traditional academic positions and an increase in applied employment opportunities.[2] In the effort to attract students and protect jobs, sociology departments have revamped their curricula by the addition of applied-oriented courses and tracks at both the undergraduate and graduate levels.

The increased recent attention accorded sociology's applied side suggests the possibility of long overdue consideration of neglected subjects—most of all the integration of pure and applied sociology.[3] As will become evident, an acceptable synthesis or formal merger is difficult because of traditional and deep seated commitment to their separation. The aim here, then, is to comb the historical record to identify the views and reasoning of those responsible for establishing prevailing conceptions of the differences and proper interrelationship between pure and applied sociology. Awareness of this material is essential for those who would make the case for deemphasizing the distinction on the grounds that its continuation is detrimental both to the development of general knowledge and to pragmatically effective social science.

Interest in differentiating between and interrelating pure and applied sociology has waxed and waned with periods of relative social and economic stability and significant instability. The first discernable period includes the years prior to World War I.

PRE-WORLD WAR I VIEWS AND PREMISES

The acknowledged originator of the notion of a sociology with pure and applied branches was Auguste Comte (1798–1857). Comte "first divided sociology into two departments or stages: the pure (abstract or static) and the applied (concrete, synthetic, or dynamic)" (Chugerman, 1965: 200).

The part of Comte's social theory that most appealed to America's budding sociologists was a product of the aftermath of the 1789 French Revolution. Born in idealistic faith in humanity's ability to practice "the golden rule" if freed from what was regarded as the arbitrary and corrupting constraints of the *ancien regime,* the revolution spawned a reign of terror and the general social chaos that eventually led to the re-centralization of power and authority.

To Comte, the lesson to be learned was that society was a much more delicate and complicated phenomenon than had been appreciated. Effective and planned social change, Comte argued, must stem from accurate knowledge acquired by the most advanced and objective means, that is, the scientific method.

Comte's Positive Philosophy

In Comte's positive philosophy (1974: 41), any science has two basic elements—"the abstract or general," the object of which is to identify invariant natural laws; and "the concrete, particular, or descriptive," the object of which is to apply identified laws to improve society. Scientific study of the abstract and general entails statical and dynamical aspects. Social statics entails identification of the laws governing the systematic interrelationship of societal structural components. "The statical study of sociology," says Comte, "consists in the investigation of the laws of action and reaction of the different parts of the social system" (1974: 457). Social dynamics is concerned with the specification of the laws governing change in societal structures and their functioning; or as Comte puts it, "social dynamics studies the laws of succession" (1974: 464).

It is important to emphasize that Comte viewed the scientific study of social statics and dynamics as theoretically interrelated activities. As he indicates,

> the distinction . . . corresponds with the double conception of order and progress; for order consists . . . in a permanent harmony among the conditions of social existence; and progress consists in social development; and [in] the conditions in the one . . . and the laws of movement of the other . . . we find again the constant relation between the science and the art—the theory and the practice. (1974: 457)

To Comte, the purpose of scientifically acquired knowledge of the laws of social order and change is to permit "prevision," or prediction. Prediction is regarded as prerequisite to the possibility of effective and accurate social planning and social engineering. When accurate prediction of complex societal events and activities becomes a reality, the rule of reason is presumed to be at hand and the human possibilities thereby unlimited. Ward accepted this line of reasoning without modification as he adopted other elements of Comte's perspective to his own purposes.

Ward's Dynamic Sociology

As Samuel Chugerman (1965: 154), Ward's biographer, points out, practically every sociologist after Comte managed to misinterpret the difference between social statics and dynamics. The tendency was to equate the study of societal structure with social statics and the study of the functions of structures with dynamics. For Ward, social statics involved the study of both societal structures and their functioning. In his words, "The investigation of structures is anatomy, that of functions is physiology, and in all sciences, including sociology, the study of both anatomy and physiology belongs to the department of statics" (Ward, 1897: 175). The study of changes in societal structures and functions belongs to the department of dynamics. Social dynamics has two branches—one which studies the influence of natural laws on social change, and the other whose aim is to improve society by application of knowledge of social change.

Ward subsumes both social statics and social dynamics under pure sociology. According to Ward, pure sociology "answers the questions What, Why, and How, by furnishing the facts, the causes, and the principles of sociology" (1906: 3). In contrast, applied sociology "answers the question What for?" (1906: 5).

Ward was convinced that any mature science must have both pure and applied stages. And following Comte, he thought the object of pure sociology was the acquisition of the exact knowledge needed to predict, and the object of applied sociology was the application of predictions in the effort to ameliorate the human condition. Ward insists that "without the pure stage all attempts at application must be wholly random" (1883: 247), and that pure science per se is useless. As Hofstadter states, Ward stressed that the human "task is not to imitate the laws of nature, but to observe them, appropriate them, direct them" (1968: 74).

Ward's position on the practical relevance of pure sociology was not consistently held to this extreme level. In a later section of the same work cited above, Ward acknowledges that "knowledge must, in great part, be pursued for its own sake" and that "it is easy to place too narrow an estimate upon apparently useless results" (1883: 509).

Clearly, however, the thrust of Ward's position is on the side of a pure sociology inspired by utilitarian motives—the isolation of societal laws that have some practical human benefit. He is not content to simply let nature take its course, that is, to adopt a non-interventionist laissez faire policy and ignore the problem of what and who should be responsible for defining and implementing relevant knowledge. In his view, "those who can see a surplus of good in things as they are, or can hope for their improvement under the laws of evolution unaided by social intelligence must be set down as hopelessly blinded by the great optimistic illusion of all life" (Loewenberg, 1957: 21). He consistently emphasized the necessity of scientifically guided social amelioration,[4] and argued that human society would inevitably be governed sociocratically.

Ward borrowed the term "sociocracy" from Comte and uses it to define a society collectively oriented and governed by the science of society. He defines sociocracy as "government by society, or the art which corresponds to the science of sociology" (Chugerman: 319). Sociology's aim is the acquisition and implementation of knowledge toward the end of improving the condition of all. Ward makes a moral choice. Individualism and laissez faire economics have ruled long enough, he argues. It is time to acknowledge the condition of the neglected and exploited masses.

Ward was careful to differentiate sociocracy from both individualism and socialism. As Ward sees it:

1. Individualism has created artificial inequalities.
2. Socialism seeks to create artificial equalities.
3. Sociocracy recognizes natural inequalities and aims to abolish artificial inequalities.
4. Individualism confers benefits on those only who have the ability to obtain them, by superior power, cunning, intelligence, or the accident of position.
5. Socialism would confer the same benefits on all alike, and aims to secure equality of fruition.
6. Sociocracy would confer benefits in strict proportion to merit, but would insist upon equality of opportunity as the only means of determining the degree of merit. (1899: 292-293)

Ward does not think a revolution or radical means are necessary to bring about sociocracy. He thinks of it as a natural extension of the evolutionary process of democratically constituted society. As he puts it, "Just as absolute monarchy passed imperceptibly into limited monarchy, and this, in many states without even a change of name has passed into more or less pure democracy, so democracy is capable of passing as smoothly into sociocracy" (Commager, 1967: 173).

The governing mechanism of sociology is to be a national academy of social science. The academy's faculty and its research assistants are to be chosen by a panel composed of the country's most esteemed intellects. As Chugerman explains,

> Ward's vision of the national academy was one without professional philosophers in abstract speculation and sitting high on a pedestal of pure science. Nor would there be any expert opinion for sale, since the state would be the only bidder. Graduates of the academy would fill all administrative posts in the government service. Politics would be integrated with social research, and all public employees would receive a thorough training in the theory and practice of government before entering the public service. (Chugerman, 340-341)

Unquestionably, Ward was among the most respected minds of the day. His productivity and intellectual range were such as to inspire some to regard him as a genius, if not the American Aristotle.[5] He was the acknowledged founder of American sociology, and he became the first president (1906) of the American Sociological Society (ASS).

At the initial meetings of the ASS, and with Ward's presidential address in mind, Albion Small, the first editor of the *American Journal of Sociology,* presented a paper titled, "Points of Agreement Among Sociologists."[6] According to Small, sociologists agreed that their primary goal was the discovery of laws as the essential means of gaining control of nature and intervening in the evolutionary process in order to improve the general physical, social, and intellectual well-being. But goal attainment required patience. "As we have come to the conclusion that the dynamic phases of life are the final terms of our intelligence," he wrote, "it follows that we must regard all phases of ability or knowledge as relatively tentative until they have yielded their meaning" (1907: 649). The business of applied sociology was to be deferred until pure sociology accomplished its purposes.

There is no evidence of interest in critical examination of Small's (following Ward's lead) line of reasoning. No one questioned Ward's conception of applied sociology as atheoretical, as that branch or stage of sociology concerned strictly with the application of theoretical principles or laws identified and verified by pure sociology. Matters of more pressing and mundane importance contributed to this lacuna. In the early years of the ASS, the major issues involved the teaching of the introductory course, the development of research standards, and academic freedom (Rhoades, 1981: 11). Formal associational interest in the application of sociological knowledge was not expressed until

1920, the year that Henry Pratt Fairchild's 1916 treatise in applied sociology was re-issued.

Fairchild's Interpretation

Fairchild (1880–1956, a president of the American Sociological Society) perpetuates the premise of an atheoretical applied sociology. He holds that most sciences have two departments: a "theoretic" or pure science and a "practical" or applied science. As does Ward, Fairchild assigns pure sociology the task of identifying the laws of human association. But contrary to Ward, who maintains that pure sociology relates the past and the present, Fairchild stresses that "pure sociology has its eye neither on the future nor the present, but on the past" (1916: 4). Also unlike Ward, who holds that applied sociology relates to the future only, Fairchild holds that applied sociology relates to the present and the future. The goal of pure sociology is to determine what society is and the goal of applied sociology what society can be. However, like Ward, Fairchild sees applied sociology as helpless without the theoretical insights of pure sociology: "It is from pure sociology that applied sociology gets all its knowledge of the fundamental facts, the basic principles and laws which it is to utilize in accomplishing its conscious purposes" (5).

Like Ward, Fairchild sees applied sociology as an evolutionary rather than a revolutionary endeavor. The aim is scientifically informed piecemeal and gradual reform rather than total and abrupt radical transformation. Fairchild ends his book with the following statement: "The study of applied sociology is the study of the problem how to provide for advance into new and better things without sacrificing the stability and soundness which inhere in the tried and proved forms, institutions, and mores of society" (1916: 332). Such ideas began to attract renewed attention after the First World War.

AFTER WORLD WAR I AND BEFORE THE GREAT DEPRESSION

The First World War compelled sociologists to reassess prevailing social theory and behavioral assumptions. Evolutionary theory—whether reform oriented in the hands of a Lester Ward or conservatively predisposed in the manner of a William Graham Sumner[7]—was based on the assumption of social progress through "the struggle for existence" and "the survival of the fittest," notions compatible with laissez faire capitalism. Many, following Ward and his predecessors, also assumed the direction of human evolution to be toward ever increasing rationality. The brutal facts of the war—the most deadly conflict in human history with at least 10 million dead and 20 million wounded—indicated the widest possible gulf between theory and fact.

There was a shift in the focal point of the sociological perspective—from the total society or macro level to the small group or micro level. A problem of some concern—the origin or creation of the "rational," "mature" adult—was something that could no longer be taken for granted or overlooked. Family interaction and the socialization process (including schooling) occupied center stage in the social-psychological movement that generated the broad theoretical orientation that Herbert Blumer[8] named "symbolic interactionism."

Interest in new theories and problems was matched by greater concern with measurement, or the identification of methods of objectively identifying and interrelating relevant social facts. Correlatively, the idea emerged that scientifically acquired behavioral and social knowledge should be applied sooner rather than later.

It is not surprising, therefore, that the Reverend S.Z. Batten was moved to present a resolution at the 1920 meeting of the ASS that read as follows:

> In view of the fact that sociology is concerned with human well-being and the progress of society; and in view of the fact that there has accumulated a vast body of knowledge of social facts and progress: Resolved, that the ASS appoint a committee of five to consider ways whereby his body of knowledge may be thoroughly socialized and interpreted to the people in such a way as to lead to necessary changes in our educational system and to bring about conscious social action; this committee to report at the next annual meeting of the Society. (Rhoades, 1981: 14)

The motion was referred to the appropriate committee for action, but no record has been found of its having been acted upon one way or another.

Among noteworthy applied oriented publications in the 1920s, two stand out—one by Franklin H. Giddings (1855–1931, a President of the ASS) and the other by one of his students, Herbert N. Shenton (1894–1942)[9]. What particularly concerned Giddings was that social workers and others were not using scientifically adequate methods of specifying what they were doing and learning. "Our social workers and our uplift organizations do not know," he said, "what results they are getting, and by what methods they are getting them" (1924: 41). He was convinced that scientific methods are the only way of discovering what is being accomplished by public policies, educational procedures, and other behavior changing efforts. And from his vantage point, experimentation is the only effective means of social amelioration aimed at accomplishing specified goals. But goal attainment is not a pure process. In the history of melioristic efforts, Giddings saw an untold amount of wasted time and energy because of the failure to ask questions such as the following: "What else probably will happen when we bring about, or try to bring about, a change that we have in view, and believe to be desirable?" (1924: 182). He felt that neglect of this sort was "the characteristic vice of legislation."

Shenton's work is more than an extension of his mentor's ideas. It is a thorough attempt to clarify what applied sociology is and is not. He emphasizes a difference between "practically useful sociology" and "the practical application of sociology." He uses the one in reference to "organized knowledge" of a certain type and the other to the actual attempt to positively intervene in social life. Thus, he defines applied sociology as "a body of sociological knowledge especially selected, presented, interpreted and organized for those who are endeavoring to use sociology effectively for the achievement of proximate social ends" (1927: 31).

The concept of "proximate social ends" was borrowed from Giddings, who distinguishes between immediate and practical goals ("proximate" ends) and long-run and ideal goals ("ultimate" ends). Proximate ends—for example, solving or ameliorating the effects of particular social problems such as poverty and crime—are preliminary to the attainment of ultimate ends. According to Giddings, the ultimate visualized ends are "Amelioration of the human lot, by security and material abundance; the survival (which security and abundance make possible) of variates from a standardized human type in whom lie our hope of discovery, of invention, and of experimentation; the socialization of entire populations, with elimination of the antisocial; and that individuation which is an evolution of intelligent, responsible, self-determining personality—of adequate man" (1927: 170–171).

Goal attainment requires the execution of three tasks, the first two by pure sociology and the third by applied sociology. The first is the identification of the general patterns of human association; discovery of the laws behind associational patterns is the second. Both are to be accomplished by application of the methods of inductive science (including qualitative studies of "co-individual phenomena" and quantitative studies of "multi-individual response to stimulation") and positive philosophy.

In Shenton's scheme, applied sociology has the task of formulating principles of human interaction and association useful for effecting social change. The functions of the applied or practical sociologist are limited to estimations of the likely course of social change in specified instances and making recommendations about the effectiveness of different ways of accomplishing desired social change. "His task ends," says Shenton, "when he has reached the limits of scientific analysis and of significant probability" (1927: 159). The agents of change are the social engineers and social artists, neither of whom are necessarily sociologists.

The societal engineer is guided by the principles of sociology, which he applies by technical methods. "He desires to have the principles and the data of sociology so stated and arranged that they lend themselves readily to the technical use for which he needs them" (1927: 223).

Social art refers to all deliberate efforts to accomplish desired social change. It is practiced by all manner of people in all types of situations and contexts. As Shenton sees it, "the social artist must not only arrange human beings in cooperative schemes so that they can achieve for themselves that which they could not otherwise achieve; he must also blend the associations so that the individuals share social experiences that could not otherwise be attained and so that they become something that they could not otherwise become" (1927: 233, note no. 13).

Shenton was well aware that what he advocated could be used by anyone—elites and nonelites, the pure of mind and the corrupt. "It is quite probable", he writes, "that an applied sociology of the sort described in these pages will increase the possibilities of social control, and these possibilities may be grasped alike by socially minded idealists or unscrupulous individualists" (1927: 165). While offering no ironclad solution to the problem, he feels, nonetheless, that development of socially scientific means of control would not only complicate public policy issues and decision making, but also improve the ability of the general public to protect itself.

As an important part of a larger discipline, then, applied sociology has a number of functions: (1) to make sociological knowledge practically useful, (2) to develop basic concepts and frames of reference useful for converting the perceptions and inferences of non-sociological practitioners into sociologically relevant terms, and (3) to "enrich and correct general sociology" via practical field expertise (1927: 236).

Shenton's ideas have yet to be given the serious and thorough attention they merit. One might think the Depression would have provoked widespread interest in his work. But such was not the case, as sociologists became preoccupied with immediately pressing problems, including their own employment needs.

BETWEEN THE DEPRESSION AND WORLD WAR II

Sociology has never manifested concern with the balanced development of pure and applied sociology. Matters of pure sociology—the quest to make sociology a respectable scholarly discipline via a graduate curriculum emphasizing preparation for academic employment and scholarly research, for example—have always been preeminent. It has been primarily during periods of decline in academic employment that sociologists have fretted about the imbalance, especially the failure to adequately emphasize preparation for non-academic employment. This trait, much in evidence in recent years, was revealed first during the Depression.

Sociologists and other social scientists were involved in important work at the federal level virtually at the onset of the Depression. In 1928, President Hoover established the President's Committee on Social Trends. Although an economist chaired the committee, its research director, William F. Ogburn, was a sociologist. In 1933, the committee published two summary volumes and thirteen monographs, many of which were written by sociologists.[10] The applied purpose of the committee's efforts is indicated by President Hoover's foreword to the initial reports. "It should serve," he said, "to help all of us to see where the social stresses are occurring and where major efforts should be undertaken to deal with them constructively" (1933: v).

In the early years of the Depression, the American Sociological Society's Research Planning Committee sought to encourage the application of sociological knowledge to New Deal Programs. In fact, sociologists were instrumental in conducting the research and compiling the evidence that led to the drafting of social security legislation. According to Hauser, "sociologists employing social statistics not only played a prominent part in establishing the framework for the social security system but also continued to play a role in the evaluation of the program and its various amendments over the years" (1967: 860).

In January 1934, the ASS committee on Opportunities for Trained Sociologists noted the danger of doctorate overproduction during a period of diminished academic employment. In 1935, the committee found that although there was an increase in the public service employment of social scientists, sociologists were not as well represented as economists, political scientists, lawyers, and social workers. The committee traced the problem to the fact "that sociology has been almost exclusively preoccupied with the training of teachers of the subject, and that until recent years it has shown a conspicuous lack of practical and applied research work—research that would be of immediate value to public administrators" (Rhoades: 20).

Although many sociologists found applied employment during the Depression, many joined the ranks of the unemployed due to academic retrenchment. As Kenneth Lutterman (1983: 430) points out, the Depression terminated academic expansion and greatly reduced job opportunities for sociologists. Writing in 1940, and after examining the record over the preceding 30 years, Jerome Davis concluded that "sociology has been becoming more theoretical, more scientific, and less preoccupied in the field of social action than formerly" (1940: 171). Davis found that although sociologists were highly committed to the study of social problems, they did not feel particularly obligated to become agents of social change. The general explanation given for this position made reference to the overriding necessity of value-neutrality in conformity with the principle of scientific objectivity.

In a systematic analysis of the content of all sociology textbooks published between 1932 and April 1938, Hornell Hart found "some seeming agreements," the most prominent of which was that sociologists, as people generally, are chiefly motivated by unscientifically acquired values. He advised his colleagues that if they wished to adhere to the scientific ideal, they must take pains to avoid selecting and interpreting data on the basis of personal evaluations. Above all, he emphasized, they should refrain from imposing their "private value-judgments upon other people" (1938: 863).

The major voice in opposition to this line of reasoning was that of Robert Lynd (1892–1970). Lynd argues that when social scientists refrain from specifying what should be done with their knowledge, they allow other less principled actors to fill the void—in the case of Depression-related problems, for example, the National Association of Manufacturers and the American Federation of Labor. Lynd finds the Depression to have dramatized as never before the inadequacy of operating a complex society by means of the "casual values" of special interest groups claiming to represent the public interest. "At this point," says Lynd, "the social sciences, the instruments for appraisal and direction-finding, plead immunity from the responsibility to guide the culture. . . . Either the social sciences know more than do the "hard-headed" businessman, the "practical" politician and administrator . . . and . . . other de facto leaders . . . as to what the findings of research mean . . . or the vast current industry of social science is an empty facade" (1939: 186).

Although no critic of the value of empiricism in social science, Lynd was convinced that there is a seductive quality about the empirical measurement of social phenomena, namely, acceptance of the values and goals of the system studied. Social scientists begin, he says, by accepting prevailing social institutions as reality, their basic datum. In turn, institutions are assumed to be part of a system, and the goal becomes the discovery of its laws. Lynd's contention is that if "order is to exist in culture, it must be built into it by science, and not merely by discovering it" (1939: 125). In his view, the task of social science is "to discover what kinds of order actually do exist in the whole range of the behavior of human beings, what kinds of functional relationships between parts of culture exist in space over time, and what functionally more useful kinds of order can be created in our contemporary culture" (1939: 125-126).

Lynd's concerns were expressed at the end of a decade during which formal interest in applied sociology waned to the point of indifference. As Walter Argow put it, "applied sociology seems to be in the pleasant state known as suspended animation" (1941: 37).

FROM WORLD WAR II TO THE PRESENT

In tracing changing conceptions of pure and applied sociology and their relative importance to sociologists at different times in American history, the years after the onset of the Second World War manifest at least two subdivisions: the period from World War II to 1960, and the years from 1960 to the present.

From World War II to 1960

During the Second World War, sociologists served both in the armed forces and a variety of federal agencies—from the OSS (Office of Strategic Services, or the forerunner of the CIA) to the OPA (Office of Price Administration). The impact on the number of college teachers was not as great as might be imagined. In 1944, the sociology college teaching faculty was down only by a fourth and the ranks of sociology graduate students were trimmed by only a third (Rhoades, 1981: 34). But by 1943, the American Sociological Society began to plan for the postwar years.

The Society created a Training and Recruitment Committee in 1943, and in 1944 the committee reported that in the immediate postwar period sociology college teaching positions would increase in the 45 to 70 percent range and sociology graduate students by some 35 percent over their pre-war high. Rhoades reports that the committee's postwar graduate curriculum recommendations emphasized increased preparation in quantitative methods and research as well as training for likely non-academic growth positions in industry, journalism, and public administration (1981: 35).

In 1945, Kimball Young, the Society's president, foresaw the emergence of greater public than private support for sociological research, and greater federal than state funding. If these trends were to come about, the question for Young was: "How much place will there be, under governmental auspices, for the more abstract, less immediately practical, and long-range research?"

(Rhoades, 1981: 35). Despite the creation of the National Science Foundation and the emergence of other federal funding sources for social science research, Young need not have worried about their leading to the ascendancy of applied over pure sociology in the foreseeable post-war period.

A major consequence of the Second World War was the elevation of the physical sciences and their technological capabilities to a position of preeminent respect, fear, and hope. If physical science knowledge could be used to produce weapons of unlimited destructiveness, it also could be used to create the products conducive to unlimited material well-being. The question was (and is), can society be so ordered as to contain the bellicose and destructive in favor of the peaceful and constructive applications of acquired knowledge of the physical world? With these ideas in mind, and writing in 1946, Philip Hauser (a living past president of the ASA; in 1959, the American Sociological Society changed its name to American Sociological Association) wondered if the social sciences were "ready for the supreme challenge of providing enough knowledge about human institutions and human relationships in time to prevent the suicide of the human race potentially inherent in the anachronism represented by our social institutions, and practices in our contemporary physical world" (1946: 80).

The social sciences were challenged to respond not only to the impending social impact of what promised to be a period of rapid technological change, but also to the imminent creation of the National Science Foundation. "If the National Science Foundation is enacted into law," Hauser wondered, "will the social sciences be ready?" (1946: 381). He thought not, but believed that deficiencies could and would be overcome. The "urgent task" was the development of "carefully planned, well-designed, far-reaching and significant research projects" (1946: 381).

Writing at the same time, and under the auspices of the ASS, Talcott Parsons (1902–1979, a president of the ASS) also emphasized the challenge posed by the impending federal legislation. He argues that the social sciences are limited both methodologically and theoretically. He thinks, however, that "during the last generation," there was "substantial development on the theoretical level which provides a much firmer foundation for research and application in a variety of fields" (1946: 663). Parsons too was convinced that research in some areas was at a level where the provision of "adequate resources and well-trained personnel" could generate "results of first-rate practical importance" (1946: 663). Examples include the ability to diagnose conflict and sources of inefficiency in industry, opinion and attitude evaluation, the analysis of demographic factors, and analysis of elements of the business cycle. Parsons ended by stressing that

> the urgency of the social problems of our time, and their close connection at so many points with technological development means that someone is inevitably going to undertake action to solve them. As experts on technology many natural scientists will tend to consider it their responsibility to attempt to intervene in

this field. The enormous popular prestige of the natural scientists will favor this tendency. . . . But in so far as social science has any validity at all, scientific competence in the field of social problems can only be the result of a professional level of training and experience in the specific subject-matter. If, that is, we are to be moving more and more into scientific age, and science is to help solve its social problems, it must be social science which does so. (1946: 665)

However great the incentive and need to develop applied sociology in the immediate post World War II period, there is little to indicate a response proportionate to the expressed interest. By all indications, sociologists preferred positions in the ever expanding academic job market over non-academic employment. Membership growth in the American Sociological Society was particularly great between 1949 to 1959—from 2,673 to 6,436 (Rhoades, 1981: 42).

By 1949, sociologists such as Parsons were stressing the dangers of over-commitment of resources to the discovery of practical solutions to social problems. In his 1949 presidential address to the ASS, Parsons expresses interest in striking "a proper balance between fundamental research, including its theoretical aspect, and applied or 'engineering' work" (1949: 368). But, he now insists,

> It is not a question of whether we try to live up to our social responsibilities, but of how. If we should put the overwhelming bulk of our resources, especially of trained talent, into immediately practical problems it would do some good, but I have no doubt that it would have to be at the expense of our greater usefulness to society in the future. For it is only by systematic work on problems where the probable scientific significance has priority over any immediate possibility of application that the greatest and most rapid scientific advance can be made. (1949: 368)

Simply put, applied sociology's time had not yet come. Pure sociology required more time to grow and mature.

Interestingly, Parsons did not entertain the possibility that neither pure nor applied sociology could properly develop without constant reciprocal input. The idea of balanced and simultaneous growth of sociology's two sides was eschewed in favor of advocacy of total commitment to what was presumed to be of greatest importance—the development of theory prerequisite to effective data synthesis and accumulation.

How much of the impetus for turning inward and focusing on disciplinary needs and concerns was supplied by purely logical considerations as opposed to conditioning factors such as the threat to academic freedom posed by the activities of HUAC (House Un-American Activities Committee) is not known. What is known is that by the mid-1950s, sociologists were beginning to question the discipline's relative isolation from practical affairs. Claude Bowman, for example, thought that sociology had become too detached. He attributed part of sociology's isolation to the "pure-science emphasis that dominates both research and theory" (1956: 563). "With all due respect," he said, "the value of [detached] scholarship . . . is now over-emphasized"(1956: 563).

Behind the practice of scholarly detachment, Bowman saw the quest for scientific objectivity. Scientific objectivity was, he felt, a quite legitimate emphasis when "facts were sparse" and prevailing means inadequate to eliminate bias in the study of controversial, value laden subjects such as social class, race, and religion. However, advance in theoretical and methodological sophistication was such that "continued devotion" to social detachment was anachronistic.

To Bowman, pure sociology had developed to the point where applied sociology was not only feasible but long overdue. He proposed the application of sociological knowledge and expertise in evaluation research to problems and issues involving public policy formation and decision making at the local level—schools and social service agencies, for example.

If Bowman challenged the logic of continued neglect of applied concerns because of alleged theoretical and methodological shortcomings, Alvin Gouldner (1920-1981) questioned the essential relevance of much of basic sociology for applied purposes. As he indicates, applied sociology, unlike pure sociology, is not concerned primarily with "values intrinsic to science" (for example, objectivity, prediction, and replication); it is oriented to the values and needs of laypeople. The knowledge sought by the applied sociologist is in the order of solutions to problems defined by clients rather than colleagues. Hence, the major theoretical orientations of pure sociology may be of little use to the applied sociologist. As Gouldner sees it, the identification of practical solutions to lay problems invariably requires knowledge of social change. The major theoretical orientation of the day, structural–functionalism, focused on the problem of social order. "Pure sociological theory," says Gouldner, "has only begun to develop models adequate to cope with the analysis of change, and is even more removed from the analysis of change tempo, involving questions of sudden transition" (1957: 96).

However accurate and well presented, Bowman's and Gouldner's views had no appreciable impact on prevailing conceptions of the proper relationship between pure and applied sociology. One might think that the timing of their presentations was to blame. But even during the turbulent 1960s, arguments for a revised conception of the nature and role of applied sociology fared no better.

From the 1960s to the Present

The time span from the 1960s to the mid-1970s united trends, movements, and events that provoked dramatic change. The civil rights movement, the controversial HUAC hearings, conservative norms seemingly more appropriate for a less informed and affluent era, and the Vietnam War are some of the factors that combined to produce a spate of social movements and leftist political activity. The effects were particularly apparent in colleges and universities, including classroom instruction and behavioral and social research. Students and professors felt compelled to become "involved" in "relevant" problems and issues.

At the beginning of the period, Alvin Gouldner presented the challenge. In his 1961 presidential address to the SSSP (Society for the Study of Social Problems), Gouldner—basically repeating Lynd's essential message, but in his own provocative style—contended that to gain true public acceptance, sociology had to clarify "the value relevances of sociological inquiry" and commit itself to involvement in "the contemporary human predicament." However,

> the manner in which some sociologists conceive the value-free doctrine disposes them to ignore current human problems and to huddle together like old men seeking mutual warmth. "This is not our job," they say. "And if it were we would not know enough to do it. Go away, come back when we're grown up," say these old men. The issue, however, is not whether we know enough; the real questions are whether we have the courage to say and use what we do know and whether anyone knows more. (1970: 73)

Over the course of the decade, and often at the risk of offending their more "purest" power-wielding colleagues, more sociologists than ever sought applied or practical outlets for their talents. Their involvement covered the broadest possible range—from active membership in political and social movements to consultation with and the conduct of research for all manner of groups and organizations.[11] Anything seemed possible, even the assimilation of applied sociology into mainstream sociology. As John Riley saw it, for example, "the ambiguity which has frequently marked the occupational status of the nonacademic sociologist is gradually being resolved. . . . And . . . the opportunities for non-academic sociologists in influential positions of relatively high status appear to be increasingly plentiful" (1967: 798–799).

But the practical talents of academic sociologists too were in demand. James Coleman, for example, was commissioned by the Office of Education to undertake the largest study ever of the educational resources available to students of diverse ethnic and racial backgrounds and at all educational levels. Others found their services in demand in President Johnson's War on Poverty program and a number of Presidential Commissions. The experiences of those involved in these endeavors are discussed in Chapter 6. For the moment it is important to note that the demand for sociologists in such nationally important policy related activities declined significantly in the 1970s. In a recent publication Nathan Glazer describes the trend as "the eclipse of social engineering." As he sees it, "when the history of American social policy is written, I think the greatest weight will have to be put on this theme: an optimistic evaluation of human and social scientific capacities marked the 1960s and 1970s, with decreasing confidence in the 1970s" (1988: 42).

A major share of the declining interest in social science must be credited to a levelling off if not a dip in the nation's economic condition. A conservative reaction, fed by the economic constriction brought about the Arab oil embargo in 1973, led to a return to more fundamental concerns in both society and the social sciences.

In sociology there was renewed concern with establishing the scientific status of the discipline. Theory construction and elaboration became secondary to the development and application of research methods. However, something important had changed; the radical period had a significant consciousness raising effect. Neither pure nor applied sociology, particularly the latter, could be any longer conducted under a secure banner of value neutrality or unquestioned scientific objectivity. Ideological intrusion and value bias were regarded as inherent features of sociological analysis. In 1976 Richard Berk and Peter Rossi, two of the foremost applied sociologists, observed that "it is simply impossible to be a neutral technician. . . . Evaluation researchers are always choosing sides even before empirical findings are produced" (1976: 348-349).

Increasingly, then, sociologists found their work evaluated not so much for its procedural limitations as its ideological tone and implications. However scientifically objective their aims and procedures, sociologists and other social scientists were judged to be less value neutral than predisposed toward a leftist theoretical perspective and policy recommendations calling for structural rather than individual change. Categories of people were invariably depicted as the victims of a system requiring surgical overhaul. In the 1980s the conservative assessment of the theoretical and social policy shortcoming of social science were detailed in widely read and politically influential treatises by George Gilder and Charles Murray. Their work and its possible significance for pure and applied sociological theory are also included in Chapter 6.

The 1990s must be considered a period of challenge for the social sciences. The practical utility and marketability of social science requires ideological accommodation with capitalism and its social institutions. But just how far most sociologists are willing to sacrifice ideological commitment, or a critical intellectual stance, in the name of economic reality remains to be seen. The recent growth and development of applied sociology courses and curricula across the country suggests that economic and political pragmatism has widespread support.

No precise data are available on the number of sociologists engaged in applied sociology or its separate branches. Without doubt, most are engaged in social research, evaluation work most of all. In a 1985 publication, Rossi and Howard Freeman (1985: 361) estimated the total number of individuals employed in evaluation work at 50,000. They did not hazard a guess at the proportion of the total accounted for by sociologists.

However long-standing and extensive the involvement of sociologists in applied work, Rossi and William Whyte contend that applied sociology continues to occupy a low status position in the discipline.[12] As they see it,

> this low status exists despite the difficulty of drawing the line between applied and pure, or basic sociology. As one of us (Rossi, 1980) has observed, the line is so fuzzy that applied research is often redefined by the passage of time, emerging as basic sociology in the disciplinary literature. . . . This lack of clear definition applies particularly to perspectives, content, and method. (1983: 6)

The difficulty of specifying a clear dividing line between pure and applied sociology led Joseph DeMartini to view them as points on a continuum. At one end is pure discipline oriented social science activity (theory construction and hypothesis testing); at the other is applied client oriented problem solving work (needs assessments and program evaluation). At the center, DeMartini places "sociology as social critique" (1982: 6) On one side are more pure activities (causal analysis of trends and problems), and on the other more applied activities (policy analyses).

As difficult as it may be to precisely identify the point of demarcation between pure and applied sociology, DeMartini contends that their connection is limited by contradictory elements. As far as he is concerned, until "theoretical concepts and principles are combined with an analysis of political decision making and intervention strategies," pure and applied sociology "will follow parallel if not separate lines of development" (1982: 213).

••••• *SUMMARY AND CONCLUSION*

Early concepts of pure and applied sociology now seem largely outmoded. The early idealistic roles assigned each have been diminished by concession to pragmatic considerations and experience. Instead of searching for general and timeless societal principles and laws, pure or basic sociology more modestly seeks the identification of patterns and trends in specified areas within and among given societies. And instead of awaiting the day when pure sociology will have made available the principles and laws preliminary to sociocratically managed society, applied sociology is guided by clients with limited tasks to be accomplished and specified problems to study and treat. The two now exist simultaneously but without adequate theoretical linkage.

Although this brief historical exploration is not sufficient to identify an obviously acceptable way of integrating pure and applied sociology, it does provoke sensitivity to neglected subjects and questions whose answers may point the way toward a profitable way of treating the subject. Thus, it seems apparent that unification of pure and applied sociology awaits identification and acceptance of a common goal or goals. If it is agreed, for example, that systematic knowledge accumulation of the nature of social order and social change is a common goal, how might the work of the two be interrelated? To what practical ends is knowledge of such subjects to be put and by whom and which means? Just as generally accepted answers to such questions are unavailable so too is an accepted conception of the process of knowledge accumulation.

As Thomas Kuhn points out, it is commonly believed that science is "the one enterprise that draws constantly nearer to some goal set by nature in advance" (1970: 171). In his view, knowledge growth in science is more accurately to be interpreted as a process of evolution from primitive beginnings rather than toward anything in particular. "If we can learn to substitute evolution-from-what-we-do-know for evolution-toward-what-we-wish-to-know," he says, "a number of vexing problems may vanish in the process" (171). With the passage of time, what we wish to know and why and by which means have become more rather than less ambiguous. Contributing to this state of affairs is the conventional view that scientific progress is accomplished best if problems and subjects examined are determined from within than without a given discipline. As Kuhn puts it,

> the insulation of the scientific community from society permits the individual scientist to concentrate his attention upon problems that he has good reason to believe he will be able to solve. Unlike the engineer, and many doctors, and most theologians, the scientist need not choose problems because they urgently need solution and without regard for the tools available to solve them. In this respect, also, the contrast between natural scientists and many social scientists proves instructive. The latter often tend, as the former almost never do, to defend their choice of a research problem . . . chiefly in terms of the social importance of achieving a solution. Which group would one then expect to solve problems at a more rapid rate? (1970: 164)

But to what degree can and should a given behavioral or social science remain aloof from or uncontaminated by individual or societal needs and problems? Is it possible that a general social science such as sociology has more to gain than lose (both in terms of knowledge growth and practical relevance) by proceeding on both pure and applied fronts simultaneously and with regard for their essential interrelatedness?

Kuhn's rationale is consistent with the position taken by nineteenth century social theorists such as Comte and Ward who believed that applied sociology should be independent of and secondary to pure sociology. Social reconstruction depended on the scientific identification of the laws of social order and change. But even if such laws can be discovered, as many, if not most behavioral and social scientists now doubt (Fiske and Shweder, 1986), how and by whom are they to be implemented? Is piecemeal social engineering the basic way? Are revolution, conflict and violence out of the question? And isn't elitism required in the traditional premise (as initiated by Comte and perpetuated in one form or another by American sociologists from Ward to Parsons) of the primacy of pure to applied sociology? If elitism is to be avoided, wouldn't it be more appropriate in democratically constituted society to emphasize amassing knowledge from the self-defined problematic world of average citizens than the problematic context of the discipline? An affirmative answer does not automatically imply neglect of the "pure" goal of systematically acquired knowledge. What it does imply is the need to link pure and applied theory. To date, pure or basic sociological theory has been oriented to the general and abstract rather than the particular and practical, and applied sociological theory just the reverse. The nature of the two types of theorizing and the possibilities of their integration are examined in the following chapters.

●   **NOTES**

1. See, for example, Jesse Bernard's "American Sociology as Moral Life," *Sociological Forum,* 1 (Summer 1986), 525-535.

2. In a recent communication with the Executive Office of the American Sociological Association, my department was told that the number of jobs advertised in the Association's Employment Bulletin had tripled between 1983 and 1988. Furthermore, the composition of the Association has changed over the past 10 years. In 1976, 85–95 percent of the membership was college-located. However, by 1983, the proportion had dropped to 75 percent. The number in business and government had doubled and is expected to rise to 30 percent of the membership within the next 10 years.

3. Marvin E. Olsen recently made a plea for the integration of pure and applied sociology and offered some ideas toward how it might be done. See his "Epilogue: The Future of Applied Sociology," in M.E. Olsen and M. Micklin, *Handbook of Applied Sociology* (New York: Praeger Publishers, 1981), 561–581.

4. Edward P. Payson, a contemporary of Ward's, developed a comparable, albeit less influential evolutionary rationale for an applied sociology. See his *Suggestions Toward an Applied Science of Sociology* (New York: G.P. Putnam's Sons, 1898).

5. In comments made after Ward's death, E.A. Ross (1913: 6), his son-in-law, observed: "If Aristotle had chanced to be born in Illinois about the middle of the nineteenth century, his career would have resembled that of Lester F. Ward more than that of any other American of our time." Perhaps Ross' comments inspired Chugerman to title his biography, *Lester F. Ward: The American Aristotle.*

6. The paper was published the following year in the *American Journal of Sociology*, 12 (March 1907), 633–649.

7. For a concise presentation of the views of reform and conservative Social Darwinists, see Bert James Loewenberg, Ed., *Darwinism: Reaction or Reform?* (New York: Rinehart, 1957).

8. See his *Sybmbolic Interactionism: Perspectives and Method* (Englewood Cliffs, NJ: Prentice-Hall, 1969).

9. In 1923, James Q. Dealey, a student of Ward's, published a text that basically reiterated his mentor's teachings. See his *Sociology: Its Development and Applications* (New York: D. Appleton).

10. President's Research Committee on Social Trends, *Recent Social Trends* (New York: McGraw-Hill, 1933).

11. For a sense of the occupational interests of sociologists at the time, see Abbott L. Ferriss, "Sociological Manpower," *American Sociological Review,* 29 (February 1964), 103–114.

12. Ellsworth R. Fuhrman makes the same point in his "Theoretical Observations on Applied Behavioral Science," *The Journal of Applied Behavioral Science,* 18 (April–May 1982), 224–225.

- ## REFERENCES

Argow, W.A. 1941. "The Practical Application of Sociology." *American Sociological Review* 6: 37–40.

Berk, R.A., and Rossi, P. 1976. "Doing Good or Worse: Evaluation Research Politically Re-Examined." *Social Problems* 23: 337–349.

Blumer, H. 1969. *Symbolic Interactionism: Perspective and Method.* Englewood Cliffs, NJ: Prentice-Hall.

Bowman, C.C. 1956. "Is Sociology Too Detached?" *American Sociological Review* 21: 563–568.

Chugerman, S. 1965. *Lester F. Ward: The American Aristotle.* New York: Octagon Books.

Commager, H.S., ed. 1967. *Lester Ward and the Welfare State.* New York: Bobbs-Merrill.

Comte, A. 1974. *The Positive Philosophy.* New York: AMS Press.

Davis, J. 1940. "The Sociologist and Social Action." *American Sociological Review* 5: 171–176.

Dealey, J.Q. 1923. *Sociology: Its Development and Applications.* New York: D. Appleton.

DeMartini, J.R. 1982. "Basic and Applied Sociological Work: Divergence, Convergence, or Peaceful Co-existence?" *The Journal of Applied Behavioral Science* 18: 203–215.

Fairchild, H.P. 1916. *Outline of Applied Sociology.* New York: Macmillan.

Ferriss, A.L. 1964. "Sociological Manpower." *American Sociological Review* 29: 103–114.

Fiske, D.W., and R.A. Shweder, eds. 1986. *Metatheory in Social Science.* Chicago: University of Chicago Press.

Fuhrman, E.R. 1982. "Theoretical Observations on Applied Behavioral Science." *Journal of Applied Behavioral Science* 18: 217–227.

Furner, M.O. 1975. *Advocacy & Objectivity: A Crisis in the Professionalization of American Social Science, 1865–1905.* Lexington, KY: University of Kentucky Press.

Giddings, F.H. 1924. *The Scientific Study of Human Society.* Chapel Hill: University of North Carolina Press.

Glazer, N. 1988. *The Limits of Social Policy.* Cambridge, MA: Harvard University Press.

Gouldner, A.W. 1957. "Theoretical Requirements of the Applied Social Sciences." *American Sociological Review.* 22: 92–102.

————. 1965. "Explorations in Applied Social Science." In A.W. Gouldner and S.M. Miller, eds., *Applied Sociology; Opportunities & Problems.* New York: Free Press.

————. 1970. "Anti-Minotaur: The Myth of a Value-free Sociology." In J.D. Douglas, ed., *The Relevance of Sociology.* New York: Appleton-Century-Crofts.

Hart, H. 1938. "Value-Judgments in Sociology." *American Sociological Review* 3: 862–867.

Hauser, P.M. 1964. "Are The Social Sciences Ready?" *American Sociological Review* 4: 379–384.

————. 1967. "Social Accounting." In P.M. Lazarsfeld, W.H. Sewell, and H.L. Wilensky, eds., *The Uses of Sociology.* New York: Basic Books, Inc.

Hinkle, R.C. Jr., and G.J. Hinkle. 1954. *The Development of Modern Sociology.* New York: Random House.

Hofstadter, R. 1944. *Social Darwinism in American Thought.* Boston: Beacon Press.

Hoover, H. 1933. Foreword in *Recent Social Trends In The United States: Report Of The President's Research Committee On Social Trends.* New York: McGraw-Hill Book Company.

Kuhn, T.S. 1970. *The Structure of Scientific Revolutions.* Chicago: The University of Chicago Press.

Lazarsfeld, P.F., W.H. Sewell, and H.L. Wilensky, eds. 1967. *The Uses of Sociology*. New York: Basic Books, Inc.

Loewenberg, B.J. 1957. *Darwinism: Reaction or Reform?* New York: Rinehart.

Lundberg, G.A. 1964. *Foundations of Sociology*. New York: David McKay Company, Inc.

Lutterman, K.G. 1983. "Changing Opportunities in Applied Sociology Education." In H.E. Freeman, R.R. Dynes, P.H. Rossi, and W.F. Whyte, eds., *Applied Sociology*. San Francisco: Jossey-Bass Publishers, 428–440.

Lynd, R.S. 1939. *Knowledge for What?* Princeton, NJ: Princeton University Press.

Parsons, T. 1946. "The Science Legislation and the Role of the Social Sciences." *American Sociological Review* 11: 653–666.

_____. 1954. The Prospects of Sociological Theory." In T. Parsons, *Essays in Sociological Theory*. New York: Free Press.

_____. 1975. "The Present Status of Structural-Functional Theory in Sociology," In L.A. Coser, ed., *The Idea of Social Structure: Papers in Honor of Robert K. Merton*. New York: Harcourt Brace Jovanovich.

Payson, E.P. 1898. *Suggestions Toward An Applied Science of Sociology*. New York: G.P. Putnam's Sons.

Rhoades, L.J. 1981. *A History of the American Sociological Association: 1905-1980*. Washington, D.C.: American Sociological Association.

Riley, J.W. Jr. 1967. The Sociologist in the Nonacademic Setting." In P.F. Lazarsfeld, W.H. Sewell, and H.L. Wilensky, Eds., *The Uses of Sociology*. New York: Basic Books, Inc.

Ross, E.A. 1913. "Lester Frank Ward." *American Journal of Sociology* XIX: 64–67.

Rossi, P.H., and W.F. Whyte. 1983. "The Applied Side of Sociology." In H.R. Freeman et al., eds., *Applied Sociology*. San Francisco: Jossey-Bass Publishers.

Rossi, P.H., J.D. Wright, and S.R. Wright. 1978. "The Theory and Practice of Applied Social Research." *Evaluation Quarterly* 2: 171–191.

Rossi, P.H., and H.E. Freeman. 1985. *Evaluation*. Third Edition. Beverly Hills: SAGE Publications.

Shenton, H.N. 1927. *The Practical Application of Sociology*. New York: Columbia University Press.

Small, A.W. 1907. "Points of Agreement Among Sociologists." *American Journal of Sociology* XII: 633–649.

Ward, L.F. 1883. *Dynamic Sociology*. New York: D. Appleton and Co.

_____. 1897. *Outlines of Sociology*. New York: Macmillan Company.

_____. 1906. *Applied Sociology*. Boston: Ginn & Company.

_____. 1968. *Dynamic Sociology, Volume 1*. New York: Johnson Reprint Corporation.

CHAPTER 2

● ● ●

Pure Sociological Theory

Pure sociological theory is a broad mixture of concepts, perspectives, assumptions and subjects. The essential unity behind the diversity is provided by basic interest in the study of human interaction as a norm creating and normatively guided activity. People behave differently when in the presence of others, and sociologists believe that the study of normative processes and their consequences is essential to understanding why. Norms may be defined as expected patterns of behavior appropriate in given situations. They include a range of rules, from simple and generally understood prescriptions involving everyday social etiquette to complex and not generally understood laws and legal formulations. Sociologists wish to know how and under what circumstances norms arise, and once created, how, when, and why they may come to have an independent effect on what people do and don't do—singly and together. The study of the behavioral effects of social interaction is, of course, the province of the social psychologist. Normative structures and their sociobehavioral, including attitudinal effects, are primary subjects of the sociologist.

The scientific study of normative patterns and social institutions has been guided by a variety of theoretical strategies and tools. In recent years, however, a split has occurred between those who advocate theory-guided research and those who would reverse the procedure. Thus, the initial pages of this chapter examine the positions of those on different sides of this issue. The bulk of the chapter is devoted to an examination of classic interpretations of the sociological perspective and the basic elements of theory building (frames of reference, conceptual schemes, hunches, hypotheses). The last section examines axiomatic or logico-deductive theory—its basic structure and uses.

THEORY OR FACT: WHICH COMES FIRST?

To study the array of problems and processes involving the general subjects of social order and change, sociologists have sought to implement accepted inductive and deductive procedures. The problem is that conceptions of the proper interrelationship of induction and deduction, the empirical and the logical, are as debatable as the proper connection between pure and applied sociology. Some are convinced that induction must precede deduction (the specification of particulars must precede generalization), others the opposite (a general idea of what to look for must precede the identification of relevant particulars), and still others fall somewhere in between.

In other words, positions taken on the proper relationship between induction and deduction take the form of points on a continuum, the poles of which may be variously specified. In general philosophy, the extremes may be represented by the distinction between indeterminism versus determinism, the idea that some "things" are subject to causal analysis and others not.

In contemporary sociology, the dichotomy is expressed by distinguishing between metaphysical and empirical modes of thinking. And metaphysical thinking has begun to be referred as the theoretical, and empirical the factual end of the spectrum. Jeffrey Alexander, for example, begins his recent four volume work by arraying the components of scientific thinking on a continuum with "metaphysical environment" at one pole and "empirical environment" at the other. "Those scientific statements closer to the right-hand side of the continuum [for example, observations, methodological assumptions, correlations]," says Alexander, "are said to be 'empirical' because their form is more influenced by the criterion of precisely describing observation. . . . Statements closer to the left-hand side [for example, presuppositions, models, concepts] are called 'theoretical' because their form is concerned less with the immediate character of the observations that inform them" (1982: 2).

What has been difficult to accept and practice is a view of the theoretical and empirical as equally independent and necessarily simultaneously interdependent. At different periods in the history of social science, one has been stressed more than the other. From roughly the late 1930s to at least the mid-1960s, for example, Parsonsian structural-functional "grand theory" held sway. To a considerable extent the current emphasis placed on inductive over deductive approaches can be interpreted as a reaction to the perceived empirical limitations of "grand theory." Barney Glaser's and Anselm Strauss's "grounded theory" is a case in point.

Glaser and Strauss open their work by observing that attempts to better interrelate theory and research consist of efforts to improve methods of testing existing theory. But instead of continuing in this vein, they thought it more profitable to devise ways of developing new rather than verifying established theory. The obstacle to their plan was the dominance of grand theory, which in their view was regarded by too many as "synonymous with theory," but basically irrelevant to their research.

Grounded theory is defined as "the discovery of theory from data systematically obtained from social research" (1967: 4). To Glaser and Strauss, generating grounded theory is "a way of arriving at theory suited to its supposed uses." They contrast their position to the generation of a set of logically deduced statements from *a priori* assumptions. In their view, "logically deduced theories based on ungrounded assumptions, such as some well-known ones on the "social system" and on "social action" can lead their followers far astray" (1967: 4).

Glaser and Strauss acknowledge the fact that when one undertakes a study, one does so from a selected sociological perspective and with a particular question or problem in mind. However, they are convinced that commitment to a pre-study theoretical orientation diminishes perceptual sensitivity. In their view too many sociologists find it difficult to "see around" their "pet theory."

What Glaser and Strauss chiefly object to, however, is not theoretically guided field research, but theory construction unguided by field research. Consequently, the concept of "grounded theory" is quite compatible with Robert Merton's much earlier concept of middle-range theory.

In the late 1940s, Merton, in reacting to Parsons' "grand" social systems theory,[1] proposed that sociological knowledge will evolve most fruitfully if it is structured by theory that strikes a middle course between all encompassing general theory on the one hand and minor everyday working hypotheses on the other. "Middle-range theory," says Merton, "is intermediate to general theories of social systems which are too remote from particular classes of social behavior, organization and change to account for what is observed and to those detailed orderly descriptions of particulars that are not generalized at all" (1967: 39).

As Alexander (1982: 13) indicates, Merton conceives of theory as something simultaneously empirically deductive and logically creative. Merton's basic definition of theory is a set of logically interrelated statements which can be empirically interpreted. However, middle-range theories "are sufficiently abstract to deal with differing spheres of social behavior and social structure, so that they transcend sheer description or empirical generalization" (Merton, 1967: 68).

Whether or not one agrees with Alexander (1982: 13) that there is a second side to Merton's statement on middle-range theory, one that supports "the . . . attempt to undercut the role of the nonempirical elements in sociological formulations." Merton is at pains to accomplish what Glaser and Strauss have in mind, that is, encouraging sociologists to collect their own data from which to derive empirically based theory. For Merton and Glaser and Strauss, there is little doubt that the ostensible aim is to challenge the dominance of a level of theorizing that is perceived to encourage separate and competing schools of thought rather than concerted effort to establish the scientific credibility of the discipline. What makes Alexander's point difficult to minimize, however, is that theory construction, in the wake of the arguments of the likes of Merton and Glaser and Strauss, has become a scarce activity. In a 1975 publication, Leon Warshay pointed out what amounted to accepted fact when he stated that:

> Probably the greater part of sociological activity does not explicitly use theory as the basis for research. Theory . . . is given lip service at best or is treated with hostility or disdain as unfounded, scientifically dangerous speculation. The role of theory is seen to follow research inductively as its product or summary rather than preceding research as its subject or organizer. (1975: 9–10)

THE ELEMENTS OF BASIC SOCIOLOGICAL THEORY

Unfortunately, and contrary to what might be expected, the ascendancy of positivism in sociology has not been associated with clarification of the ambiguous status and meaning of theory. Bernard Cohen goes so far as to say that "there is still no agreed-upon view of what a theory is" (1989: 177). The problem is the vast range of the term's applicability. As indicated elsewhere (Larson, 1967: 4), theory may refer to a single thought or all thought. It may refer to the initial phases of the thinking process or only to its results and conclusions. Theorizing includes the precise work entailed in discovering a single phenomenon, hitting upon a new analytical perspective on or a different interpretation of a subject, the discovery of a pattern or patterns among identified phenomena, and the synthesis of disparate detail that leads to the specification of a law.

To clarify the situation, some distinguish between metatheory and theory proper. To David Wagner, for example, metatheory includes "discussion about theory—about what concepts should be included, about how . . . concepts should be linked, and about how theory should be studied" (1984: 26). In his view, theories of this sort are in fact best described as orienting strategies as they indicate the phenomena of importance and how they are to be approached. To Wagner, theory proper is referred to as "unit theory." A unit theory is a set of logically interconnected statements that can be empirically interpreted—what is also referred to as axiomatic or logico-deductive theory.

Whatever differences sociologists might have as to the best way of differentiating among the essential types or stages of theorizing, most would probably agree that theory building begins with a particular frame of reference and set of concepts that identify phenomena to be studied; frames of reference and conceptual schemes enable the derivation of testable hypotheses concerning possible connections among relevant phenomena. And perhaps a majority would also agree that the goal, at least ideally, is the construction of axiomatic or logico-deductive theory.

FRAMES OF REFERENCE AND CONCEPTUAL SCHEMES

Empirically oriented theory, as any sort of systematic thinking, must begin by focusing on some things rather than others and from a certain angle. One cannot examine something of any complexity from all possible angles at once. The multifaceted character of human behavior, for example, requires analysis from a variety of viewpoints. Viewpoints, perspectives, or frames of reference differentiate the pursuits of the several sciences and are vital to the scientific process.

Identification of a unique frame of reference and set of basic concepts to study a problem of concern are inextricably intertwined. A frame of reference generates concepts and a concept may generate a frame of reference. And the articulation of one frame of reference may provoke the development of another, particularly one which reverses the visual angle. For example, the natural opposite of looking at behavior from "the inside out," or from the vantage point of the acting individual toward the world, is to look at it "from the outside on or in," or from a view emphasizing the effects of externally imposed norms, sanctions, and values. The individual oriented "internal" perspective is generally referred to in sociology as symbolic interactionism. The group oriented "external" perspective may be referred to as structuralism or structural-functionalism. Both frames of reference have pure and applied aspects, and the following sections review major varieties of each in preparation for applied interpretations in following chapters. Exemplary structural perspectives and conceptual schemes were developed by Karl Marx (1818–1883) and David Emile Durkheim (1858–1917). Because Marx's theory antedates Durkheim's, his will be discussed first.

Structural Perspectives and Conceptual Schemes

According to Marx,

> In the social production of their life, men enter into definite relations that are indispensable and independent of their will, relations of production which correspond to a definite stage of development of their material productive forces. The sum total of these relations of production constitutes the economic structure of society, the real foundation, on which rises a legal and political superstructure and to which correspond definite forms of social consciousness. The mode of production of material life conditions the social, political and intellectual life process in general. *It is not the consciousness of men that determines their being, but, on the contrary, their social being that determines their consciousness.* (Freedman, 1968: 126)

The statement contains several terms that are key components of Marx's conceptual scheme: "mode of production," "relations of production," "productive forces," and "social consciousness." In the concluding sentence, which is one of, if not the earliest concise expressions of the sociological frame of reference, Marx tells us that the concepts are to be interpreted from a vantage point in which "consciousness" is determined by "social being." That is, the origin of our self awareness is to be traced to group life and social interaction. Specifically, and because he wished to understand how and when capitalism might be overthrown, Marx is interested in a particular kind of consciousness, that is, awareness of one's revolutionary social class affiliation. Because he wrote at a time when people routinely worked twelve or more hours a day at least six days a week, "social being" refers to those similarly situated workers in the division of labor with whom one regularly interacts and shares common political and economic interests.

To study the relationship between social being and consciousness, Marx developed a conceptual scheme that he thought pinpointed the variables to analyze within a given economic system or mode of production. Any mode of production has two essential parts—forces of production and relations of production. The forces of production, that is, the driving force behind the production of the essential goods meeting basic human needs, are people and technology. The relations of production are the various divisions or levels within the division of labor—management and labor and all the various subdivisions within and between each. Marx posits that changes in the forces of production lead to conflict with existing relations of production. People implementing technology discover new methods of production that challenge established practice. As Maurice Cornforth explains it,

> For example, . . . the development of manufacture—and, we should add, the development also of new techniques in agriculture—required and led to the employment of wage-labor. Only with capitalist relations could the newly-developed forces of production be more fully employed. But the existing feudal relations, which tied the laborer to the land and to the service of his lord, were a barrier to the development of the new productive forces. Hence, these relations, within which production had once flourished, now began to act as a fetter. A contradiction arose between the old production relations and new productive forces. (1971: 60)

Contradictions lead to questions and questions may lead to conflict between defenders of the status quo and their challengers. For example, a contradiction that developed in capitalist society is the persistence of extensive poverty despite the ability to produce more than enough to satisfy the basic needs of all citizens. Different views on the proper public response to the problem have long generated heated debate and a variety of programs. But the persistence of poverty exposes a larger contradiction—that between the nation's political ideals and its economic realities. All citizens are alleged to be politically equal, but because of economic inequality some have significantly more political influence than others. The preoccupation of the Marxist is how and when such contradictions expand and combine with others to polarize a population to the extent of causing a revolution.

To Marx, the social problem of the day was economic exploitation, the domination of the working-class, or proletariat, by the capitalists, or bourgeoisie. Exploitation has a devastating personal effect, indicated by its alienation of workers from their work and themselves. As Marx sees it,

> the worker is related to the product of his labor as to an alien object. For on this premise it is clear that the more the worker spends himself, the more powerful

the alien objective world becomes he creates over-against himself, the poorer he himself—his inner world—becomes, the less belongs to him as his own. . . . [L]abor is external to the worker, i.e., it does not belong to his essential being; that in his work, therefore, he does not affirm himself but denies himself, does not feel content but unhappy, does not develop freely his physical and mental energy but mortifies his body and ruins his mind. The worker therefore only feels himself outside his work, and in his work feels outside himself. He is at home when he is not working, and when he is working he is not at home. (Freedman, 1968: 69, 71)

Because a reading of social history indicated that social class conflict was the essential means to the elimination of exploitation and its alienating effects, Marx sought to specify how and when the proletariat would come to realize that its historical mission is to overthrow the bourgeoisie and found an advanced social order that would elevate work to a self-selected, self-satisfying activity—initially socialism and eventually communism. To identify and study relevant phenomena, Marx prescribes an analytical perspective based on social determinism, or the premise that what people value and do are a product of interaction with group members similarly situated in society. Emile Durkheim developed virtually the same frame of reference, but for the study of the diametrically opposite problem.

As a citizen of France—a country still reeling from the effects of revolution—Durkheim was obsessed with the nature of social order or with what binds people together to promote the day-to-day order apparent in any civilization. Following the lead of predecessors such as Comte, Durkheim postulates that social bonding is the product of social facts. Social facts are defined as all ways of thinking, acting, and feeling that are externally imposed and, therefore, coercive. Of course, when doing the expected thing, one is less likely to feel coerced. Social facts, then, are the likes of language, norms, roles, values, and the entire range of social institutions that antedate our existence and that one becomes exposed to in the lifelong process of socialization.

Durkheim's first rule for the observation of social facts is to treat them as "things," that is, to regard them as in the nature of empirically verifiable entities. "To treat phenomena as things," he says, "is to treat them as data which provide the starting point for science" (Thompson, 1985: 74).

Durkheim's basic rule for the causal analysis of social facts identifies his version of the sociological perspective. "The determining cause of a social fact," says Durkheim, "must be sought among antecedent social facts, and not among the states of individual consciousness" (Thompson, 1985: 86). The sociologist is to study human behavior from a vantage point that is quite independent of intrasomatic factors, psychological factors most of all. Social facts, Durkheim asserts, exist independently of their individual manifestations. "It may be objected," he says, "that a phenomenon can only be collective if it is common to all members of the society, or at the very least, to a majority. . . . This is certainly so, but if it is general it is because it is collective. . . . It is a group condition. . . . It is found in each part because it is in the whole rather than it being in the whole because it is in the parts" (Thompson, 1985: 71).

Social facts are not directly observable. As Durkheim states, "social solidarity is a completely moral phenomenon which, taken by itself, does not lend itself to exact observation nor indeed to measurement. . . . [W]e must substitute for this internal fact which escapes us an external index which symbolizes it and study the former in the light of the latter" (1933: 64). Social facts are to be discerned by indications of their coerciveness—for example, the application of negative sanctions, or punishment and correction for the violation of group norms. Negative sanctions range from some form of simple disapproval for failing to observe some form of social etiquette—a frown from one's spouse for making what is perceived as a sexist comment—to court-ordered execution for commission of a heinous crime.

Durkheim initially applied his social fact frame of reference to the analysis of the historical development of the division of labor in society. He sees human society as having evolved two types of social solidarity. The earliest type is mechanical solidarity. In the small roving bands of hunters and gatherers of humankind's distant past, the division of labor was slight. What one man or woman did was pretty much what all other men and women did. In such a group, what binds people together is their similarity and homogeneity.

The second type is referred to as organic solidarity. This type of social cohesion stems from the interdependence created by the complex division of labor characteristic of life in the large cities of the industrial era. What binds people together in the modern metropolis is not their similarity but their dissimilarity. No one is entirely self sufficient. Virtually everyone is dependent on innumerable others for the provision of essential goods and services.

Durkheim assumes that both forms of social solidarity are expressions of a collective conscience—the beliefs and sentiments common to societal members. Violations of the collective conscience provoke sanctions indicative of a breech of one type of solidarity or the other. Application of repressive or penal sanctions indicate a threat to the integrity of mechanical solidarity. An offense against one is an offense against all. Where organic solidarity is dominant, the division of labor is extensive and an offense against one is not necessarily an offense against anyone else. In "post-modern," "post-industrial" society, civil cases vastly outnumber criminal offenses. Therefore, the most evident sanctions are restitutive rather than repressive. "Damage-interests," says Durkheim, "have no penal character; they are only a means of reviewing the past in order to reinstate it, as far as possible, to its normal form" (1933: 111). If someone damages our automobile, we want the damage repaired. Punishing the offender is secondary.

Unlike Marx, who viewed the history of human society as the emergence of a series of modes of production caused by social class conflict, Durkheim simply incorporated all societies—past and present—in a continuum, with mechanical solidarity at one pole and organic solidarity at the other. He did not foresee the emergence of a third qualitatively unique type of solidarity. Instead, he suggests that social solidarity becomes increasingly problematic with the inevitable advancement of a complex division of labor. His goal is to ensure care for the maintenance of an essential degree of mechanical solidarity to offset growing impersonality and social isolation. To Durkheim, then, social bonding is an end in itself, not a means to engage in class conflict to effect envisioned radical social change or anything else.

Durkheim devised a number of conceptual distinctions to specify the unique phenomenal realm of the science of society. A distinction that inspired the development of a unique frame of reference was one Durkheim made between the identification of the causes of social facts as opposed to their functions.

It is Durkheim's position that "when one undertakes to explain a social phenomenon, one must study separately the efficient cause which produces it and the function it fulfills" (1985: 84). The efficient cause of a social fact would be an immediately preceding social fact—for example, an abrupt loss of important social bonding preceding suicide. The function of a social fact is defined as the contribution it makes to the social order of which it is a part. The seemingly unlikely subject of crime was analyzed to make the point.

Crime, for very good reasons, is generally regarded as something pathological rather than normal. However, because crime is a general feature of human society, might it not have certain positive functions, that is, in some way contribute to social health? Durkheim presumes that a healthy society is one open to change and continuous adaptation to innovation. He thinks positive social change impossible without individual freedom and a healthy degree of toleration for social deviancy. "In order that the originality of the idealist whose dreams transcend his century may find expression," says Durkheim, "it is necessary that the originality of the criminal . . . shall also be possible" (1938: 71).

But crime per se has positive social benefits. When people identify and punish the criminal, they reinforce common norms and remind one another of the limits of acceptable behavior. In Durkheim's words, "the social reaction which constitutes punishment is due to the intensity of the collective sentiments that the crime offends. . . . [I]ts useful function is to maintain these sentiments at the same degree of intensity, for they would soon diminish if the offenses committed against them went unpunished" (1985: 85).

Social fact functions are not to be construed as ends or purposes. Durkheim emphasizes that he chose the term function over purpose because it was apparent to him that the existence of social facts is independent of their uses or social consequences. Thus, the functions of a social fact are not the causes of a social fact. As Durkheim put it,

> Showing how a fact is useful does not explain how it arose nor how it is what it is. The uses which it serves presuppose specific properties which characterize it but do not create them. Our need for things cannot give them a specific nature

and, consequently, that need cannot produce them from nothing and endow them with existence (1985: 84).

As indicated above, Durkheim clearly differentiated between functional and causal analysis. As he saw it, the functional perspective aided the identification of social facts and assessment of their role and importance in the whole of which they are a part. As Menzies puts it, "functionalism works by showing that activities which, seen in isolation, do not make sense do make sense in the context of the social system in which they occur" (1982: 9). In distinguishing between the causes and functions of social facts Durkheim showed that his concerns were both pure and applied. "For what good is it to strive after a knowledge of reality," he said, "if the knowledge we acquire cannot serve us in our lives" (1982: 85). He aimed not only to place sociology on a sound theoretical footing, but also to identify how society's several components interrelate to effect social organization. When general social fact, or functional configurations have been specified, the sociologist would be in a position to recommend changes with predictably positive benefits. Unfortunately, at least in terms of our awareness of the details of his hopes for humankind via social meliorism, Durkheim did not expatiate on the applied side of his thinking.

Interestingly, Talcott Parsons (1902–1979), the one most responsible for elaborating on Durkheim's concept of functional analysis, was motivated to develop a more general or pure than applied theoretical orientation. Parsons thought of theory as a term used to describe a number of things sharing "only the element of generalized conceptualization." He referred to his own "generalized conceptualization" as a system to differentiate it from "discrete theories" concerning "particularly phenomena or classes of them." To Parsons, a theoretical system "is a body of logically interdependent generalized concepts of empirical reference" (1954: 12).

He views theory as having two general purposes: to enable systematic description, and analysis. Prerequisite to detailed analysis is identification and description of relevant structural phenomena by means of a frame of reference or "the most general framework of categories in terms of which empirical scientific work makes sense" (1954: 214). He advocates the study, of social phenomena within a social systems frame of reference. As Edward Devereux points out, Parsons defines a social system as two or more people "occupying differentiated statuses or positions and performing differentiated roles, some organized pattern governing the relationships of members and describing their rights and obligations with respect to one another, and some set of common norms, or values, together with various types of shared cultural objects and symbols" (Devereux, 1961: 39).

The essential structures of any social system are any set of relations among two or more individuals that can be empirically demonstrated to endure. Functions are those effects of social structures that either contribute toward or detract from the continuation of a given social system. As Parsons summarizes his theoretical orientation,

> The logical type of generalized theoretical system under discussion may thus be
> called a "structural-functional system." . . . It consists of the generalized categories
> necessary for an adequate description of states of an empirical system. . . . One of
> the prime functions of system on this level is to ensure completeness, to make it
> methodically impossible to overlook anything important, and thus explicitly to
> describe all essential structural elements and relations of the system. (1975: 218)

The structural-functional perspective as introduced by Parsons and elaborated on by Merton (1949) was dominant in American sociology from roughly 1945 to the mid-1960s. Toward the end of the 1950s, however, critical reaction to the prevailing one-sided emphasis on the study of social order began to be challenged, particularly by Marxist oriented scholars such as Ralf Dahrendorf.

Dahrendorf advocated adoption of a coercion theory of society to complement the structural-functional or integration perspective. Thus, whereas integration theorists conceive of "social structure in terms of functionally integrated system held in equilibrium by certain patterned and recurrent processes," coercion theorists view "social structure as a form of organization held together by force and constraint. . . . For sociological analysis, society is Janus-headed, and its two faces are equivalent aspects of the same reality" (1959: 159). Not long after Dahrendorf presented his neo-Marxist conflict theory, another Marxist influenced perspective—critical theory—began to attract considerable attention. Critical theory describes the viewpoint espoused by members of the Frankfurt school of thought.

The Frankfurt school emerged in Weimar Germany. A Marxist oriented but independent group of intellectuals and scholars obtained private funding to establish an Institute for Social Research at the University of Frankfurt in 1924. Because its members were mainly Jewish, the Nazis rise to power impelled the institute to relocate to Columbia University in New York City in 1934. Major figures in the Frankfurt school included the institute's first director, Max Horkheimer (1895-1973),[2] Theodor Adorno (1903-1969),[3] and Herbert Marcuse (1898-1979).[4]

What united the three was reliance on Hegelian dialectical thinking, most of all the antithetical or negative phase. Indeed, their thought frame has been described as "negative dialectics."[5] Due to factors such as the excesses of the Stalinist regime in Russia, the three came to share an abiding distrust of theoretical syntheses such as Marx's because of their tendency to become dogmas, or tools for the domination rather than emancipation of humankind. They determined to react critically to any thesis or synthesis (whether in the form of a mode of production such as socialism or capitalism, a social theory such as Marx's, or a philosophy of science such as positivism) that inhibited either individual or intellectual initiative and creativity.

The major living product of the Frankfurt school is Jürgen Habermas, who has been described as "the most influential thinker in Germany today."[6] He joined the Institute for Social Research after its return to Germany following

World War II. His work is much too complex and far-ranging to analyze here, but it can be said that his aims are compatible with his Frankfurt school predecessors, that is, the perpetuation of a critical mode of thinking and the development of emancipatory social theory.

Recently, Habermas has turned his attention to the study of symbolic interaction and language. As John Thompson and David Held indicate, "Habermas's concern with language stems both from its centrality in the formation of consciousness and from its capacity to provide a foundation for critique" (1982: 8). Furthermore, they add, "language is the medium of ideology *qua* systematically distorted communication; and . . . to make sense of the notion of systematically distorted communication, one must have some idea of what rational or non-distorted communication would be" (1982: 8). Habermas refers to this Work as "a theory of communicative action or interaction." For insight, he has scanned the contributions of the symbolic interactionists.

Symbolic Interactionist Views and Conceptual Schemes

Among the first and most influential sociologists to stress the symbolic element in interaction was George Herbert Mead (1863–1931). In Mead's View, the unit of behavioral analysis is "a social act." A social act is interaction between two or more individuals who are in some way mutually obligated; that is, their relationship is part of an on-going pattern. Mead emphasized language as the basis of social interaction, and *gestures* as the essential building blocks of language. Gestures, says Mead, are "any part of a social act which stands for, or is a sign of, those parts of the social act yet to occur" (Stryker, 1964: 109). He sees gestures as either preparatory indications of acts to come or expressive means of releasing tension.

Enduring gestures may become "significant symbols," those known by all societal members. They are prerequisite to intellectual activity. As Mead put it, "only in terms of gestures as significant symbols is the existence of mind or intelligence possible; for only in terms of gestures which are significant symbols can thinking . . . take place" (1934: 7).

But it was not the thinking process or intellectual endeavors per se that chiefly interested Mead. For him and many others, the subject of particular concern was the origin and nature of the rational, self-aware adult, something that experience taught them should not be taken for granted. Self-awareness, they assumed, is an outgrowth of the socialization process, the interaction of parent or surrogate parent and child.

A contemporary of Mead's, Charles H. Cooley (1864–1929), stressed the interpretive, creative, and individualistic nature of self awareness. For him, "the imaginations which people have of one another are the solid facts of society, and that to observe and interpret these must be a chief aim of sociology" (1902: 121–122). To Cooley, the self is a looking-glass image, a three step interpretation of who one is through the eyes of others. Thus, we imagine how we appear to others, how they judge us, and we react with feelings of "pride or mortification."

As Mead put it, and consistent with Cooley's viewpoint, the self has the unique quality of being an object to itself. Put another way, mature, self-reliant adults are those capable of appropriately timed and conceived behavior and interaction.

In Mead's scheme, self-growth occurs in three stages. It begins with *imitation,* the aping of the expressions and mannerisms of "significant others." Imitation is followed by the *play stage*, a point when the child plays a variety of roles. The play stage leads to the *game stage,* a point when one is able to synchronize behavior in conformity to "the generalized other," or group expectations. At the game stage, one speaks of *role taking* rather than role playing. The individual learns to anticipate what is expected and to do the right thing at the right time and place.

Focusing on the latter element, one of Mead's students, William I. Thomas (1863-1947), and a colleague, Florian Znaniecki (1882-1968), developed what they refer to as the "situational" frame of reference.

In the opening volume of their five volume work, *The Polish Peasant in Europe and America* (1918), Thomas and Znaniecki outline their theoretical orientation. They observe the omnipresence of two problems confronting the student of human interaction: (1) the dependence of the individual on social organization and culture, and (2) the dependence of social organization and culture on the individual. Hence, two types of data must be taken into account: (1) *values,* or "objective" socio-cultural elements, and (2) *attitudes,* or "subjective" individual factors. Values include both material items—for example, certain foodstuffs and clothing—as well as immaterial factors, such as honesty and thoughtfulness.

The study of attitudes is the particular province of social psychology. Sociology is assigned the task of studying values, especially those encompassed within Durkheim's concept of social facts (norms, laws, social institutions). Both social psychology and sociology are viewed as branches of social theory. The aim of social theory is to isolate the causes of social change, which they refer to as the process of becoming.

The process of becoming is to be studied by means of a situational perspective. Thomas and Znaniecki are convinced that behavior must be studied where and when it occurs, not in contrived or imagined circumstances. Behavioral situations are thought of as the closest approximation to a laboratory setting available to the behavioral scientist.

Situations are viewed as having three basic components: objective values, the subjective attitudes of the individuals present, and the individual's "definition of the situation." According to Thomas, "if men define situations as real, they are real in their consequences" (1927: 72). The classroom, for example, is a behavioral situation. It contains certain objective values—blackboards, chalk, erasers, desks, and so on. The student brings to the classroom certain attitudes, perhaps a certain level of fear and insecurity. When first entering a college or university classroom, a student may have a sense of uneasiness that leads to a search for something familiar and comforting, a vacant chair in a certain position, a friend or acquaintance to sit next to.

In contrast to Durkheim who emphasized that the determining cause of a social fact should be sought among the social facts preceding it rather than the states of individual consciousness, Thomas and Znaniecki emphasized that "the cause of a social or an individual phenomenon is never another social or individual phenomenon alone, but always a combination of a social and an individual phenomenon" (1927: 44).

Erving Goffman's (1922–1982) dramaturgical viewpoint is an influential variation of Thomas's and Znaniecki's situational perspective. According to Goffman, "all the world is not, of course, a stage, but the crucial ways in which it isn't are not easy to specify" (1959: 72).

One of Goffman's particular interests was how people "manage impressions" to accomplish their purposes. Despite the negative implications of the idea, he thought it important to acknowledge the ambiguous and problematical nature of communication. Everyday acts may or may not be sincere or honest, and it is often difficult to differentiate the sincere from the insincere. One's assessment of the behavior of another is largely dependent on indicators (gestures, mannerisms) of consistency coupled with a sincere or contrived act. As Goffman saw it, "these dichotomous conceptions are by way of being the ideology of honest performers, providing strength to the show they put on, but a poor analysis of it" (1959: 72). The con artist, in other words, may be more adept at manipulating the symbols of integrity and sincerity than the honest person. But even the honest may act to influence others to do what they might not have a mind or wish to do.

To analyze impression management, Goffman developed a conceptual scheme composed of the following terms: *performance, front, setting, appearance,* and *manner.* A performance is anything done by an actor that may influence others. Repeated performances are routines. That part of an actor's performance that enables others to put it in context is a front. The "expressive equipment" in a situation—"props" such as chairs, desks, rugs, and so on—represent the setting. The elements that compose an actor's front indicate his or her appearance. Manner describes the actor's interpretation of a role.

From Goffman's vantage point, one must be prepared to interpret and study role behavior, to work at differentiating its different possible meanings by means of the available symbolic evidence as the true motives of others are not directly accessible. As he put it,

> to undercover fully the factual nature of the situation, it would be necessary for the individual to know all the relevant social data about others. . . . Full information of this order is rarely available. . . . In short, since the reality that the individual is concerned with is unperceivable at the moment, appearances must be relied upon in its stead. (1959: 240)

Recent Developments

In recent years, sociology has been influenced by a variety of philosophical perspectives—in particular, hermeneutics, semiotics, structuralism and post-structuralism, and structuration theory. With the exception of structuration theory, the others were initiated by non-sociologists. While this is not the place to dissect and comparatively analyze each of these complex viewpoints (basic hermeneutics is an important part of the discussion in Chapter 4), it is important to note some of their similarities in light of the above discussion. A common theme in recently sociologically relevant philosophical perspectives is an effort to analyze human behavior by means of a frame of reference taking into account both the objective or structural and the subjective or individual realms.

Generally, individuals and society, "actors" and social structures, are thought of as mutually influencing elements in a constantly changing social process. Some perspectives—structuralism (see Piaget, 1970; Levi-Strauss, 1963), post-structuralism (see Chapter 4 in Giddens, 1987) and semiotics most of all—emphasize the mediating role of shared symbolic means of expression, perception and communication. Of the above, semiotics, a perspective developed within the field of linguistics, is the outstanding example. Citing Umberto Eco (1976) as her source, Kaja Silverman states that the semiotic field embraces "zoology, olfactory signs, tactile communication, paralinguistics, medicine, kinesics and proxemics, musical codes, formalized languages, natural languages, visual communication, systems of objects, plot structures, text theory, cultural codes, aesthetic texts, mass communication, and rhetoric" (1983: 5).

Sociologist Peter Manning defines semiotics as the science of signs. The concept signs denotes all those physical gestures, oral and written expressions, that have meaning to oneself and others. As a form of sociological analysis semiotics seeks to identify the implicit and explicit codes and rules that structure symbolic modes of expression and pattern human interaction. According to Manning, "sociology can be seen as a subfield of semiotics." As he sees it,

> Social practices, indicated by signs, are like language bits . . . , connected as they are and subject, therefore, to the same kinds of analytic techniques. The aim of semiotic analysis is not mere description, but rather to uncover or discover the systems that the parts constitute. . . . The purpose is to identify the elements of a system, and the system of which they are parts, in order to produce explanations of those constraints in formal and differentiated terms. (1987: 34)

Manning sees semiotics as lending itself to qualitative methodological application and a more practical understanding of important subjects such as the meaning of the social policy statements and formulations of political influentials. Through awareness of the codes and rules of symbolic expression and communication, one is in a position to develop testable theoretical hypotheses concerning human behavior, likely interpretations of oral and written statements, and a host of other important subjects.

Anthony Giddens' structuration theory includes a unique interpretation of the source and nature of the means of communication. He contends that structuralism and the critical movement that it provoked called post-structuralism are "dead traditions of thought." "Notwithstanding the promise they held in the fresh bloom of youth," he says, "they have ultimately failed to generate the revolution in philosophical understanding and social theory which once was their pledge" (1987: 73). But, says Giddens, the two were based on certain common assumptions and points of departure relevant to issues important in contemporary sociology, in particular "the thesis that linguistics (or more accurately, certain aspects of particular versions of linguistics) are of key importance to philosophy and social theory as a whole" (1987: 74).

Giddens' structuration concept is based on a view of social structure as something subject to continuous change and development. He stresses the "duality of structure," the idea that social facts both constrain and enable social interaction. "According to the notion of the duality of structure," says Giddens, "rules and resources are drawn upon by actors in the production of interaction, but are thereby also reconstituted through social interaction" (1979: 71). Individuals may be restricted by social facts or rules but they also shape and change their meaning as they employ them in everyday life. Linguistic rules are of particular importance in Giddens' scheme. As he emphasizes,

> To understand a sentence which a speaker utters means knowing an enormous range of rules and strategies of a syntactical and semantical kind, which are not contained within the speech act. . . . It is such a notion of structure (as an absent totality) which I hold to be important as a concept for the social sciences as a whole and basic to the notion of duality of structure. (1987: 61)

Basic to Giddens' view of the actor as a dynamic interpreter and shaper of social structure is the concept of power. He insists that social theory must include not only structural analyses of modes of communication and interaction but also examination of the nature of "power transactions." "Power is expressed," he says, "in the capabilities of actors to make certain 'accounts count' and to enact or resist sanctioning processes; but these capabilities draw upon modes of domination structured into social systems" (1979: 83). As is evident, the lessons of both structuralists such as Marx and Durkheim as well as symbolic interactionists such as Mead, Thomas, and Znaniecki are integral to Giddens' structuration theory. It is a theory in development and one likely to attract greater future attention.

Section Summary

The above, then, are among the most basic structural and symbolic interactionist frames of reference and conceptual schemes in mainstream sociology. Frames of reference and conceptual schemes have more than one use. Some of those discussed above are more useful for causal or explanatory analysis and others for heuristic purposes. The functional perspective, for example, is primarily a heuristic device, a way to discover something unique about society and the operation of its structural components. Its application sensitizes the observer to the value and importance of social facts that might otherwise be missed or ignored.

Causally relevant frames of reference and conceptual schemes have the same essential utility as a highway map. A highway map is obtained in order to solve a problem—for example, how to get from one place to another in a logical and predictable manner. The map delimits the area of concern and specifies the relevant categories or terms of interest (towns, cities, miles and average driving time between places, alternative routes, airport locations, railroad routes, and so on). Frames of reference and conceptual schemes provide a means of deriving testable assumptions or hypotheses. With a map and its conceptual scheme, one may hypothesize that if leaving a certain place at a certain time, one can expect to arrive at a given destination at an approximate time. Similarly, with a sociological perspective and related concepts, such as Durkheim's notions of mechanical and organic solidarity, one may hypothesize connections between type of social bond and the prevalence of various forms of social deviancy and crime. The essential point here is that a frame of reference and a conceptual scheme are prerequisite to systematic scientific analysis and experimentation.

FROM HUNCHES TO AXIOMS

Testable ideas quite often begin with a hunch, an intuitive impression or an inkling about the relationship between two or more variables (quantities that can have more than one value, for example, city size). A hypothesis may be nothing more than the formalization of a hunch by means of a written statement or other symbolic means. Following another lead suggested by Durkheim, one might, for example, sense a connection between size of place and the rate of crime. Stated as an hypothesis, the hunch might read: the larger the city, the higher the crime rate. As it happens, the hypothesis has been tested and found valid in some instances but not others.[7] When aggregate data are examined, the hypothesized relationship is invariably confirmed. But the rank order correlation between city size and crime rate can be so slight as to be trivial. Using 1980 data, for example, the rank order correlation between population size and crime rate for America's twenty largest metropolitan areas is .31. If one were to assume the same rank order in crime rate as city size for these twenty places, one would be wrong 69 percent of the time.

Hypotheses that cannot be confirmed when analyzed from different vantage points have limited applicability. A major goal in science is to discover those that have the broadest, most general application. Certain generally relevant hypotheses may be referred to as propositions or laws and used as major premises in logically deductive theory. Theory building in this vein is commonly referred to as the "covering law" model of explanation or axiomatic theory (see, for example, Homans, 1982: 286).

Axiomatic or Logical-Deductive Theory

Bernard Cohen defines logical-deductive theory as "a set of interrelated universal statements, some of which are definitions and some of which are relationships assumed to be true, together with a syntax, a set of rules for manipulating the statements to arrive at new statements" (1989: 178). By universal statements, Cohen refers to propositions that have the potential of general relevance. The syntactical model for this type of theory is the tripart Aristotelian syllogism:

$$\text{If } A = B$$
$$\text{and } B = C$$
$$\text{then } A = C$$

The three statements constitute a major premise, a minor premise, and a conclusion. They connect any three possible referents by means of the rule that things equal to the same thing are equal to each other. If one accepts the rule and the validity of the major and minor premise, the conclusion must follow. Knowledge of some relationships makes others logically possible.

As Hans Zetterberg indicated some years ago, the advantage of axiomatic theory for social research is that it offers a "parsimonious summary of anticipated or actual research findings" (1955: 534). Suppose, following Durkheim, one is interested in the bearing of group size on the amount of deviancy. Other variables one may be aware of that must be considered include extent of the division of labor and degree of social cohesion. From the formula $\frac{N(N-1)}{2}$, we know that there are six possible relationships among the four variables. However, available research may indicate that only the following three have been established: (1) the larger the group, the greater the division of labor, (2) the less the social cohesion, the greater the amount of deviancy, and (3) the larger the group, the greater the amount of deviancy.

To show how the remaining three possibilities may be deduced from these three, let A stand for group size, B for the division of labor, C for social cohesion, and D for deviancy. Interpreting the three known relationships as A=B, C=D, and A=D, and assuming that things equal to the same thing are equal to each other, then the following deductions may be made:

(4)	if A=B	(5)	If A=D	(6)	If B=D
	and A=D		and C=D		and C=D
	then B=D		then A=C		then B=C

Thus, the fourth possibility is, the greater the division of labor, the greater the amount of deviancy; the fifth, the larger the group, the less the social cohesion; and the sixth, the greater the division of labor, the less the social cohesion. Zetterberg would refer to the first three statements as the theory's postulates and the three derived statements as its theorems. Of course, the three deduced statements may or may not be new testable hypotheses. They may be newly discovered by oneself, but an established part of the research agenda of someone whose work we are not aware of. The best one can do is peruse the relevant literature and determine to the best of one's ability what may be known about them.

In any event, the validity of the entire theory depends on how well each of the six meets the test of empirical examination. If any one is not upheld, the validity of all six may be in doubt. Still, the aim should be to add as many new variables to the scheme as seem relevant in order to push the theory to its limits. It makes sense to explain as much as possible with an existing theory before bothering to invent a new one.

Of course, axiomatic theories may be constructed at such a high level of abstraction as to virtually preclude the possibility of validation or invalidation by generally accepted empirical standards. Marx's theory of revolutionary social change by means of social class conflict is a case in point. While there is much that is debatable in Marx's theory, it is indisputable that Marx employed deductive logic in organizing ideas and drawing conclusions. The theory is quite susceptible to axiomatic interpretation such as that presented in Figure 2-1.

However logical, the theory is difficult to assess empirically because the variables are difficult to specify. What are the real world entities that compose the forces of production, the relations of production, and the other several variables that compose the conceptual scheme? Following their master's lead, Marxists are inclined to judge efforts to quantify his ideas or concepts as vulgarizations of his theory. One might assume, for example, that a measured change in the forces of production should, by the terms of the theory, lead to a measurable change in ideas relevant to class consciousness. However, according to Marxist scholar Maurice Cornforth this is an example of vulgar Marxism because "while it is true that there exists a certain correspondence between ideas and institutions on the one hand, and forces of production on the other, it is not true that the former can ever be explained directly from the latter" (1971: 91). Why not? Because when "employing their forces of production people enter into relations of production, and it is on the basis of the relations of production that they create their ideas and institutions" (1971: 91). If this is true, the deterministic or causal foundation of the theory, that which makes it compelling, is undermined. Of course, as in the case of any theorist, what Marx thought or wished is not the last word in the matter. If his theory is more than a private possession or select philosophy, if it is to be scientifically meaningful, it must be subjected to empirical and independent assessment. "Vulgarization" is the necessary fate of any conventionally regarded scientific theory, regardless of its level of abstraction, alleged uniqueness, or the personal wishes of its creator or defenders. The problem is that Marx considered his theory to be based on a unique approach, the dialectical method, and not susceptible to appraisal by the canons of conventional empirical science.

- **FIGURE 2-1**

An Axiomatic Interpretation of Marx's Theory of Revolutionary Social Change

I   (a) Changes in the forces of production are prerequisite to changes in the relations of production

     (b) Changes in the relations of production are prerequisite to changes in attitudes & values

     (c) Therefore, changes in the forces of production arc prerequisite to changes in attitudes & values

II   (a) Changes in the forces of production are prerequisite to changes in attitudes & values

     (b) Changes in attitudes & values are prerequisite to the rise of revolutionary class consciousness

     (c) Therefore, changes in the forces of production are prerequisite to the rise of revolutionary class consciousness

III   (a) Changes in the forces of production are prerequisite to the rise of revolutionary class consciousness

     (b) The rise of revolutionary class consciousness is prerequisite to the rise of revolutionary class conflict

     (c) Therefore, changes in the forces of production are prerequisite to the rise of revolutionary class conflict

IV   (a) Changes in the forces of production are prerequisite to the rise of revolutionary class conflict

     (b) The rise of revolutionary class conflict is prerequisite to the rise of revolutionary social change

     (c) Therefore, changes in the forces of production are prerequisite to the rise of revolutionary social change

V   (a) Changes in the capitalistic forces of production are prerequisite to the rise of revolutionary social change

     (b) Revolutionary social change is prerequisite to the rise of socialism

     (c) Therefore, changes in the capitalistic forces of production are prerequisite to the rise of socialism

VI   (a) Changes in the capitalistic forces of production are prerequisite to the rise of socialism

     (b) The rise of socialism is prerequisite to the rise of communism

     (c) Therefore, changes in the capitalistic forces of production are prerequisite to the rise of communism

Exactly how his theory might be tested and either confirmed or denied Marx did not say. As Robert Heilbroner notes, what is lacking in Marx's theory is

> a rule for separating valid procedures from invalid ones; a test, however difficult to achieve in fact, that would enable us to discard some dialectical results as false. The dialectical approach . . . leaves us with no means of appraising its results other than by the tests of conventional science, or those of ordinary logic. (1980: 49-50)

To briefly summarize, it is clear, as Zetterberg indicates, that axiomatic theory is a convenient way of systematically organizing thought and uncovering possibly new research leads from available data. Nonetheless, it is in fact a seldom employed research tool. Its drawback is the difficulty of precisely measuring the connection between specified variables. It is one thing to postulate a relationship between variable A and variable B; it is another to exactly quantify what it may be. Instead of being able to measure precise quantities of social facts in relation to each other, the social scientist must rely on statistical interpretations. The use of statistical methods, random sampling, correlation techniques, significance testing, and so on, are necessary because social scientists are not able to manipulate people and behavior under controlled experimental conditions. And even if they could, there are good reasons to believe that the scientific results would be no less difficult to assess. Experimentation entails a certain amount of distortion, influencing behavior in "unnatural ways," something difficult to control for or eliminate in the complex, constantly changing phenomenon that is human interaction.

The failure to resolve the measurement problem limits the possibilities of axiomatic theory. Until hypotheses can be assumed to be verifiable and regarded as axiomatic, social scientists are loathed to express their knowledge in such a format. Axiomatic theory remains an ideal whose time has not and may not come. If it cannot be realized, the possibilities of systematically accumulated knowledge are highly limited. Scientific facts do not simply add up, or automatically accumulate; they must be synthesized in an agreed upon format and by means of accepted rules whose interpretation can be independently validated. Until a methodological breakthrough occurs or a substitute is found, axiomatic theory remains the most promising synthesizing device available.

One can, of course, promote axiomatic theorizing by severing its ties to empiricism, or the necessity of solving "the measurement problem." A current example is "analytical theory." Among its advocates is Jonathan Turner, who calls for a rejection of prevailing empirical assumptions regarding theory building and a return to a major tenet of Auguste Comte's positive philosophy. As Turner points out, Comte advocates a science of society whose goal is the identification of societal laws. In Comte's view, the identification of laws is independent of the specification of causes. Indeed, to Comte, the search for the causes of societal phenomena is a fruitless endeavor. "Our business," says Comte, "is—seeing how vain is any research into what are called *Causes* . . .—

to pursue an accurate discovery of [natural] Laws, with a view to reducing them to the smallest possible number" (Turner, 1987: 157). To Turner it is clear that Comte emphasizes the primacy of theory, a conception of theory as an independent endeavor. Accordingly, Turner believes that sociological theory should "loosen the requirements of logical positivism." His conception of sociological theory, which he says is shared by most analytical theorists, is as follows:

> we can develop abstract laws of invariant properties of the universe, but such laws will need to be supplemented by scenarios (models, descriptions, analogies) of the underlying processes of these properties. Moreover, explanation is in most cases not going to involve precise predictions and deductions, primarily because experimental controls are not possible in the tests of most theories. Explanation will consist, instead, of a more discursive use of abstract propositions and models to understand specific events. Deductions will be loose, and even metaphorical. (Turner, 1987: 159)

As Turner acknowledges, however, the position of the analytic theorist is in the minority. Along with sociological theory generally, its future status remains to be specified.

• • • • • ## SUMMARY AND CONCLUSION

Basic sociological theory includes a range of orientations, from those useful for the structural analysis of society to those designed to study social interaction. Theoretical orientations are composed of frames of references and conceptual schemes that facilitate the identification of social phenomena and their functional and causal analysis. Causal analysis entails not only theoretical specification but also research methods. Methodological precepts (rules and procedures for the collection and analysis of data) now exert greater influence than theoretical orientations over the direction and conduct of social research.

While some continue to stress the interdependence of theory and research, others emphasize the primacy of one or the other. The tendency has been for the primarily theoretically or empirically oriented to go their separate ways. But for some time the commanding position has been occupied by the methodologically inclined. Theory testing has all but disappeared. The methodological requirements for the articulation and assessment of empirically relevant theory have become so stringent as to deter most from the attempt, and encouraged the submergence of theoretical predisposition in the choice of problem studied and research methods. One tends to study well defined and generally acknowledged problems by means of prescribed methods.

The secondary status of theory in basic or pure sociology has undoubtedly contributed to the neglect of theory in applied sociology. Both branches of the discipline suffer from the same problem: the absence of systematically accumulated knowledge. Some have begun to question the likelihood of knowledge accumulation without data synthesis by means of systematic or axiomatic like theory. As will be brought out in a later chapter, the absence of knowledge accumulation is a problem of growing importance throughout the social and behavioral sciences. For the moment, it is important to assess the nature and status of theory in applied sociology.

● **NOTES**

1. In his most recent statement on middle-range theory, Merton states that it expands on material developed in a critique of a paper presented by Parsons at the 1947 meetings of the American Sociological Society and subsequently published in 1949 in the *American Sociological Review.*

2. Horkheimer's major works include *Critical Theory: Selected Essays* (New York: Seabury Press, 1972) and *Critique of Instrumental Reason* (New York: Seabury Press, 1974).

3. Adorno's contributions to critical theory include *Dialectic of Enlightenment* (New York: Seabury Press, 1973), with Max Horkheimer, and a co-edited work, *The Positivist Dispute in German Sociology* (London: Heinemann, 1976).

4. Marcuse's relevant works include *One-Dimensional Man* (Boston: Beacon Press, 1964) and *Negations: Essays in Critical Theory* (Boston: Beacon Press, 1968).

5. See Susan Buck-Morss, *The Origins of Negative Dialectics* (New York: The Free Press, 1977).

6. John B. Thompson and David Held, eds. *Habermas: Critical Debates* (Cambridge, MA: The M.I.T. Press, 1982), 1.

7. See, for example, Keith D. Harries, "Cities and Crime: A Geographical Model," *Criminology,* 14 (November 1976), 369–386.

● **REFERENCES**

Alexander, J.C. 1982. *Positivism, Presuppositions, and Current Controversies.* Berkeley: University of California Press.

Buck-Morss, S. 1977. *The Origin of Negative Dialectics.* New York: Free Press.

Catton, W.R., Jr. 1966. *From Animistic to Naturalistic Sociology.* New York: McGraw-Hill.

Cohen, B.P. 1989. *Developing Sociological Knowledge: Theory and Method.* Chicago: Nelson-Hall.

Cooley, C.H. 1902. *Human Nature & The Social Order.* New York: Scribner's.

Cornforth, M. 1971. *Historical Materialism.* New York: International Publishers.

Dahrendorf, R. 1959. *Class and Class Conflict in Industrial Society.* Stanford, CA: Stanford University Press.

Devereux, E.C. Jr. 1961. "Parsons' Sociological Theory." In M. Black, ed. *The Social Theories of Talcott Parsons.* Englewood Cliffs, New Jersey: Prentice-Hall.

Durkheim, D.E. 1933. *The Division of Labor in Society.* Glencoe, Illinois: The Free Press.

_____. 1938. *The Rules of Sociological Method.* New York: Free Press.

_____. 1960. *The Division of Labor in Society.* New York: Free Press.

_____. 1961. *Suicide.* New York: Free Press.

Eco, U. 1976. *A Theory of Semiotics.* Bloomington, IN: Indiana University Press.

Freedman, R. 1968. *Marxist Social Thought.* New York: Harcourt, Brace and World.

Giddens, A. 1979. *Central Problems in Social Theory: Action, Structure and Contradiction in Social Analysis.* London, England: The Macmillan Press Ltd.

————. 1987. *Social Theory and Modern Sociology.* Cambridge, England: Polity Press.

Glaser, B.G., and A.L. Strauss. 1967. *The Discovery of Grounded Theory: Strategies for Qualitative Research.* Chicago: Aldine Publishing Co.

Goffman, E. 1959. *The Presentation of Self in Everyday Life.* New York: Doubleday.

Habermas, J. 1984. *The Theory of Communicative Action, Vol. 1.* Boston: Beacon Press.

Harries, K.D. 1976. "Cities and Crime: A Geographical Model." *Criminology* 14: 369–386.

Heilbroner, R.L. 1980. *Marxism: For and Against.* New York: W.W. Norton.

Homans, G.C. 1982. "The Present State of Sociological Theory." *The Sociological Quarterly* 23: 285–299.

Horkheimer, M. 1972. *Critical Theory: Selected Essays.* New York: Seabury Press.

Horkheimer, M., and T.W. Adorno. 1972. *Dialectic of Enlightenment.* New York: Seabury Press.

Larson, C.J. 1977. *Major Themes in Sociological Theory.* New York: David McKay Company, Inc.

Levi-Strauss, C. 1963. *Structural Anthropology.* New York: Basic Books, Inc.

Lukes, S., ed. 1982. *Durkheim: The Rules of Sociological Method and Selected Texts on Sociology and its Method.* New York: Free Press.

Manning, P.K. 1987. *Semiotics and Fieldwork.* Newbury Park, CA: SAGE Publications.

Marcuse, H. 1964. *One-Dimensional Man.* Boston: Beacon Press.

————. 1968. *Negations: Essays in Critical Theory.* Boston: Beacon Press.

Mead, G.H. 1934. *Mind, Self and Society.* Chicago: University of Chicago Press.

Meltzer, B.M., J.W. Petras, and L.T. Reynolds. 1975. *Symbolic Interactionism.* Boston: Routledge & Kegan Paul.

Menzies, K. 1982. *Sociological Theory in Use.* Boston: Routledge & Kegan Paul.

Merton, R.K. 1949. *Social Theory & Social Structure.* New York: Free Press.

Parsons, T. 1937. *The Structure of Social Action.* New York: McGraw-Hill.

————. 1951. *The Social System.* New York: Free Press.

————. 1954. *Essays in Sociological Theory.* New York: Free Press.

Piaget, J. 1970. *Structuralism.* New York: Basic Books, Inc.

Polanyi, M. 1958. *Personal Knowledge.* Chicago: University of Chicago Press.

Silverman, K. 1983. *The Subject of Semiotics.* New York: Oxford University Press.

Stryker, S. 1964. "The Interactional and Situational Approaches." In H.T. Christensen, ed., *Handbook of Marriage and The Family.* Chicago: Rand McNally & Co.

Thomas, W.I., and F. Znaniecki. 1927. *The Polish Peasant in Europe and America Vol. 1.* New York: A.A. Knopf.

Thompson, J.B., and D. Held, eds. 1982. *Habermas: Critical Debates.* Cambridge, MA.: M.I.T. Press.

Thompson, K., ed. 1985. *Readings from Emile Durkheim.* New York: Tavistock Publications.

Turner, J. 1987. "Analytical Theorizing." In A. Giddens and J. Turner, eds., *Social Theory Today.* Stanford, CA: Stanford University Press, 156–194.

Wagner, D.G. 1984. *The Growth of Sociological Theories.* Beverly Hills: SAGE Publications.

Warshay, L.H. 1975. *The Current State of Sociological Theory.* New York: David McKay Company, Inc.

Zetterberg, H. 1965. *On Theory and Verification in Sociology.* Totowa, NJ: The Bedminster Press.

CHAPTER 3

● ● ●

*Applied Sociological Theory**

Unlike pure sociological theory, applied sociological theory lacks a variety of distinctive, readily available and generally acknowledged examples to outline and interrelate. Applied sociological theory is an occasionally discussed subject rather than a carefully and systematically defined one. There is, in fact, a range of opinion as to the difference between pure and applied sociological theory and whether theory is either present in or relevant to applied sociology. Some who perceive the neglect or absence of theory in applied sociology question its sociological relevance. Behind the situation lies an absence of consensus on the difference between pure and applied sociology and what is and is not applied sociology. Some would claim applied sociology primarily concerns the study of social problems to determine practical solutions and influence public policy. Others would stress discipline versus client oriented work and research. The initial pages of this chapter examine the different views on these and related subjects in order to gauge the current status of theory in applied sociology.

Central portions of this chapter are devoted to a discussion of such subjects as the bearing of basic theory on applied social research (and vice versa), and

---

*Major portions of this chapter were published under the title "Applied/Practical Sociological Theory: Problems & Issues" *Sociological Practice Review* 1 (June 1990): 8–19.

49

the nature and theoretical structure of major types of applied sociology—for example, social engineering and clinical sociology. The concluding section explores the nature and qualities of practically relevant sociological theory. Of particular significance is the possible influence of applied sociological theory on basic theoretical concerns, such as general knowledge growth.

APPLIED VERSUS PURE SOCIOLOGY

Applied sociology usually is defined by comparing and contrasting its aims and characteristics with those of pure sociology. Among the first to examine the subject in this way was Alvin Gouldner. As he saw it, applied social science, in contrast to pure social science, is not primarily concerned with aims and values such as objectivity and prediction. Instead, it is oriented to the values of laymen, values that are "extrinsic to science as such" (1957: 93). That applied sociology is lay-client rather than discipline-oriented is the major theme in attempts to differentiate applied from pure sociology. Joseph DeMartini's recent effort is an outstanding example.

DeMartini defines applied sociology as "the use of sociological theories and/or methods to address issues of practical concern identified by a client for which this use is intended" (1982: 204). Nonetheless, he finds "very little" development of theory for practical purposes, and concludes that "applied work will continue—at least in the short run—to stress research design and data collection/manipulation skills" (1982: 204).

To DeMartini, applied sociology involves work done on behalf of individuals or groups who need certain information and knowledge to accomplish desired ends. Pure sociology is strictly oriented to the perceived needs, interests, and concerns of the profession. Applied sociology is concerned with problem solving and "the persuasive use of available information"; its reference groups are political interest groups. Pure sociology is concerned with knowledge production, hypothesis testing, and the "qualification of conclusions"; its reference group is "fellow professionals" (1982: 204).

In contrast to pure sociologists, who are employed primarily by academic institutions, applied sociologists are employed by all manner of clients—from private sector firms wishing to sample public opinion about a new or old product to government agencies wishing to assess the effectiveness of such programs as those aimed at treating prison overcrowding and homelessness. Undoubtedly, most applied sociologists are employed temporarily (as consultants, therapists, expert witnesses, and so on), but increasing numbers are finding full-time employment as researchers, human relations experts, human service providers, middle-management bureaucrats, and social planners.

As Peter Rossi et al. point out, the difference between pure and applied sociology is generally thought of as depending on who chooses the dependent variable (1978: 172). If the individual scholar makes the choice, it is pure sociology; if the client decides, it is applied sociology. The problem, they add, is that there is "considerable overlap" among the individuals and groups involved in pure and applied endeavors. Consequently, they think a better differentiating criterion is the purpose of the work to be done. "Applied social research," they state, "is directed to the solution of some real world problem; basic research, in contrast, is conducted to enhance the body of knowledge of the discipline" (1978: 173). But, they add, the distinction might not apply in individual cases. On the one hand, one must understand a problem before it can be solved; and on the other, an understood problem is one whose solution can be contemplated. In essence, they claim it is difficult to clearly differentiate between pure and applied sociology because the two may be inextricably intertwined. They stress the idea that research activity of any sort is generally a combination of science and art or "craftlore." Science includes basic theoretical and methodological principles, and art the "workable techniques, rules of thumb, and standard operating procedures." As they see it, "basic and applied social research share the science and craftlore of the social science disciplines, but differ in their artful aspects: the theories, methods, and procedures of basic and applied research are quite similar, but the style of work encountered in each camp is not" (1978: 173).

In another paper, Freeman and Rossi emphasize the view that pure and applied sociology have "qualitatively different" outlooks. They acknowledge the fact that the two share common methodological and theoretical means, but argue that "there the similarity ends."

Freeman and Rossi identify six "clear differences" between pure or conventional and applied sociology: (1) pure sociologists pursue self-satisfying work and are evaluated by their peers; applied sociologists work for and are evaluated by non-academic clients; (2) although constrained by funding sources and publishers interests and requirements, pure sociologists explore problems and subjects of their own choosing; applied sociologists do not have the same freedom of choice because they must heed the wishes of clients and sponsors; (3) regardless of problem or subject, pure sociologists must conform to rigid scholarly standards; applied sociologists comply with such standards only if necessary to attain practical ends; (4) pure sociologists are chiefly interested in identifying general patterns and principles relevant to restricted groups and subjects; applied sociologists seek broadly applicable generalizations; (5) pure sociologists are theoretically oriented; applied sociologists are practically oriented; and (6) the goal of the pure sociologist is scholarly journal publication; the goal of the applied sociologist is to aid sponsors understanding of subjects they advocate and their ability to influence decision makers and decision making (1984: 572-573).

While quite aware that their conception of applied sociology is more narrow than some would accept, Freeman and Rossi contend that "applied sociologists generally are committed to two major tasks": extricating the policy and action relevant implications from primary and secondary data sources, and advising policy makers on the basis of their theoretical and methodological expertise (1984: 575).

Instead of emphasizing the qualitative uniqueness of applied social science, some stress its interrelatedness with pure social science. As R. K. Merton sees it, for example, the goal of basic or pure social research is to discover new and shed light on known patterns and uniformities. The goal of applied research is to effect new practical results by means of basic theoretical and empirical knowledge (Rosenblatt and Gieryn, 1982: 21).

For Merton, the key difference between pure and applied research is the different role possibilities of their practitioners. In basic research, the worker's role provides (1) virtual freedom in problem selection, (2) freedom to change the problem focus because something different appears more interesting or promising, and (3) a "reference group" of peers as evaluators. As he points out, "the role of workers in applied research tends toward the other extreme" (1982: 215). That is, in applied research (1) the worker's problem choice is determined by the practical needs and interests of others, (2) the worker is not generally free to alter or change the problem focus, and (3) the relevant reference group is outside the worker's field of expertise.

Nonetheless, Merton finds theory and research highly interrelated activities. In articles published during the 1940s, he identified the chief functions of theory for research as the synthesis and accumulation of scattered facts, the suggestion of possibly unconsidered and fruitful lines of inquiry, the prediction of empirical possibilities, and the precise combination of thought and fact that promotes precision and measurement. "Above all," says Merton, "it [formal theory] prepares the way for consecutive and cumulative research rather than a buckshot array of dispersed investigations" (1967: 154).

Merton insists, however, that research has a larger role to play than the mere evaluation or testing of theory. In his view "it *initiates,* it *reformulates,* it *deflects,* and it *clarifies* theory."

To Merton, a common feature of social research is a serendipity pattern—the tendency to encounter unanticipated and apparently anomalous facts and details. Science is rife with examples of "accidental" discovery via research and experimentation. Quite often something is perceived that is not predicted or supposed to occur. Wilhelm Roentgen's discovery of x-rays is a case in point. Where others saw only a glowing screen, Roentgen saw the useful form of radiation that has become an integral part of medical diagnosis and treatment. An example in social science is R. J. Roethlisberger's and William Dickson's discovery of the importance of the structure of informal relationships in the quality of work performed by employees in an electrical plant. They discovered that some parts of the plant's organization could be more readily changed than others: "The technical organization can change more rapidly than the social organization; the formal organization can change more rapidly than the informal; the systems of beliefs and ideas can change more rapidly than the patterns of interaction and associated sentiments, of which these beliefs and ideas are an expression" (1949: 695). It was this anomalous finding that led to a more effective way of influencing worker productivity than could have been anticipated.

The discovery of anomalous fact may lead to the recasting of theory—that is, the introduction of new variables can make a significant difference in the explanatory power of a theory. Merton provides the example of Bronislaw Malinowski's theory of magic. As Merton tells it, when Malinowski's subjects, the Trobriand islanders,

> fished in the inner lagoon by the reliable method of poisoning, an abundant catch was assured and danger was absent. Neither uncertainty nor uncontrollable hazards were involved. And here, Malinowski noted, magic was not practiced. But in the open-sea fishing, with the uncertain yield and its often grave dangers, the rituals of magic flourished. Stemming from these pregnant observations was his theory that magical belief arises to bridge the uncertainties in man's practical pursuits, to fortify confidence, to reduce anxieties, to open up avenues of escape from the seeming impasse. (1949: 162)

In addition to the initiation and recasting of theory, research may lead to a shift in theoretical focus. Merton thinks that developments in research methods often have this effect. Examples include the interest shown in the bearing of social structure on the formation of personality and character that followed in the wake of the construction of projective methods such as the Rorschach test and the thematic apperception test.

Lastly, empirical research often leads to concept clarification. As Merton points out, "in non-research speculations, it is possible to talk loosely about 'morale' or 'social cohesion' without any clear conceptions of what is entailed by these terms, but they must be clarified if the researcher is to go about his business of systematically observing instances of low and high morale, or social cohesion or social cleavage" (1949: 169).

In the mid-1970s, William Snizek examined the relationship between theory and research by evaluating over 1,400 articles in nine major journals from 1950 to 1970. He found that choice of research method was much more likely to determine theoretical orientation than vice versa. "One hopes," he observed, "that we have not reached that point in the history of sociology when . . . the 'methodological tail is wagging the theoretical dog'!" (1975: 425).

In applied areas, methodological rather than theoretical sophistication is emphasized. Freeman and Rossi, for example, begin their description of the educational needs of applied sociologists by stating: "It is especially critical . . . that applied sociologists be conversant with and well grounded in the range of research methods that constitute our craft" (1984: 576). They make no reference to any kind of theoretical skill training that may be either needed or useful in the education of applied sociologists. Nonetheless, basic sociological theory influences the work of applied sociologists, and the work of applied sociologists most certainly has implications for basic sociological theory.

In the latter vein, Darnell Hawkins has explored the bearing of applied social research on social theory. He argues that applied social research can lead to a closer awareness of the following "aspects" of the relationship between theory and research:

> (1) basal and metatheoretical assumptions that underlie a given social theory, including nations of "human nature," human motivation, and the like; (2) conceptions of "social structure," including the assumed primacy of certain social structural parts; (3) the link between application and theory, and a fuller examination of rules of proof and nonproof of theory; and (4) the ideological and institutional "climate" in which given theory, research, and application exist. (1978: 144)

Any theory of directed behavioral or social change, notes Hawkins, is based on either an explicit or implicit assumption about human nature. Some social scientists, for example, presume that people are essentially rational, while others believe that people are essentially creatures of their emotions. Consequently, as Hawkins points out, differences of opinion among applied researchers as to which policy is likely to produce desired change are frequently the result of different views of human nature. He describes these as "metatheoretical disagreements rather than disagreements over issues of data analysis, proof, and other aspects commonly associated with the testing of theory" (1978: 142).

Further, applied research often exposes unexamined assumptions about social structure—for example, that a given group is composed of systematically interrelated parts that have an equilibrium tendency, homeostatic mechanisms, and so on. Hawkins insists that it is crucial for the applied researcher to have a clear understanding of social structural assumptions. It may be, for instance, that goal attainment (for example, the change of a given system) must be accomplished by the most direct means available. In such cases, Hawkins suggests, it may be crucially important to have a clear understanding of which parts of a given system are more important than others "in effecting change in the whole" (1978: 143).

Applied social research contributes to the ongoing process of the formulation and reformulation of theory by putting it to a practical test. As Hawkins states:

> In contemporary social science, the testing of theory is usually conceived as involving the use of sophisticated mathematical models and precise measurement. Such a detached, quantitative simulation of the social world, especially when aided by modern technology, may provide valuable insight into the inner workings of society; however, it will never serve to replace completely the need for a "real" world application and testing of social theory. (1978: 143)

Lastly, applied research provokes awareness of the ideological predilections of the investigator and the ideological climate of society. Sensitivity to ideology is important for any number of reasons, says Hawkins, but particularly because latent if not manifest ideological commitments may determine the applied researcher's assumptions regarding human nature and social structure.

Instead of stressing the bearing of applied research on theory, Hilde Nafstad emphasizes the importance of theory to applied research. She refers to applied social science as "systematic attempts to contribute to the solution of practical social problems through research and theoretical-empirical activity based on the traditionally academic established disciplines of social science" (1982: 260). As she explains it, her intention is not to "provoke" the image of a competitive relationship between the two, but to emphasize "their mutual interdependence" and "how they may ideally supplement each other" (1982: 260).

According to Nafstad, pure social scientists are free to study problems and subjects consistent with their theoretical interests. Applied social scientists, however, must study contemporary social problems. The pure social scientist can justify problem choice on the basis of contributing something new to a standing subject or to clarify a theoretical issue. In contrast, the applied social scientist is generally compelled to conduct research to uncover solutions to practical problems.

But Nafstad finds one overriding "asymmetric relationship" between pure and applied social research: "While basic researchers are free to more or less ignore the practical relevance of their research, it is evident that the applied researchers cannot disregard the demand for theoretical relevance and justification" (1982: 210).

Nafstad contends that applied social research must be just as well theoretically grounded as pure social research. "A weak or inadequate theoretical basis in traditional academic research will, at worst," she says, "have undesired effects on one's personal academic career, while lack of theoretical knowledge on the part of the applied researcher may have disastrous effects on the social groups the particular research is designed to assist" (1982: 261).

Nafstad's thesis is important but difficult to evaluate because only a small portion of applied research is published or in other ways made public. Much of it is in the form of written reports designed for the needs and interests of non-scholarly audiences. The extent to which such documents and the research behind them is structured by theory of one kind or another is unknown and unknowable (a good deal is confidential). Consequently, it is not possible to assess the impact of the general theoretical quality of applied research on the lives and situations of those it is ostensibly meant to effect.

Later, examples of applied research conducted from certain theoretical perspectives and with the aid of selected sociological concepts will be discussed and analyzed. For the moment, it is worth noting that Nafstad's basic contention of theoretical unity between pure and applied research, which suggests the dependence of the latter on the former, is consistent with Lester Ward's vision of the proper relationship between the discipline's two branches.

ARE PURE AND APPLIED THEORY THE SAME?

Alvin Gouldner was the most outspoken critic of the notion that applied sociology is "nothing more" than the use of the theories and methods of pure sociology to solve or treat practical problems. Because he could find "few validated laws or broad generalizations" in contemporary sociology, it seemed to him that there is "no close correlation . . . between the development of generalizations by the pure disciplines and the multiplication of opportunities for, and varieties, of applied sociology" (1965: 7).

Gouldner acknowledges the fact that the applied social sciences use the contributions of the pure social sciences, but claims that the following better describe the relationship between the two:

> (a) Applied social scientists are more likely to use the concepts than the generalized propositions of their basic discipline. (b) Not all concepts or theoretical models of pure social science are equally useful to applied social scientists. (c) Applied social scientists will more likely borrow from their basic disciplines those concepts and theoretical models which aid them in understanding or producing changes. (d) When the basic discipline does not provide theoretical systems or concepts aiding the applied social scientist to deal with change, the latter will develop these himself. (1965: 9–10)

As noted in Chapter 1, Gouldner was convinced that the "prediction and production" of social change is the primary purpose of applied social science. "Applied social science," in his view, "requires concepts enabling it to deal with change, while much of pure social science today is oriented to the analysis of stable social institutions in their equilibrium" (1965: 8).

The emphasis that Gouldner placed on the dearth of social change models and the dominance of social order oriented structural-functional theory reflected the major current of opinion during the period in which he wrote. Ralf Dahrendorf,[1] C. Wright Mills,[2] and contributors to what came to be referred to as the "sociology of sociology"[3] hammered the point home in what must be regarded as one of the most persistent and thorough critiques of a prevailing social theory in the history of social science.

But much applied social research has little or nothing to do with social change. And probably most that does is not sufficiently conclusive to justify clearly beneficial behavioral, structural, or policy modification. Perhaps the most important point Gouldner made was that the theories and concepts of basic sociology are neither necessarily applicable nor readily adaptable to applied purposes. In the words of Snizek and Fuhrman, "in many instances a theory which is appropriate to the interest of the academic social scientist has little or no bearing on the applied behavioral situation" (1980: 98).

TYPES OF APPLIED SOCIOLOGY

Different views of the bearing of theory on practical matters have spawned different models of applied work. James Rule has identified a broad and general range of what he refers to as "models of relevance"—ideal-type approaches toward the practical implementation, of sociological knowledge. The first is the "no net effects" viewpoint. Those of this persuasion reject the idea that acquired knowledge of society can be applied to effect more good than harm. The classic statement on the subject, as Rule notes, is that of W.G. Sumner (1840–1910). In an anti-reformist article published in 1894, Sumner stated:

> The great stream of time and earthly things will sweep on just the same in spite of us. It bears with it now all the errors and follies of the past, the wreckage of all the philosophies, the fragments of all the civilizations, the wisdom of all the abandoned ethical systems, the debris of all the institutions, and the penalties of all the mistakes. It is only in imagination that we stand by and look at and criticize it and plan to change it. Everyone of us is a child of his age and cannot get out of it. . . . The men will be carried along with it and be made by it. The utmost they can do by their cleverness will be to note and record their course as they are carried along, which is what we do now, and is that which leads us to the vain fancy that we can make or guide the movement. That is why it is the greatest folly of which a man can be capable, to sit down with a slate and pencil to plan out a new social world. (Loewenberg, 1957: 15)

As Rule notes, few contemporary sociologists are likely to adhere to the extreme version of the model, primarily because it is difficult to defend. To make the attempt, he points out, one would have to contend that "perceptions of the social world" have no appreciable impact on behavior related to social betterment. The fact is, however, that social science does have some influence on such perceptions. Further, as Rule notes, even awareness of the absence of an available effective problem remedy may have positive consequences. As Sumner was well aware the implementation of empirically unproven social remedies may exacerbate existing and provoke new problems.

Rule's second ideal-type is the natural opposite of the first. He calls it the "direct and positive effects" model. Its outlook is at the heart of sociology, past and present. It is based on the assumption of a broad-based consensus among people that life in general would be better if certain problems were solved, crime and poverty most of all.

The third, fourth, and fifth models address the problems of "special constituencies." The third model is "predicated on the assumption that . . . one category of 'consumers' of social insight has the power to act effectively in the . . . interest of all society" (1978: 45). Marx's conception of the historic role to be played by the proletariat in capitalist society is the outstanding example. "Marx's model of relevance," says Rule, "represents an ingenious attempt to address a special constituency with the unique ability to bring about a better, more rational world" (1978: 48).

The fourth model includes "uncoopted" special constituencies. During the 1960s, for example, "the most promising 'consumers' of insights for social innovation" were the "outsiders"—racial and ethnic minorities, the poor, the deviant. As Rule states: "Adherents to [this] model lack the Marxist faith in the ultimate historical triumph of their special constituency, while they also lack [model two adherents'] assurance that the conditions which they find unacceptable will meet with universal disapproval" (1978: 51).

The special constituency of model five is "government officialdom." This is, as Rule notes, among the oldest of models of relevance. Clients are representatives of any government agency. "The message is clear: Those in power, aided by the proper social science techniques, can determine the needs of society more efficiently than ever" (1978: 56). Consulting work concerned with what Karl Popper refers to as "piecemeal social engineering" fits this model.

Most attempts to specify the nature and types of models combining theory and practice have been more narrowly conceived than Rule's. What makes his particularly important is its fundamental sensitivity to the value commitments of sociologists and social scientists generally. Most are chiefly concerned with delineating or defending the importance of either pure or applied sociology or some particular aspect of one or the other. Rule accentuates the idea that sociology is a blend of the pure and the applied, the theoretical and the practical, and that most sociologists adhere to some combination of the two. The point is often missed in the effort to specify the difference between the discipline's two sides.

Social Engineering

Gouldner identifies two types of applied sociology: social engineering and clinical sociology. The two are described via "a typical case." To illustrate the engineering approach, Gouldner provides the example of an industrial firm contracting with a consulting firm to survey employee attitudes as to satisfaction with wages, working conditions, hours, and quality of supervision. As he sees it, typically, the consulting firm's task is to compile a report detailing the percentage of employees who are pleased and displeased with the four factors. The report generally contains a set of recommendations about which the hiring firm usually requests a meeting or two to discuss and clarify. In the usual case, said Gouldner, the report is afterward filed and left to collect dust.

To Gouldner, the distinguishing feature of the engineering model is that consultants accept without question terms determined by the client. Typically, he suggests, consultants neither require clients to identify the precise reasons and problems behind a requested survey nor indicate whether the proposed social research will solve the ostensible problem(s). Behind the requested survey, says Gouldner, is the likelihood of "a number of vaguely sensed tensions." Perhaps, he observes, there has been a breakdown in communication between labor and management. The problem is, of course, that the survey may not reveal the fact and nature of possible underlying tensions. As he notes, management may initiate a survey of employee attitudes and opinions to "outflank a union." In such instances, value indifferent applied social research may lead to a worsening rather than an improvement in management-employee relations (1965: 12).

Paul Lazarsfeld and Jeffrey Reitz little appreciated Gouldner's negative portrait of the social engineer. As they indicate, Gouldner begins his essay by stating that:

> Not so long ago the words "social engineer" were a term of opprobrium. They carried with them the suspicion that such a social scientist had somehow betrayed his vow of dispassionate objectivity and had sold his scientific heritage for a tasteless mess of popularity. (1965: 5)

"So Gouldner's paper," state Lazarsfeld and Reitz, "which starts with the plan of giving the term 'social engineer' some respectability, ends by using the same concept as a symbol of the poor performer" (1975: 13-14). Lazarsfeld and Reitz trace the apparent inconsistency to Gouldner's known commitment to efforts to bridge the gap between theory and social problems, thought and action. As critical as he was of the theoretical conservatism of the academic sociology of his day, Gouldner was particularly disdainful of those who would practice uncommitted, technically correct, "value free" pure or applied sociology. As Gouldner saw it, "legitimated by references to the conceptions of a 'value-free' social science, . . . many applied social scientists have claimed that all they can properly do is to study the diverse consequences of different policies, or to suggest efficient means for the realization of ends already specified by their client (1965: 13).

The question Gouldner wished to emphasize is: "in the event of employment by a client whose values differ from those of the group whom the applied social scientist is asked to change, with whose values and to whose ends shall the scientist conform?" (1965: 13). Framed during a volatile period in American history, the question remains of primary concern to anyone concerned with or involved in applied social science and the uses and abuses of its tools, techniques, and knowledge. It is a question seldom posed and examined in times of needed applied employment by sociologists unable to find academic employment or requiring additional income.

Some include the role of change agent as an integral part of social engineering. Rossi and Whyte, for example, define social engineering as the attainment of a goal by application of sociological knowledge to "the design of policies of institutions." Further, they say, "social engineering can be accomplished for a mission oriented agency or for some group opposed to the existing organizational structure, or it may be undertaken separately from either" (1983: 10).

The polar extremes, then, may be referred to as reformist versus revolutionary, or in Popper's terms, piecemeal versus utopian social engineering. According to Popper, the piecemeal engineer, in contrast to the utopian, adopts "the method of searching for, and fighting against, the greatest and most urgent evils of society rather than searching for, and fighting for, its greatest ultimate good" (1962: 158). The piecemeal engineer is one who seeks to solve a specific problem within a delimited segment of society by means consistent with prevailing disciplinary and social standards. Utopian engineering is concerned with the radical reconstruction of society in the image of a predetermined ideal. Only when the ideal aim is specified does the Utopian consider the selection of proper means. As Popper sees it, the Utopian aim of blueprint guided total societal reconstruction requires centralized leadership and is, therefore, predisposed toward dictatorship.

Popper's preference for piecemeal over holistic social engineering is rationalized on a number of grounds. One of the more important of which concerns the identification of relevant social problems. In his view,

> blueprints for piecemeal engineering are comparatively simple. They are blueprints for single institutions, for health and unemployed insurance, for instance. . . . If they go wrong, the damage is not very great, and a readjustment not very difficult. They are less risky, and for this very reason less controversial. (1962: 159)

As Rule has indicated, such a seemingly logical position actually masks a "flight from social theory." As he explains, Popper "implausibly implies that 'the most intolerable evils' of society are unconnected to one another, that efforts at their alleviation require no over-arching analysis of larger social forces generating the offending conditions" (1978: 93).

Rule also finds an implicit ideological predilection in Popper's viewpoint. According to Rule, Popper "arbitrarily" rejects all radically oriented social change theory in favor of "positions long associated with conservative and centrist positions" (1978: 98).

However valid and cogent Rule's criticisms, Popper's views on social engineering appear to approximate the prevailing American viewpoint. Holistic social engineering seems unmistakably idealistic, utopian, and worst of all, impractical. The general social theory prerequisite to guided holistic engineering is neither evident nor encouraged. Perhaps the closest recent example is Parsonsian structural-functional social systems theory, and it was soundly criticized for being utopian and ideologically biased. When social engineering is mentioned, the image conveyed is of the piecemeal variety, which is generally regarded as atheoretical and concerned with the application of social science research methods to the solution of non-academically defined "real world" problems.

Morris Janowitz once proposed a dichotomy somewhat similar to Popper's. He distinguished between two professional perspectives among sociologists, a social engineering and an "enlightenment" model. To Janowitz, social engineers "are skilled in on-the-spot data collection and have the interpersonal orientations and skills to communicate their findings in direct terms to policymakers and professional practitioners" (1970: 248). Hans Zetterberg's following depiction illustrated what Janowitz had in mind: "If eighteenth-century physics gave us the modern engineer to deal with technological problems, and nineteenth- century biology gave us the modern physician to deal with health problems, so twentieth-century social science dreams that it shall give mankind the social practitioner to deal scientifically with social problems" (1962: 15).

In contrast, claims Janowitz, advocates of the enlightenment model do not accept the premise that sociological knowledge per se is a sufficient basis for the construction of general social policy or guiding professional practice. Sociology is regarded as one among several social sciences, and social science information only one of several needed types for general practical purposes. When operating under the enlightenment model, sociologists must be cognizant of the fact that they are responsible to the diverse clientele and publics with whom they interact. Succinctly put, the engineering model seeks "definitive answers to specific questions and particular hypotheses in order to make concrete recommendations." In contrast, the enlightenment model emphasizes creation of "the intellectual conditions for problem solving" (1970: 252).

Because Janowitz singled out the work of Paul Lazarsfeld as indicative of the social engineering model, it was predictable that Lazarsfeld would respond to Janowitz's conceptions. Lazarsfeld and Reitz interpreted Janowitz as saying that "the social engineer is one who fails to see the gap between knowledge and action," and that "the counterimage to the social engineer is not the 'true' scientist, but the enlightener with his breadth of view and his high level of aspiration" (1975: 12). They "admired" Janowitz's enlightenment model but disagreed "with his characterization of a rigid, self-confident social engineer who thinks he has all the answers" (1975: 12).

The enlightenment model has been little discussed since Janowitz introduced it. However, interpretations of clinical sociology place it somewhere between Janowitz's two models.

Clinical Sociology

Encouraged by the increasing participation of sociologists in child guidance clinics during the 1920s, Louis Wirth was the first to identify and discuss the rudiments of clinical sociology. He defines clinical sociology "as a convenient label for those insights, methods of approach, and techniques which the science of sociology can contribute to the understanding and treatment of persons whose behavior or personality problems bring them under the care of clinics for study and treatment" (1931: 10). It was not his intention to propose the creation of an alternative to clinical psychology or psychiatry. Because he believed that any single scientific viewpoint was inadequate to solve behavioral problems, he proposed the addition of sociological knowledge and insight to prevailing modes of treatment. "It is not desirable," he says, "that the sociologist should displace the physician, the psychiatrist, the psychologist, or the social worker, but he should bring to them the insights which his approach furnishes not merely in order to modify their viewpoint but to understand the child's behavior more completely as a social phenomenon" (1931: 59).

What Wirth thought the sociologist could bring to the treatment process is a "cultural approach." As Wirth described it, the cultural approach is based on the idea that a behavioral problem is viewed as a deviation from prevailing custom. Hence, its understanding and correction is dependent on an understanding of the cultural milieu in which it occurs.

In addition to the possibility of direct participation in case evaluation and treatment, Wirth's conception of the scope of clinical sociology included research as well as specialist training and general consultation with treatment personnel.

Unfortunately, and as Roger Straus states, the clinical sociology movement "collapsed under the stresses of the Great Depression and then the Second World War" (1979: 478–479). Alvin Gouldner's writings in the late 1950s and 1960s signaled revived interest in clinical sociology.

Gouldner's conception of the clinical approach is the equivalent of the dialectical opposite of social engineering. A case in applied anthropology provided the contrasting example. The problem concerned an Indian community in Peru that was experiencing considerable internal strife due to conflicts over cattle ownership. The anthropologists involved, after noticing that the Indians hadn't thought of it, proposed the practice of branding. Once accepted and implemented by the community's wealthier leaders, branding resolved the problem. According to Gouldner, the clinicians "took their clients' complaints and self-formulations as only one among a number of 'symptoms' useful in helping them to arrive at their own diagnosis of the clients' problems" (1965: 13). The key point for Gouldner was that where "the engineers studied what they were told to do," the clinicians relied on their own knowledge and skills to define and treat the problem.

Gouldner closed his paper by slightly tempering his negative view of social engineering and positive view of clinical sociology by observing: "If the engineer lacks a sophisticated conception of the client relation and an adequate appreciation of the depth and meaning of client resistance, the clinician typically lacks a sophisticated conception of research design and technology" (1965: 20).

Contemporary clinical sociology (which has its own professional organization and journal) includes a broad range of concerns, of which those of Wirth and Gouldner are an integral part. According to John Glass,

> In the broadest sense, clinical sociology is the bringing of a sociological perspective to intervention and action for change. The client may be an individual, family, school system, medical center, work group, or the like, and the task may involve a redefinition of self, situation, or the creation of healthier and more humane environments. (1979: 524)

Clinical sociology now operates on both the micro and macro levels of analysis. Further, the "clinic" is not generally a detached professional office area but the natural setting of individual and group clients. Hence, participant observation and qualitative methods are frequently employed.

Clinical sociologists have been highly sensitive to the possible practical uses of basic sociological theory. According to D.P. Johnson, for example, knowledge of sociological theory increases practitioners' flexibility "in terms of the types of problems they can diagnose and potential interventions they can implement" (1986: 58). And to Cheryl Anderson and Linda Rouse (1988: 137), sociological theories (1) provide behavioral models useful in determining counseling goals and identifying treatment techniques, (2) aid the identification and critical analysis of tacit assumptions in applied work concerning the nature of reality, (3) provide analytical perspectives for determining why certain change strategies fail or succeed to accomplish desired aims, and (4) furnish a way of developing an organized and systematic plan of action. Anderson and Rouse applied symbolic interactionist and critical theory to the problem of women battering with interesting results.

The self concept is particularly useful. The question is, how does the abuse sustained by the victim influence her sense of self? As they point out, "repeated abuse" can alter a previously positive self concept, and that "when the batterer accompanies physical assault with verbal abuse the victim's sense of self is further eroded" (1988: 138).

The clinician's role in cases of family violence is not, insist Anderson and Rouse, the "impartial mediator." The clinician "needs to serve as a significant other in unambiguously defining violence as inappropriate" (1988: 138-139). And a basic goal of counseling is assisting the victim to self restructuring by "recalling positive identities prior to the relationship; recapturing lost social identities outside of the marriage; recognizing competencies on which to rebuild self-esteem" (1988: 139).

Also of particular use to Anderson and Rouse is the concept of "systematically distorted communication" in Jürgen Habermas's critical theory. As they see it, in Habermas's theory, "battering can be regarded as a communication disorder symptomatic of unequal power relations. . . . In shelter programs, efforts to empower battered women typically include providing a critique of sexist assumptions about family relations, particularly the husband's right to dominate by force" (1988: 142). The effect is "consciousness raising" and an inducement to action.

The problem is, of course, that increasing the victim's assertiveness may not only decrease distorted communication but also provoke the offender to renewed violence. Thus, the batterer must be taught to assert himself communicatively rather than violently. But, "[w]here the battering spouse is not changing, empowerment for the victim means developing the emotional resources and social supports that will enable her to perceive alternatives and leave the relationship, if she chooses." It is Anderson's and Rouse's conclusion that basic sociological theories are practically useful for the study and analysis of domestic violence: "In addition to providing guidelines for institutional level change, sociological theories offer perspectives with implications for clinical practice" (1988: 144).

Empowerment, active intervention, resocialization, behavioral and social change are of fundamental importance to clinical sociologists. They are as evident in micro-level work such as Anderson's and Rouse's as well as macro-level endeavors. An example of the latter is Charles Kleymeyer's work in Cali, Colombia, during the 1970s.

Kleymeyer was part of a research team investigating "the use and nonuse of ambulatory care service" in local hospitals. He organized a team of interviewers to observe "the quality and consequences of interpersonal interaction" between patients and hospital personnel. From approximately 2000 recorded instances of "problematic interactions," Kleymeyer discovered that nonuse of ambulatory care services was related to impersonal, stressful, and generally negative patient experiences with hospital personnel. The finding led to changes such as the institution of "in house client advocates" or "patient representatives," human relations courses for hospital employees, and incentives for humane and competent patient treatment. "From a theoretical standpoint," notes Kleymeyer, "program objectives . . . included raising client power . . . , making adjustments in the reward structure, crystallizing new institutional values, adding competing role models, providing technical retraining, and resocialization into alternative roles and social processes" (1979: 595). From Kleymeyer's study it is apparent that "grounded theory" is particularly applicable to qualitative research methods and, therefore, clinical sociology. An interesting example is "grounded encounter therapy."

Grounded encounter therapy is a type of sociotherapy—therapy involving interacting parties. It stresses the conduct of therapy in social context and appropriate milieu. Social context refers to all the social relationships that have a bearing on clients' problems. Milieu refers to the setting or "situations" in which relevant social interaction has occurred between patients and those implicated in their problems. To L. Alex Swan, grounded encounter therapy involves

1) Confronting the social context of the clients, designating the social situation and the milieu of the context, and encountering the clients: within the situation, with each other, and with the sociotherapist;
2) Interpreting and analyzing the situation and, thus, verifying the apparent and the real problems and difficulties;
3) Connecting the emerging explanations and meanings with the situation of the client; and
4) Devising strategies for therapy. (1988: 78)

Grounded theory also has been used in the conduct of organizational research and analyses. Examples include studies of psychiatric institutions (Strauss et al., 1964), hospitals (Trimble et al., 1972), business corporations (Johnson, 1981), and the academic world (Conrad, 1978). According to Patricia Martin and Barry Turner: "In the field of organizational studies, grounded theory is likely to interest those concerned with the pilot stages of large-scale survey inquiries, those conducting case studies of organizational behavior who wish to produce more than an impressionistic account from their inquiries, those interested in features of the organizational world—such as corporate cultures—that lend themselves . . . to qualitative investigation, and those concerned about carrying out the detailed, locally based fact gathering and interpretation essential to conducting excellent organizational research" (1986: 143).

A highly "grounded" organizational theory involving confrontational tactics was developed by the late Saul Alinsky, an acknowledged pioneer in clinical sociology.[4] During the 1960s, he helped black communities across the country apply the organizational weapon to accomplish desired ends. His last work, *Rules for Radicals* (1971), contains the clearest statement of his theory of community organization.

Although he described himself as a radical seeking revolutionary social change, Alinsky advocated working within the system. "We will start with the system," he declared, "because here is no other place to start except political lunacy" (1971: xxi). He insisted that the organizer must begin with the world not as it should be but as it is.

Alinsky stressed the absence of a set theory, that is, a fixed set of procedures to effect community organization for change. Community organization was not an exact science. The organizer's sense of truth was of something relative to changing conditions and circumstances. Above all, he said, "the free-society organizer is loose, resilient, fluid, and on the move in a society which is itself in a state of constant change" (1971: 11).

Dogma had no place in Alinsky's scheme. He referred to it as "the enemy of freedom." He was, however, mindful of the value of ideological commitment on the part of those involved in community organization. The problem was that ideology had a way of "deteriorating into dogma." To avoid this possibility, he stressed that "no ideology should be more specific than that of America's founding fathers: 'For the general welfare'" (1971: 4).

The organizer's aim was to help people help themselves on the assumption that "if people have the power to act, in the long run they will, most of the time, reach the right decisions" (1971: 12). The alternative was unacceptable, some form of political elitism—dictatorship or political aristocracy.

To assist people attain their ends, the organizer was guided by tactical rules. Alinsky defined power tactics as "doing what you can with what you have." Among his thirteen tactical rules are the following:

1. Power is not only what you have but what the enemy thinks you have.
2. Never go outside the experience of your people.
3. Whenever possible go outside of the experience of the enemy.
4. Make the enemy live up to their own book of rules. (1971: 127–130)

Alinsky's last years were devoted to an attempt to mobilize the middle class, those whom he liked to refer to as the "have-a-little-want-mores." John Glass attributes the shift away from the "have-nots" to declining interest in white organizers by the black community. Whatever the case, Alinsky was convinced that future "organization for action" would focus on the middle class. As he reasoned "when more than three-fourths of our people from both the point of view of economics and of their self-identification are middle class, it is obvious that their action or inaction will determine the direction of change" (1971: 184).

The organizational means was "a proxies for people" movement. The idea was to encourage progressive corporate stockholders to donate their proxies to concerned groups to influence company decisions for any number of purposes—to challenge investments and encourage humane and socially beneficial decisions and actions. "The way of proxy participation," said Alinsky, "could mean the democratization of corporate America" (1971: 183).

According to Glass,

Today, more than a decade after his death, Alinsky remains a controversial figure. His tactics have become commonplace among small neighborhood groups across the country. In Los Angeles, for example, the United Neighborhoods Organization (UNO) operates in the barrios largely on the Alinsky model of an issue-oriented mass membership organization to pressure business and government for change and action. (1984: 37)

Clearly, clinical sociology, unlike other types of applied sociology, is both highly theoretically oriented and substantively diverse. The clinical sociologist is required to treat or solve practical human, social, and organizational problems by means of the most situationally relevant theory available. As Jonathan Moreno and Barry Glassner put it, "the choice of theoretical perspectives in particular cases depends . . . on the nature of the client and the problem being addressed" (1979: 537).

While any theory may have some clinical or applied relevance, not all types and elements of theory may be suitable for applied purposes. Applied sociologists have provided some idea of the generally desired qualities of practically relevant theory.

APPLIED SOCIOLOGICAL THEORY: DESIRED QUALITIES

William Snizek and Ellsworth Fuhrman (1980: 98) contend that a theory selected for practical use should be simple, causal, and manipulable. By simple, they mean the absence of the complexity and open-endedness that excites the academic mind but is frustrating and intolerable to those requiring timely solutions and answers to immediate problems and issues. The reference to causality addresses the practical need to specify which factors are responsible for a given problem so they can be manipulated to effect predictable results. Snizek and Fuhrman believe that the one generally accepted criterion for selecting one from a number of theoretical alternatives is predictive ability. The higher the predictive ability, the greater the control "over some future event(s)" (1980: 100).

Other factors Snizek and Fuhrman believe necessary to consider in selecting a relevant theory are time constraints and available resources. Any combination of the two is likely, of course, to be influenced by cost. Generally, the most desirable applied theory is one that costs the least and promises to be most effective in accomplishing desired results in a delimited time span. As Snizek and Fuhrman summarize their position, "the practical demands of theory in an applied context require that the applied scientist, in consultation with the client, examine the cost, effectiveness, and effects of various theories" (1980: 102).

If behavioral change is involved, Curt Tausky believes that an effective applied theory is one that incorporates "a healthy dose of tangible rewards." As he explains: "When a performance problem is at issue, employees are much more likely to alter their behavior if benefits (e.g., pay, promotion, time off) are offered" (1980: 233).

Others seek more general qualities. Stanley Seashore, for example, wants an applied theory that helps "guess where the best facts might be" (1980: 234). Along the same lines, Harry Triandis (1980: 229) looks for a theory that helps answer four questions: what to study, the interrelated variables to take into account, subjects' likely responses, and the determining conditions.

According to Triandis, the applied social scientist must adapt available theoretical means to accomplish a particular purpose. All theory, he says, must have three essential traits: accuracy or validity, generality, and parsimoniousness. The problem is that unlike their pure counterparts, applied social scientists must invariably sacrifice one or more to attain a given goal. Accuracy, for example, may be antithetical to parsimony. And in instances where budget and time constraints are high, parsimony may be the overriding consideration.

An example of what Triandis suggests is provided by the work of Peter Rossi, Richard Berk, and Kenneth Lenihan. Their research was sponsored by the U.S. Department of Labor and referred to as TARP (the Transitional Aid Research Project). The problem of concern was the bearing on the recidivism rate when ex-felons received financial aid in the form of unemployment insurance benefits for up to six months after prison discharge. Those eligible for unemployment assistance after release were compared to those from the same institution who were not. As the authors indicate, existing criminological theory had to be modified to take into account the following facts about TARP participants: (1) all were convicted felons, and many were recidivists; (2) most had been convicted for property offenses, crimes that were either a primary or supplemental source of income; (3) many had long association with the "criminal subculture"; (4) they represented the lowest status level of their local communities; and (5) their backgrounds made them incomparable to their age peers in that few had responsibilities for family support. Borrowing elements from utilitarian criminological theory and theories regarding work and occupations, testable hypotheses such as the following were constructed: "Employment will reduce all arrests by withdrawing time from illegal activities, by opening up new options, and by shaping the preferences and enhancing the self-regard of employed ex-offenders"; and "TARP payments will compete with employment and will therefore reduce the time spent on employment" (1980: 215).

The essential findings were that compared to those who did not receive financial assistance, those who did obtained better paying jobs and had a lower rate of rearrest.

The TARP study is exceptional for the way the authors skillfully used theory to examine a problem of considerable practical importance. Unfortunately, sociological theory and theory construction are all too often neglected in the survey research conducted by applied sociologists.

In brief, the desired qualities of applied sociological theory identify an ideal type whose outstanding characteristics include: accuracy, inclusiveness, predictability, simplicity, specificity, and generality. A concerted effort to construct and test theories with as many such strengths as possible could yield invaluable information both for practical and basic knowledge purposes. Whether or not applied sociologists believe it feasible and desirable to participate in such a task for other than immediate practical ends remains to be seen.

• • • • • *SUMMARY AND CONCLUSION*

The nature and purpose of applied sociological theory remains to be clarified. Its specification is dependent on determination of the extent to which pure and applied sociology are independent and interdependent. Should applied sociology be thought of as primarily independent or an integral part of a larger endeavor? Should pure sociology be thought of as something whose primary interests are independent of or directly concerned with everyday "real world," non-academically defined problems and issues? Should each side have a branch of the other? That is, if pure sociology can be thought of as having an applied side, can applied sociology be thought of as having a pure side? If desired, how is systematic unification of the two to occur?

As indicated at the close of Chapter 1, if unification of pure and applied sociology is desired, common goals must be agreed upon. If it is agreed that systematic knowledge accumulation is a common goal, there must be integration of theory, method, and problem. But which theories, methods and problems have the greatest promise of productive integration? If real world problem solving is a common ground, is the approach to be primarily reform oriented piecemeal engineering or revolutionary oriented activist intervention? If some combination of the two, of what use is clinical sociology? Until greater closure is reached on such questions than is presently the case, one must determine the nature of applied sociological theory from the way it is conceived and used by those variously engaged in sociological practice.

To some, theoretical skill is secondary to statistical and methodological expertise in the repertoire of the applied sociologist. Depending on the problem, the client's needs and interests, and a host of other factors, accurate measurement of the extent of a problem, identification of a trend and its probable consequences, and the like may be all that matters. However, in instances where diagnosis and treatment of an interpersonal or organizational problem is involved, theoretical knowledge, insight, and guidance may be crucial.

It is doubtless the case that theory needed to address everyday problems may be entirely different from that required to address problems in pure sociology. The theoretical guidance useful to a probation officer in search of services for a client, for example, is of remote relevance, at best, to one seeking the discovery of the general laws of social order and social change. But is it of no less importance to build scientifically relevant social theory from sociology's applied than pure side? Are Alinsky's principles or tactical rules of community organization any less theoretically significant than the prevailing principles of pure sociology? Such questions must be resolved if applied sociological theory is to develop and contribute to knowledge accumulation as useful to the discipline as society.

In one form or context than another, many of the questions raised here emerge in the general re-examination of basic principles that is presently occurring throughout the behavioral and social sciences. As will become evident in Chapter 4, problems and issues involving disciplinary aims such as the search for behavioral and societal laws, the merits of quantitative versus qualitative research methods, the integration of pure and applied work, and the bearing of theory on knowledge accumulation are generally pervasive.

● NOTES

1. Among the major critical works of the day was Ralf Dahrendorf's "Out of Utopia: Toward a Reorientation of Sociological Analysis," *American Journal of Sociology,* 64 (September 1958), 115-127.

2. See C. Wright Mills, "Grand Theory," Chapter 2 in his *The Sociological Imagination* (New York: Oxford University Press, 1959), 25-49.

3. See, for example, Larry T. Reynolds and Janice M. Reynolds, eds. *The Sociology of Sociology* (New York: David McKay Company, Inc., 1970).

4. See Janet M. Billson, "Saul Alinsky: The Contributions of a Pioneer Clinical Sociologist," *Clinical Sociology Review,* 2 (1984): 7-11.

● REFERENCES

Alinsky, S.D. 1971. *Rules for Radicals.* New York: Random House.

_____. 1984. "A Sociological Technique in Clinical Criminology." *Clinical Sociology Review* 2: 12-24.

Anderson, C., and L. Rouse. 1988. "Intervention in Cases of Woman Battering: An Application of Symbolic Interactionism and Critical Theory." *Clinical Sociology Review* 6: 134-147.

Billson, J.M. 1984. "Saul Alinsky: The Contributions of a Pioneer Clinical Sociologist." *Clinical Sociology Review* 2: 7-11.

Conrad, C.F. 1978 . "A Grounded Theory of Academic Change." *Sociology of Education* 51: 101-112.

DeMartini, J.R. 1982. "Basic and Applied Sociological Work: Divergence, Convergence, or Peaceful Co-existence?" *The Journal of Applied Behavioral Science* 18: 203-215;

Freeman, H.E., R.R. Dynes, P.H. Rossi, and W.F. Whyte, eds. 1983. *Applied Sociology.* San Francisco: Jossey-Bass Publishers.

Freeman, H.E., and P.H. Rossi. 1984. "Furthering the Applied Side of Sociology." *American Sociological Review* 49: 571-580.

Fuhrman, E.R. 1982. "Barriers to Applied Theory: Historical and Contemporary." *The Journal of Applied Behavioral Science* 18: 217-227.

Glass, J.F. 1979. "Reviewing An Old Profession: Clinical Sociology." *American Behavioral Scientist* 23: 513-528.

_____. 1984. Saul Alinsky in Retrospect." *Clinical Sociology Review* 2: 35-38.

Glassner, B., and J.A. Freedman. 1979. *Clinical Sociology*. New York: Longman.

Gouldner, A.W. 1956. "Explorations in Applied Social Science." *Social Problems* 3: 169-181. Reprinted in A.W. Gouldner and S.M. Miller, eds. *Applied Sociology: Opportunities & Problems*. New York: Free Press, 1965, 5-22.

_____. 1957. "Theoretical Requirements of the Applied Social Sciences." *American Sociological Review* 22: 92-102.

Hawkins, D.F. 1978. "Applied Research and Social Theory." *Evaluation Quarterly* 2: 141-152.

Janowitz, M. 1970. "Sociological Models and Social Policy." In his *Political Conflict: Essays in Political Sociology*. Chicago: Quadrangle Books.

Johnson, D.P. 1986. Using Sociology to Analyze Human and Organizational Problems: A Humanistic Perspective to Link Theory and Practice." *Clinical Sociology Review* 4: 57-70.

Johnson, G. 1981. "The Application of Grounded Theory to a Study of Corporate Growth." Working Paper 212. Birmingham, England: University of Aston Management Centre.

Kleymeyer, C.D. 1979. "Putting Field Methods to Work: A Case in a Latin American Health Setting." *American Behavioral Scientist* 23: 589-608.

Lazarsfeld, P.F., and J.G. Reitz. 1975. *An Introduction to Applied Sociology*. New York: Elsevier.

Loewenberg, B.J., ed. 1957. *Darwinism: Reaction or Reform?* New York: Rinehart.

Martin, P.Y., and B.A. Turner. 1986. "Grounded Theory and Organizational Research." *The Journal of Applied Behavioral Science* 22: 141-157.

Merton, R.K. 1949. *Social Theory and Social Structure*. New York: Free Press.

_____. 1967. *On Theoretical Sociology*. New York: Free Press.

Moreno, J.D., and B. Glassner. 1979. "Clinical Sociology: A Social Ontology For Therapy." *American Behavioral Scientist* 23: 531-542.

Nafstad, H.E. 1982. "Applied versus Basic Social Research: A Question of Amplified Complexity." *Acta Sociologica* 25: 259-267.

Popper, K.R. 1962. *The Open Society and Its Enemies, Volume I: Plato*. London: Routledge & Kegan Paul.

Rosenblatt, A., and T.F. Gieryn, eds. 1982. *Robert K. Merton: Social Research and the Practicing Professions*. Cambridge, MA: Abt Books.

Rossi, P.H., J.D. Wright, and S.R. Wright. 1978. "The Theory and Practice of Applied Social Research." *Evaluation Quarterly* 2: 171-191.

Rossi, P.H., R.A. Berk, and K. Lenihan. 1980. *Money, Work, and Crime*. New York: Academic Press.

Rossi, P.H., and W.F. Whyte. 1983. "The Applied Side of Sociology." In Freeman et al., eds., *Applied Sociology*. San Francisco: Jossey-Bass Publishers, 5-31.

Rossi, P.H., and H.E. Freeman. 1985. *Evaluation: A Systematic Approach*, 3d ed. Beverly Hills: SAGE Publications.

Rule, J.B. 1978. *Insight & Social Betterment: A Preface to Applied Social Science*. New York: Oxford University Press.

Seashore, S.E. 1980. "The Data Grubber and the Rosy-Eyed Theory: A Fable." *The Journal of Applied Behavioral Science* 16: 233-235.

Snizek, W.E. 1975. "The Relationship between Theory and Research: A Study in the Sociology of Sociology." *The Sociological Quarterly* 16: 415-428.

_____. 1982 . "Bringing Theory Back In: A Three-Year Retrospective." *The Journal of Applied Behavioral Science* 18: 495-503.

Snizek, W.E., and E.R. Fuhrman. 1980. "The Role of Theory in Applied Behavioral Science Research." *The Journal of Applied Behavioral Science* 16: 93-103.

Straus, R.A. 1979. The Reemergence of Clinical Sociology." *American Behavioral Scientist* 23: 477-486.

_____, ed. 1985. Using Sociology: An Introduction from the Clinical Perspective. New York: General Hall, Inc.

Strauss, A., L. Schatzman, R. Bucher, D. Ehrlich, and M. Sabshin. 1964. *Psychiatric Ideologies and Institutions*. New York: Free Press.

Sumner, W.G. 1957. "Why Man Could Not Remake the World, 1894." In B.J. Loewenberg, ed., *Darwinism: Reaction or Reform?* New York: Rinehart, 12-15.

Swan, L.A. 1988. "Grounded Encounter Therapy: Its Characteristics and Process." *Clinical Sociology Review* 6: 76-87.

Tausky, C. 1980. "Prediction in Applied Settings." *The Journal of Applied Behavioral Science* 16: 230-233.

Triandis, H.C. 1980. "Theoretical Reflections on Applied Behavioral Science." *The Journal of Applied Behavioral Science* 16: 229-230.

Trimble, E.G., A.B. Cherns, B.C. Jupp, and B.A. Turner. 1972. *The Effectiveness of Cost Planning and Other Cost Control Techniques in Hospital Construction*. Loughborough, England: Loughborough University of Technology.

Wirth, L. 1931. "Clinical Sociology." *The American Journal of Sociology* 37: 49-66.

Zetterberg, H.L. 1962. *Social Theory and Social Practice*. New York: Bedminster Press.

CHAPTER 4

• • •

Philosophical Problems and Issues in Contemporary Social Science

As Richard Shweder and Donald Fiske point out, increasing numbers of social scientists have expressed uneasiness about the progress of their respective disciplines (1986: 1). To many, for example, acquisition of the kind of definitive knowledge prerequisite to isolation of behavioral and societal laws seems as remote a possibility as ever. The consequence is a growing literature critical of positivism, the common philosophical source of prevailing epistemological principles and assumptions.

As indicated in Chapter 1, positivism, introduced by Comte and elaborated upon by Ward, provided the basic premises concerning the nature and interrelationship of pure and applied sociology. As the doctrine evolved at the hands of philosophers and social scientists, it became synonymous with science. The scientific study of human behavior and society required adoption of positivistic assumptions as to observation, measurement and experimentation. And the fact is, as philosopher Richard Miller states, "positivism remains the dominant philosophy of science" (1987: 3).

From the positivist viewpoint, human behavior and society are to be measured and analyzed in the same manner as all other natural phenomena. Positivists emphasize a unified view of science. Major non-positivist alternatives, such as hermeneutics and semiotics, often subsumed under the general label of interpretivism, stress the need to take account of the unique and symbolic nature of human behavior. To interpretivists, human behavior may be causally influenced by objectively quantifiable antecedents, but the subject is a decision-making entity capable of change, adaptation, and variable responsiveness. Those who practice this view are as much if not more interested in detailing the creative and idiosyncratic as they are the patterned and commonplace side of human activity.

Essential differences between devotees of positivism and interpretivism are traceable to premises concerning the differences between the natural and the human or cultural sciences. Therefore, the opening paragraphs of this chapter examine the positions of those who have influenced thought about this important subject. This is followed by a discussion of the basic elements of contemporary positivism and the major criticisms that it has incurred—particularly those directed at its "covering law model" of phenomena. Later sections consider philosophical alternatives to positivism, such as hermeneutics, and their implications for pure and applied sociological theory.

NATURAL VERSUS HUMAN SCIENCE

Major ideas concerning similarities and differences between the natural and human sciences emerged most strongly in nineteenth-century German philosophy. The subject attracted the interest of those who were inclined to be either idealists or empiricists. Idealists presumed free will to be a distinctive human trait and emphasized the variability if not the unpredictability of human behavior. Empiricists stressed the application of the methods of the natural sciences to the study of all phenomena.

The two philosophical outlooks presumed different methods and aims, the *nomothetic* versus the *idiographic*. According to Wilhelm Windelband (1848–1915), the initiator of the distinction,

> we may say that the experiential sciences seek in the knowledge of reality either the general . . . or the particular. . . . The former are sciences of laws, and the latter are sciences of events; the former teach what always is, the latter what once was. If we may be permitted to coin new artificial terms, scientific thought is *nomothetic* in the former case and *idiographic* in the latter. (Plantinga, 1980: 25)

The idealistic approach was thought to be confined to idiographic methods, such as description and comparison and the identification of similarities and differences among human behavior and events, whereas the empirical approach applied nomothetic methods, such as experimentation aimed at identifying laws.

Heinrich Rickert (1863–1936), Windelband's student, did not accept the nomothetic and idiographic distinction. He presumed that reality is composed

of objects that are either repetitive or unique. "In reality," he writes, "there are
. . . only individual objects no general objects at all; there is only the unique
and nothing that really repeats itself" (Plantinga, 1980: 26). Any science, natural or human, may search for the general (patterns, laws) or the particular (the
unique, idiosyncratic). As Don Martindale summarizes Rickert's position: "Phenomena are phenomena and science is science" (1981: 377).

Wilhelm Dilthey (1833–1911) took a more idealistic position. He distinguishes between *naturwissenschaften* (the natural sciences) and *geisteswissenschaften* (the human sciences or sciences of the mind). The essential difference between the two is that the aim of the former is to explain and the latter
to understand.

The philosophical foundation of the natural sciences are to be found in the
tenets of naturalism and positivism. Naturalism is based on the assumption of
the causal priority of the physical, the "outer," or "external world." Dilthey
holds that in naturalism "the process of nature is the sole and entire reality;
there is nothing else; mental life is only formally distinguished from physical
nature by the characteristics of consciousness which, having no content of its
own, is causally determined by physical reality" (Rickman, 1976: 146).

Positivism is defined as an attempt to interpret "mental and historical reality" from the perspective, used to study "the natural-external world" (Ermarth,
1978: 18). Dilthey describes positivism as "the philosophy of the scientists; all
cool, scientifically trained minds accept it" (Rickman, 1976: 113).

Fundamental to idealism is the assumption of the mind as an independent
and creative force or power. Dilthey regards the mind as "a unitary formative
power working from its own depths over the material of the real, a power
which constructs the real in thought" (Ermarth, 1978: 18). Thought, as an
expression of the mind, or the "inner-world," is to be plumbed by the science
of understanding, hermeneutics.

The practice of hermeneutics entails application of a particular method,
Verstehen. By *Verstehen,* Dilthey means learning to interpret the meaning of
events and objects (human and non-human) through the eyes of others. In
Dilthey's opinion the goal of the cultural sciences is an empathic understanding of individuals' "mental states." He thinks it possible to convert the commonplace and routine practice of empathy into an objectively and scientifically cultivated technique for understanding motives and goals. According to
Dilthey, "starting from life, understanding penetrates ever new depths; only by
reacting to life and society do the human studies achieve their highest significance. . . . But the road to such effectiveness must pass through the objectivity
of scientific knowledge" (Rickman, 1976: 183).

Nonetheless, understanding is always to be regarded as an ideal to strive for
rather than a fact to isolate. From Dilthey's vantage point, understanding is "a
constant process of approaching." It is something relative and partial rather
than absolute and complete. But through systematic study, understanding may
in time yield concepts of general validity.

All concepts are, of course, symbolic representations or interpretations of
something. Dilthey feels that all knowledge is essentially symbolic. When

studying human behavior, the observer perceives "expressions" indicative of "mental content." Expressions include signs and symbols but also indications of meaning not necessarily intended by the actor. Dilthey does not further specify what he has in mind here, but it may be surmised that he means particular mannerisms that people who know each other learn to interpret as indicative of mood, disposition, and the like. Whether we like it or not, our friends and relatives often sense how we really feel at a given moment despite our best efforts to conceal the truth. This fact notwithstanding Dilthey emphasizes that all understanding of another entails introspective interpretation, or criteria, from our own life experiences.

In Dilthey's theory of hermeneutics, then, understanding is based on perception. However, as Theodore Plantinga tells us, because the cultural sciences study "expressions" rather than cold, hard physical facts, "they must be based on a mode of knowledge that goes beyond perception" (1980: 103).

In brief, and instead of a hierarchy of the sciences, Dilthey envisions a dichotomy—the historical human sciences (*geisteswissenschaften*) and the natural physical sciences (*natureswissenschaften*). The subject of the former is facts that enter consciousness from "within" and the latter those that "enter consciousness from without." The *natureswissenschaften* study nature inferentially by means of hypotheses subjected to experimental validation. In the *geisteswissenschaften,* the natural subject is the human mind whose contents are grasped by means of intuition and introspection. "We explain nature," says Dilthey, "but we understand mental life." As Ermarth states, explanation, to Dilthey, means "knowledge of the laws of the causal order of natural phenomena," and understanding "knowledge of the inner life of man" (246).

Interestingly, Dilthey was concerned to seek applied or practical outlets for his theoretical and philosophical contributions. In his view, people were put on earth not merely to exist, but to act. To Dilthey any theory is "a theory of *praxis.*" Dilthey, who referred to himself as "old Praktikus," was highly active in political affairs and a member of a reformist group of intellectuals concerned with implementing knowledge to improve German society generally.

Among the most influential interpreters of Dilthey's and others' views on the difference between the natural and social sciences was Max Weber (1864-1920). He based his viewpoint on the assumption that social science emerged in response to "practical considerations." "Its most immediate and often sole purpose," he says, "was the attainment of value judgments concerning measures of State economic policy" (1949: 51). That is, the social sciences were intended to operate in the manner of "the clinical disciplines of the medical sciences" in the sense of being expected to diagnose perceived social and economic ills and prescribe a cure in the form of effective treatment policy. In time, however, the search for solutions to immediate practical problems yielded to the search for generally relevant, "immutably existent" natural laws, the presumed goal of any science. It is Weber's considered opinion that the discovery of laws "cannot be conceived as the ultimate goal of any science: neither a 'nomological' nor an 'historical' science, neither a 'natural' science nor a 'sociocultural' science" (1975: 63).

Weber is convinced that the aim of science is to determine the causes of particular events or subjects—for example, why an economic depression or political upheaval occurred where, when, and how it did. He thinks general laws irrelevant to this purpose. In his opinion, the search for natural laws results in the isolation of general concepts which reduce phenomena to "purely quantitative categories of some sort." From the methodological side of the problem, he finds inferential generalizations (lawlike formulae) irrelevant to empirical estimation of "individual causal complexes" (1975: 64).

Weber thought that if natural laws could be considered means rather than ends, they could be of use for causal analysis in the social or cultural sciences. As far as he is concerned, causal laws of cultural phenomena are useful only in so far as they help identify what he referred to as the "concrete causes of those components of a phenomenon the individuality of which is culturally significant" (1949: 79).

From Weber's standpoint, the human sciences should aim to identify not only general behavioral, social, and cultural patterns, but also the particular reasons, the causes of individual behavior. Weber believes that human behavior, society, and culture could and should be analyzed scientifically, that is, objectively and quantitatively. But the uniqueness of the study of human behavior by humans was that it can be both objectively interpreted and subjectively explained. We can seek to account for not only the general pattern in the particulars, but also the unique, particular motives behind individual expression.

Weber defines sociology as "a science which attempts the interpretive understanding of social action in order thereby to arrive at a causal explanation of its course and effects" (1947: 88). Action refers to "meaningful" behavior, that is, behavior based on consideration of alternative courses of action and decision making. Action is social when the behavior of another or others is taken into account. For Weber, the concept of social action captures what is uniquely distinctive and complex about the study of human behavior: the fact that it is not essentially automatic or instinctive but capable of variation, even in regard to the same stimulus or stimuli. This is not to say that Weber sided with those on the free-will side of the indeterminism versus determinism debate. Human behavior may be complex and variable, but it is subject to causal analysis.

In the manner of Dilthey, Weber prescribed the technique of *Verstehen*, or employment of the art of sympathetic introspection, in the effort to understand "meaningful" behavior and social action. It should be noted, however, that Weber did not accept intuition as a valid part of the practice of empathic understanding. He warned, for example, that the feelings one may have for another or others generally "fail to provide a verifiable standard for distinguishing the causally essential from the causally inessential" (1975: 180). It must be assumed, he argued, that an observer can only understand some part of the conduct of another or others, certainly never the totality. To Weber, as Julien Freund observes: "We can . . . never relive through empathy more than a few aspects of our own or another's experience; instead of reproducing or

repeating an earlier state of being, our intuitive cognition of it simply constitutes another original experience" (Freund, 1969: 45).

Application of sympathetic introspection is not, then, sufficient for causal
analysis. All empathically derived understanding is presumed to be based on
interpretation requiring independent empirical verification by statistical means
or otherwise. As Freund notes,

> Weber's position on this point never varied. Consequently, his theory cannot
> possibly be assimilated to Dilthey's, who regarded explanation and interpreta-
> tions as two independent methods. According to Weber, any relationship which
> is intelligible through interpretation should also be capable of causal explana-
> tion. It is not surprising, therefore, that he should have made frequent use of the
> expression "interpretative explanation." (1969: 100)

In brief, Weber was as concerned to temper a one-sided subjectivist as
objectivist approach to the study of human behavior and society. Human phenomena are indeed susceptible to scientific causal scrutiny, but not toward the
end of uncovering all inclusive natural laws of timeless relevance. Fundamentally, the causes of individual and social phenomena are to be regarded as of
historically restricted validity because of the uniquely creative and adaptive
abilities of the "actor." Oakes (Weber, 1975: 23) suggests that much of
Weber's "relativistic" position developed in response to positivistic ideas and
assumptions, those of John Stuart Mill in particular.

THE POSITIVIST POSITION

Mill, although critical and skeptical of much of Comte's positive philosophy,
gained much from its conception of unified science. Mill's basic assumption is
that science is a unitary approach. Scientific aims and premises, he contends,
are the same regardless of subject matter. In his view, any order of facts may
be the subject of scientific investigation. He holds an equally unequivocal position on the possibility of the scientific study of human behavior.

In Mill's view, one's position on the subject is invariably determined by the
side taken in the ancient free will versus determinism controversy—the dispute between those who believe the human will is self–determining and those
who believe that human behavior is determined in the same manner as all
other natural phenomena, that is, by empirically specifiable antecedent causes.
Mill left no doubt that he considered the latter position to be "the true one."

Mill holds the goal of the sciences of human nature, like that of any scientific endeavor, to be the discovery of general natural laws. He thinks of a scientific law as a uniformity holding true under specified conditions and confirmed
by available means of measurement. In the study of human nature, the immediate goal is identification of "the universal laws of the Formation of Character," that is, to determine (1) how different ways of thinking, feeling, and acting are formed, and (2) why individuals think, feel, and act similarly or

differently in comparable situations. Mill reasoned that if all social phenomena are "phenomena of human nature" produced by the pressure of "outward circumstances upon masses of human beings," and if ways of thinking, acting, and feeling are determined by fixed laws, then social phenomena too must be determined by fixed laws. Mill's optimistic practical hopes for the science of society are captured in the following statement:

> There is nothing chimerical in the hope that general laws, sufficient to enable us to answer these various questions for any country or time . . . really admit of being ascertained; and moreover, that the other branches of human knowledge, which this undertaking presupposes, are so far advanced that the time is ripe for its accomplishment. Such is the object of the Social Science. (1870: 549)

Methods of determining societal laws are hampered by limited means of applying the experimental method. Nonetheless, according to Mill, four types of inductive measures are possible.

The first is the *Method of Difference.* It can be used to compare groups to determine why one exhibits a more meaningful or desirable trait than another—for example, an obviously more productive economy. Mill provides the hypothetical example of two nations comparable in all respects except that one, the richer of the two, avoids protective tariffs in favor of freedom of industry. But, as might be expected, Mill thought the *Method of Difference* easier to define than apply because of the likelihood of subtle, difficult to specify causes in any given real world instance.

In the *Method of Agreement,* two or more nations may be compared and found to be different in every respect but one—for example, in having a restrictive economic system and economic prosperity. But here, too, any number of difficult to control for factors may be causally relevant. Thus, one might find use for the *Method of Concomitant Variations.* Here the goal is to uncover instances of the coexistence of like effects (what would today be referred to as a statistical correlation) in subjects of concern.

If all else fails, one might consider the *Method of Residues*—that is, by "making allowance . . . for the effect of all causes whose tendencies are known, the residue which those causes are inadequate to explain may plausibly be imputed to the remainder of the circumstances which are known to have existed in the case" (554). Mill does not mention how this application of the principle of "other things being equal" might be refined or used to make more refined estimates or measures of a factual nature.

Mill's positivism and methodological contributions variously influenced those responsible for the development of sociology in Europe and the United States. The most aggressive and literal advocate of what he and Comte had in mind was George A. Lundberg.

In an article published in 1939, Lundberg assesses the status of positivism in contemporary sociology. He contended that major elements of Comte's positive philosophy were just beginning to have an effective impact on sociology.

Among the most important assumptions in Comte's work is that the aim of all science is the discovery of "invariant natural laws." Lundberg finds sociologists generally to give at least "lip service" to the doctrine. However, he regarded "many, if not most" sociologists as unwilling to commit themselves to the kind of research methods required to identify societal laws. A second major principle of Comte's is the essential unity of science; that is, that all science not only has the same general goal but the same basic method. Comte refers to the scientific method as positivistic. It is presumed to be a component of a general stage of intellectual growth which succeeds a metaphysical stage.

A staunch advocate of the concept of science as a unified positivistic endeavor, Lundberg rigorously challenged allegedly "metaphysical" notions such as the subjective-objective, qualitative-quantitative dichotomies in the human sciences. Following Comte, he defines science as consisting of logically interrelated, empirically verifiable propositions. Propositions state relationships among variables which are symbolically interpreted phenomena. Lundberg postulates that all science is based on responses to environmental stimuli, and that symbols are invented to identify and interpret responses. Constructed symbols, in his view, are the building blocks of all communication and "the immediate data" of all science. It follows, therefore, "that for scientific purposes all attempted distinctions, hypotheses, or assumptions regarding differences in the *ultimate* 'nature' of so-called 'physical' as contrasted with 'social' data, between 'material' and 'immaterial,' 'mental,' 'spiritual,' or 'cultural' phenomena are ruled out" (Lundberg, 1964: 6).

Lundberg was convinced that the limited progress of sociology and other human sciences are the product of the unwillingness of many to fully accept scientific precepts and reject "metaphysical" assumptions. A fundamental feature of all science, he insisted, is objective measurement of units of analysis, or phenomena of concern. In the social sciences, this means "operational" definitions of social and behavioral facts. Operational definitions involve specification of replicable means used to identify what is being discussed or referred to—for example, the measurement of space by a ruler or social class by a scale of detailed attributes. "The individual sociologist," according to Lundberg, "seldom defines his terms in this manner. . . . Most of the current terms cannot be defined operationally because they are mere verbalisms derived from metaphysical postulates incapable of operational definition" (65).

A "metaphysical" position Lundberg was particularly obliged to challenge is the doctrine of free will, which means to some that human behavior is not susceptible to scientific scrutiny in the same manner as other phenomena. A position taken by Lundberg's contemporary, Robert MacIver (1882–1970), illustrates the point. As MacIver put it,

> one writer seems to object to our drawing a distinction between the type of causality involved when a paper flies before the wind and that revealed when a man flies from a pursuing crowd. When we mention the surely obvious fact that "the paper knows no fear and the wind no hate, but without fear and hate the

man would not fly nor the crowd pursue," this writer takes it as an illustration of "the tendency to regard familiar words as essential components of situations." . . . He suggests that because we can describe the amoeba's approach to its food without reference to fear and hate we should learn to abandon such references when applied to human beings! And he expresses an almost mystical hope that by resort to "operationally defined terms" science may attain this goal. Presumably in this new synthesis science will still have goals, but not human beings. (1942: 299–300)

From Lundberg's vantage point,

if anyone wishes to interpret the flying of a paper before the wind in terms of hate and fear . . . , I know of no way of refuting the analysis for it is determined by the terms, the framework, and the meanings adopted. These categories are not given in the phenomenon. . . . In fact, I have no objection to the words "fear" and "hate" if they are defined in terms of physico-chemical, biolinguistic, or sociological behavior subject to objective verification. (1964: 8)

A colleague of Lundberg's, William Catton, sees the interchange as illustrative of the difference between *animistic* and *naturalistic* thinking. Animistic thinkers believe that humans have certain qualities which exempt them from the laws of nature—that they (1) can act "without being acted upon," (2) "can be acted upon without responding," and (3) can change their behavior without cause. To those who are part of a culture that believes in free will, "such propositions," says Catton, "seem self evident." As he points out, naturalists—that is, those who practice natural science—postulate that there is no such thing as "an unmoved mover," for example, a behavioral act that does not have objectively verifiable antecedents. Furthermore, "a study is naturalistic only"

1. to the extent that it asks questions whose answers depend on sensory observations (with the aid of instruments when necessary). Thus naturalism stresses "objectivity"—in the sense that the conclusions of a study are subject to corroboration . . . by other investigators;
2. if it seeks to explain given phenomena by reference to data that are or could be available prior to (or at least concurrently with) observations of the phenomena to be explained . . . ; and
3. if it considers change, rather than continuity, to be the problem requiring explanation. (1966: 5)

When Catton's analysis was published, positivism had assumed a commanding position in sociology and all the behavioral and social sciences. If overshadowed by positivism, so-called animistic thinking maintains a steady following. Within the human disciplines is a deep sense that while all science may be of a piece, it is, nonetheless, important to study human behavior and its products as unique phenomena requiring particular methods and special theoretical orientations (frames of reference, conceptual schemes) for this purpose. As

Leszek Kolakowski reminds us, positivism is "a normative attitude" and a set of procedural rules rather than a theoretical perspective (1969: 2).

Kolakowski finds positivism to be based on four basic rules. The first is the rule of *phenomenalism*, which denies a difference between "essence," or "spirit," and "phenomena," or "things." To the phenomenalist, only that which is actually experienced may be validly recorded. Opinions regarding "occult entities" as the cause of "experienced things" are unacceptable.

The second is the rule of *nominalism,* that is, the assumption that the data of science are singular items rather than imagined, idealized, or constructed wholes or totalities of which they may be presumed to be a part. Thus, one must remember that the only real referents of any scientific generalization are "individual concrete objects" (1969: 5).

The third rule is the scientific invalidity of all value judgments and normative statements. Experience, Kolakowski emphasizes, does not contain object or event qualities that may be described as good or bad, beautiful or ugly. Further, experience also does not oblige us to heed commandments or prohibiting statements of any kind. The final rule is commitment to the essential unity of the scientific method. That is, "all spheres of experience" are presumed to be susceptible to study and analysis on the basis of the same "naturalistic principles" and as exemplified by physics. As Kolakowski sees it, positivism may be defined as "a collection of prohibitions" against accepting anything called scientific knowledge that is not tied to precisely specified operations and procedures capable of objective replication. As he states, "throughout its history positivism has turned a polemical cutting edge to metaphysical speculation of every kind, and hence against all reflection that either cannot found its conclusions on empirical data or formulates its judgments in such a way that they can never be contradicted by empirical data" (1969: 9).

POSITIVISM: CRITICAL REACTIONS

Critical reactions to positivism particularly relevant in the present context are those focusing on (1) the subordination of the theoretical to the factual, (2) general reliance on "objective" methods, such as survey research, which treat "subjective" impressions (attitudes, opinions) as empirical fact, and (3) the failure to identify the laws of society upon which systematic knowledge accumulation is presumed to be based.

The Subordination of Theory

The positivist position on the proper relationship between the theoretical and the factual is evident in the position taken on debatable questions such as the role of the human intellect in knowledge acquisition. Is the human intellect to be regarded primarily as an original and creative mechanism or as an especially sensitive reflective instrument? Does the human intellect add something to knowledge, or is it nothing more than a receptor and processor of stimuli? The classic opposing positions are those of William Whewell and J.S. Mill.

According to Whewell,

> When the Greeks, after long observing the motions of planets, saw that these motions might be rightly considered as produced by the motion of one wheel revolving in the inside of another wheel, these wheels were creations of their minds, added to the facts which they perceived by sense. . . . The same is the case in all other discoveries. . . . The pearls are there, but they will not hang together till someone provides the string. The distances are periods of the planets were all so many separate facts; by Kepler's Third Law they are connected into a single truth; but the conceptions which this law involves were supplied by Kepler's mind, and without these, the facts were of no avail. (1843: 207)

However, as the positivistically inclined Mill saw it,

> Whewell expresses himself as if Kepler had put something into the facts by his mode of conceiving them. But Kepler did no such thing. The ellipse was in the facts before Kepler recognized it, just as the island was an island before it had been sailed around. Kepler did not put what he had conceived into the facts, but saw it in them. (Mill, 1950: 177-178)

To Whewell, in other words, theoretical synthesis of previously disparate facts is a unique and creative phenomenon. To Mill, it is the product of perceptual awareness, the eventual recognition of a natural pattern awaiting discovery. One would emphasize the independence of theory; the other its dependence.

In science generally, the tendency has been to side with Mill, or to emphasize the empirical and inductive over the theoretical and deductive side of the argument. In reference to developments in physics, for example, Michael Polanyi points out that with positivism's rise to prominence at the end of the nineteenth-century, existing physical theory was "condemned as metaphysical and mystical" if it did not conform to certain standards (1958: 9). Any theory which could not be, or which appeared incapable of being "tested by experience" required revision to align predictions with "observable magnitudes." According to Polanyi, twentieth-century thinking about science has been dominated "almost entirely" by positivist philosophy.

Polanyi reports that from the positivist viewpoint, Einstein was stimulated to develop the theory of relativity to account for the results of an experiment conducted by Michelson and Morley. Polanyi could find no support for the claim. On the contrary, a review of Einstein's autobiography showed that he discovered relativity when he was sixteen and quite unaware of Michelson's and Morley's work. Polanyi states that the findings of the Michelson-Morley experiment were, "on the basis of pure speculation, rationally intuited by Einstein before he had ever heard about it" (10).

Fundamentally, Polanyi aims to refute the positivist presumption of a disjunction between subjectivity and objectivity. Scientific theory, in his eyes, is a passionate, rational and objective endeavor. As he sees it, it is commonly assumed that science is based on a set of logically interrelated statements based on observation. Polanyi believes this view is the expression of a deeply rooted cultural "craving" that "would be shattered if the intuition of rationality in nature had to be acknowledged as a justifiable and indeed essential part of scientific theory" (16). In the manner of Dilthey, he is convinced that knowing involves evaluation, and that this personal factor not only "shapes all factual knowledge," but also provides the bridge "between subjectivity and objectivity." In contrast to those who fear fictionalization or worse if the empirical does not determine the theoretical, Polanyi affirms the potential of theory to rationally and accurately synthesize the discovered and anticipate the future. As he points out, Einstein's theory of relativity not only made sense of the seemingly inexplicable, but also implied empirical possibilities that generated a continuous stream of research.

In Ernest Gellner's terms, the factually oriented are inclined to emphasize a *phenomenalist* position ("the outer world is nothing more than experience") and the theoretically predisposed a *realist* position ("the outer world is more than experience") (1986: 15). Gellner sees merit in both positions. He argues that the phenomenalist position would so restrict theory as to prevent it from generating promising leads conducive to discovery and the identification of new problems and variables worthy of examination. From Gellner's standpoint, the merit of the "phenomenalist reductionism" is that it reminds us that our data cannot show us "that there is something in the world over and above our data" (1986: 16).

However, Gellner well realizes the weakness of a relativistic stance. While its strength lies in acknowledgement of the value of the independence of both the theoretical and the factual, a relativistic position may militate against the quest for agreement on the integrated theoretical and methodological standards presumed prerequisite to knowledge accumulation. "Unless the deep questions are arbitrarily prejudged," says Gellner, "science cannot proceed, it appears" (1986: 111). Particularly in the United States, "arbitrary prejudgment" has stressed the primacy of positivistically rooted quantitative methodology.

Objectivity versus Pre-Understanding

Predictably, members of the "negative dialectically" inclined Frankfurt School have been among the most vociferous critics of the dominance of quantitative research methods in social science. Theodor Adorno, for example, contended that the allegedly objective research methods of the positivistically inclined social scientist rely on "subjectivism," the feelings and impressions of respondents. In his view, "the objectivity of empirical social research is an objectivity of the methods, not of what is investigated" (1976: 71). That is, the true object of investigation is not society but individual perception. As he put it: "The empirical methods—questionnaire, interview and whatever combination and supplementation of these is possible—have ignored societal objectivity, the embodiment of all the conditions, institutions and forces within which human beings act" (1976: 71).

As Habermas summarizes his mentor's point, "without recourse to a preunderstanding of the social lifeworld we cannot know what we are grasping with measurement operations" (1988: 104). Accepting the positivist claim that all science is dependent on symbolic interpretation of phenomena, Habermas insists that "scientific concepts must be linked to the interpretive schemata of the actor himself." Aaron Cicourel, whose viewpoint Habermas finds compatible with his own, has put it thusly: "The frequent assumption made is that the tests and surveys or interview schedules employed are self-contained. . . . The use of these instruments has not been accompanied by an explicit effort to study the subjects' or respondents' language, reasoning, and comprehension while being tested, completing a questionnaire, or responding to interview questions that are open-ended" (1986: 246–247).

The critical dissection of positivism has focused not only on the validity of its research means but also its aim of discovering universally applicable natural laws. Further, some of those most critical of the appropriateness of "the covering law" model for the behavioral and social sciences either are or have been positivistically inclined.

The Covering Law Model and Its Critics

The covering law model is essentially what was described in Chapter 2 as axiomatic theory. As Carl Hempel defines it, a scientific law is a generally relevant conditional statement subject to empirical evaluation. It is a causal explanation of why certain events occur at specified times and places. Thus, identification of a scientific law entails identification of (1) the determining conditions of the event or subject in question, and (2) a set of logically interrelated "if-then" statements. Hempel provides the following example:

> Let the event to be explained consist in the cracking of an automobile radiator during a cold night. The sentences of group (1) may state the following initial and boundary conditions: The car was left in the street all night. Its radiator, which consists of iron, was completely filled with water, and the lid was screwed on tightly. The temperature during the night dropped from 39°F. in the evening to 25°F. in the morning; the air pressure was normal. The bursting pressure of the radiator material is so and so much. Group (2) [statements] would contain empirical laws such as the following: Below 39.2°F, the pressure of a mass of water increases with decreasing temperature, if the volume remains constant or decreases; when the water freezes, the pressure again increases. Finally, this group would have to include a quantitative law concerning the change of pressure of water as a function of its temperature and volume.
>
> From statements of these two kinds, the conclusion that the radiator cracked during the night can be deduced by logical reasoning; an explanation of the considered event has been established. (1942: 36)

Hempel equates the explanation and prediction of an event via the covering law model. "If the final event can be derived from the initial conditions and universal hypotheses stated in the explanation," he writes, "then it might as well have been predicted, before it actually happened, on the basis of a knowledge of the initial conditions and the general laws" (38).

A well known interpretation of Hempel's covering law model has been provided by Rom Harre. He takes as the subject to be explained (the *explanandum*) the finding that copper conducts electricity. The explaining factor (the *explanans* or covering law) would be the general proposition that "all metals conduct electricity." Harre demonstrates the diverse theoretical possibilities of the covering law model as follows:

> For example if the law is
> All metals conduct electricity,
> then one theory could be
>   All materials which have free electrons are
>   conductors,
>   All metals have free electrons,
>   therefore
>   All metals conduct electricity.
> But another theory would be
>   All wooden things are conductors,
>   All metals are wooden,
>   therefore
>   All metals are conductors. (1985: 55)

The obvious caveat here is that logical deduction per se is not sufficient to differentiate a "good" from a "bad" theory, a valid from an invalid covering law. A second warning Harre issues is that the causal explanation of something may not be sufficient for predicting exactly "what will happen." "We know the causal mechanism of evolutionary change pretty well, but until we actually observe what happens we are unable to predict the appearance of new forms of plants and animals because of the presence of the random (unpredictable) element of mutation. . . . Explanation is always possible but prediction is not" (56).

Hempel's way out of such difficulties is, of course, the requirement of empirical testing of all elements of the covering law model by means capable of confirming or disconfirming any theoretical assumption or proposition. Whatever the theoretical or methodological complications, Hempel accepts the positivist principle of the unity of the sciences; he thinks the covering-law model as applicable to the historical and social sciences as the physical and natural sciences.

Hempel anticipated methodological difficulties, including the tendency of social and behavioral scientists to assume what required careful empirical scrutiny. In his view, explanations in history and sociology are noteworthy for failure to identify the regularities upon which they are based. He offers two reasons for the problem. The first is that because the hypotheses in question often have to do with individuals or social psychology, they are presumed to

be generally familiar to everyone and, therefore, "tacitly taken for granted."
The second is that

> it would often be very difficult to formulate the underlying assumptions explic-
> itly with sufficient precision and at the same time in such a way that they are in
> agreement with all the relevant empirical evidence available. It is highly instruc-
> tive, in examining the adequacy of a suggested explanation, to attempt a recon-
> struction of the universal hypotheses on which it rests. Particularly, such terms
> as "hence," "therefore," "consequently," "because," "naturally," "obviously," etc.,
> are often indicative of the tacit presupposition of some general law: they are
> used to tie up the initial conditions with the event to be explained; but that the
> latter was "naturally" to be expected as "a consequence" of the stated conditions
> follows only if suitable general laws are presupposed. (40)

A methodological solution to the tacit assumptions that may be involved in
social research has yet to be developed. Some attribute this fact to certain tacit
assumptions of the positivist perspective.

Roy Bhaskar, for example, finds that positivism presupposes a world consisting of closed systems composed of discrete facts, events, and processes
that are subject to empirical identification. In this frame, relationships
between measured items are regarded as predictable because it is assumed
that they are determined by generally prevalent, timelessly operable, naturally
inherent causal agents, that is, laws specifiable by means of a series of logically
deductible statements. To Bhaskar, positivism is a variety of empiricism that
denies the possibility of non-scientific knowledge and that emphasizes the
unity of science and "a strict value/fact dichotomy" (1986: 226).

For any number of reasons (invalid philosophical premises, methodological
limitations, impatience, and so on), and despite devoted application by its
adherents, positivism is generally perceived as having so far failed to identify
scientifically acceptable behavioral or societal laws. As Donald Fiske and
Richard Shweder point out, social science generalizations tend to be limited in
time and scope and dependent on the particular methods used to identify
them (1986: 4-5).

In consequence, social scientists have begun to question such basic positivistic assumptions as the unity of the sciences. Examination of the evidence
suggests to some that the covering law model is more appropriate for some
sciences than others. Roy D'Andrade, for example, finds certain disciplines to
have quite different world views, corresponding to three divisions: (1) the
physical sciences (physics, chemistry, astronomy), "and related engineering
fields," (2) the natural sciences (biology, geology), "some aspects of meteorol-
ogy and oceanography, much of economics and psychology, and some fields
of anthropology and sociology," and (3) the semiotic sciences ("linguistics and
some fields of psychology, anthropology, and sociology") (1986: 20).

The covering law model has proven most applicable in the physical sciences. According to D'Andrade, the physical science world view pictures "an
almost completely homogeneous universe" influenced by timeless forces sus-

ceptible to quantitative mathematical interpretation: "Quantitative statements using only a few terms, and with minimal restrictions on boundary conditions, serve as the prototype for the concept 'law'" (1986: 20–21).

As D'Andrade sees it, compared to that of the physical sciences, the natural science world view seems "lumpy or patchy." The nature of the DNA molecule is a case in point. On different planets with different environments, one would expect the DNA molecule to be composed of different elements and assume different forms. To D'Andrade, knowledge of the structure of the DNA molecule does not describe a scientific law but certain qualities of "a complex contingent mechanism."

The covering law model seems least applicable to the semiotic sciences. Disciplines or subjects such as linguistics and semantics in his view are based on a world view stressing the study of the ways people "impose order" on life and relationships by symbolic means of interpreting what is "meaningful" to them. Meaningful symbols, and their complex linguistic combinations, are, of course, boundary restricted (culturally, geographically, historically). "Semiotic-social science generalizations," says D'Andrade, "typically sound like interpretations totally contingent on time, place, and person" (1986: 26).

D'Andrade's basic point is that the most applicable general science model is one based on the view that appropriate theoretical generalizations are those based on "the kinds of order and regularity" found in a particular domain. As far as he is concerned, the domains of the physical, natural, and semiotic sciences are such as to require analysis by means of different scientific models that yield different forms and levels of knowledge. In D'Andrade's opinion, the emphasis placed on the identification of general laws consistent with Hempel's model has established an ideal that only physics seems capable of approaching. As he sees it, criticizing the behavioral and social sciences for failing to isolate natural laws is misdirected because the phenomena studied are complex systems unlikely to manifest basic and timeless "noninteractive" patterns.

In brief, the social science critique of positivism has stressed its (1) subordination of theory construction to determination of fact (the primacy of induction to deduction), (2) commitment to quantitative research methods dependent on the subjective views, opinions. and attitudes of respondents, and (3) assumption that all phenomena (whether inanimate or animate) are subject to examination and analysis by means of a common scientific approach aimed at uncovering invariant natural laws.

Recent positivistic philosophy (as initiated by Comte and developed by Ward and Lundberg) arose in reaction to perceived shortcomings and errors in deductive and other "subjective" interpretations of human behavior and society. Philosophical positions antithetical to positivism may be subsumed under what William Catton refers to as varieties of animism—orientations that regard human behavior as a unique natural phenomenon requiring analysis by means of singular theoretical and methodological strategies. Since World War II, the dominant perspective in this vein has been hermeneutics, whose list of diverse contributors includes Dilthey and Weber. Despite their basic differences, which will be brought out in a later section, both hermeneutics and positivism reject the possibility of what Richard Shweder refers to as "a science of subjectivity" (1986: 176).

HERMENEUTICS: INTERPRETIVE UNDERSTANDING

Although hermeneutics is primarily an outgrowth of eighteenth and nineteenth century German philosophy, its basic elements have been traced to very beginning of Western philosophy. Hans Gadamer, a major hermeneutic philosopher, credits Aristotle with having specified its essential point of departure. "According to Aristotle," says Gadamer, "the idea of a single method, a method which could be determined before even having penetrated the thing, is a dangerous abstraction; *the object itself* must determine the method of its own access" (1979: 114).

The object in question in this instance is the willing, acting human being—the subject of symbolic interactionists and social action theorists. Unlike traditionally ahistorical American symbolic interactionists, however, devotees of hermeneutics stress a conception of the actor as an integral part of historical development in the broadest possible sense. The individual is thought of as both a product of and a contributor to nothing less than what has been referred to in Western social thought as "the great chain of being."

Individuals are thought of not as objects in space determined by all manner of forces beyond their control, but as complex organisms continuously influenced by and influencing all that they are part of—and this includes all past and present social and cultural networks. The individual is seen as a continuously developing component of the ever evolving process of historical change.

Hermeneuticists aim to "understand" individuals from their own acting vantage points. "Understanding" is variously defined, but generally refers to what Weber meant by the concept of *Verstehen:* how and why given individuals attach "meaning" to some things (objects and values) rather than others. The goal is to understand what is meaningful to particular individuals and how and why they decide to orient themselves to certain meaningful objects and values at certain times and places. While here too there is a parallel between social action theory and hermeneutics, the latter emphasizes not only what is meaningful to particular individuals at a given time and place, but also—and primarily—how meaning changes. It is the seemingly indefinite adaptive potential of humans that captures the hermeneutic imagination.

Understanding is never complete; it is a consequence of interpretation that is subject to indefinite revision. Echoing Dilthey, Gadamer insists that interpretation is intended to be something approximate, "clearly never definitive" (1981: 195). Hermeneutics, then, is not to be viewed as an alternative means to positivism in the quest to obtain exact knowledge via measurement of relationships among precisely definable quantities. It is a perspective of a different order, one whose advocates are ostensibly motivated less to objectively analyze or understand human behavior toward the end of acquiring the knowledge prerequisite to scientifically guided social change than freeing individuals from the fact or possibility of dominance via science or anything else. Because critical theorists, too, espouse the goal of human emancipation, it is not surprising to find them among the major contributors to hermeneutic thought. Both hermeneuticists and critical theorists view positivism as conducive to scientism, which they view as an effective means of social control and oppression in complex industrial societies of any kind (Marxist, capitalist, or whatever). In a nutshell, hermeneutics includes an analytical (pure or theoretical) and a political (applied or political) agenda.

The analytic means of interpretation (whether the object is a written text or oral expression) is common language. It is via everyday language that understanding is achieved in routine discourse and science. The hermeneutic emphasis on ordinary language analysis becomes evident when contrasting the theoretical aims of the hermeneutic and the empirical sciences. As Habermas explains it, the empirical sciences seek abstract general categories (laws) to interpret known particulars. The hermeneutic sciences reverse the process. That is, hermeneutics "grasps individual life experience in its entire breadth but has to adapt a set of intentions centered around an individual ego to the general categories of language" (1971: 162–163).

Hermeneuticists are particularly concerned to relate specific interpretations of the meaning of any element of ordinary language to a "concrete life context." A concrete life context is to be construed as not only a given "situation," but also a given point in time, in the history of a particular socio-cultural tradition. Individuals and their language are parts of larger wholes, and the hermeneuticist interprets the meaning of each side of the equation in relation to the other. The "part-whole" analytical frame is referred to as "the hermeneutic circle." Dilthey's description of the process of interpreting written text illustrates the concept.

> The whole of a work must be understood from individual words and their combination but full understanding of an individual part presupposes understanding of the whole. The circle is repeated in the relation of an individual work to the mentality and development of its author, and it recurs again in the relation of such an individual work to its literary genre. (1976: 259)

Hermeneuticists regard social behavior and knowledge ("common" and scientific) as based on "dialogical" language and thinking. That is, interaction between two people (ego and alter) or an individual and a written document (a reader and a text) is based on learned preconceptions of diverse possible meaning. Through interaction, which may, and often is, of an experimental or trial and error nature, individuals seek and generally achieve a level of understanding of one another's messages. In hermeneutic thinking, as in symbolic interaction theory, interpretative understanding is based on self-development and awareness. In the manner of Charles Cooley and George Mead, self-growth is a presumed product of interaction and the ability of ego to view himself or herself through interpretations of the reactions of others. Self-understanding is viewed as a lifelong process and "something" never either fully or accurately achieved. "Self-understanding is always on the way; it is on a path whose completion is a clear impossibility" (Gadamer, 1981: 103).

The hermeneutic political agenda is based on the ideal of freedom, the right of every individual to pursue self-understanding and knowledge as he or she sees fit. "To be free," notes Roy Bhaskar, "is: (1) to know one's real interests, (2) to possess both (a) the ability and the resources, that is, generally the power, and (b) the opportunity to act in (or towards) them; and (3) to be disposed to do so" (1986: 170). For the ideal to occur individuals must become aware of the variety of constraints (particularly the nature and extent to which scientism intrudes in modern life) that limit and prevent choice. The necessary prerequisite of freedom is, then, human emancipation aided and abetted by engaged social science. Bhaskar contends that regardless of commitment to the ideals of value neutrality and scientific objectivity, the human sciences

> are necessarily non-neutral. . . . It is my contention that special qualitative kind of becoming free or liberation which is emancipation . . . is both causally presaged and logically entailed by explanatory theory, but that it can only be effected in practice. Emancipation . . . depends upon the transformation of structures, not the alteration or amelioration of states of affairs. In this special sense an emancipatory politics or practice is necessarily both grounded in scientific theory and revolutionary in objective or intent (169, 171).

However revolutionary in theory the objectives of traditional social science, Josef Bleicher makes the case for a hermeneutically and dialectically oriented sociology as an actual and effective way of working toward human emancipation. According to Bleicher social analysis should focus on the relationship between the conditions under which different types of communication occur and given social, economic and political conditions. As he sees it, "Only through freeing communicative processes from obsolete domination through a release of our hermeneutic imagination can we be in a position to tackle internal social problems and thereby also to progress towards a lessening of the dangers of international confrontation and possible self-extinction" (1982: 152).

To summarize this brief interpretation of an exceptionally wide-ranging and complex philosophical viewpoint, hermeneutics, in contrast to positivism, stresses the study of behavior and society through the deliberately imprecise method of individual interpretations of the meaning of the common language of people generally. Instead of emphasizing the unity of science and a universal phenomenological approach, hermeneuticists accent the uniqueness of human behavior and its analysis by means that acknowledge its creative and adaptive potential. Concern with the open-ended side of human behavior is conducive to commitment to the value of individual freedom, the release of the individual from anything which may arbitrarily restrict self initiative and decision making. Consequently, politically sensitive hermeneuticists have been inclined to adopt the negative dialectical stance of the critical social theorist.

Lastly, as noted in the discussion above, the hermeneutic perspective has much in common with symbolic interactionist thought. The interest in behavioral analysis by learning to see the world through the eyes of the individual actor, the emphasis on learning as an interaction process between ego and alter, and a definition of learning and knowledge as based on increasing self awareness are merely some of their noted common themes. But hermeneutics differs from interpretive sociology in important ways. A major difference occurs in regard to the concept of objectivity. As Habermas has explained it,

> From the point of view of hermeneutic self-reflection, the phenomenological and linguistic foundations of interpretive sociology belong with historicism. Like the latter, they fall prey to objectivism, for they claim a purely theoretical attitude for the phenomenological observer and the linguistic analyst when in fact both of them are bound up with their object domain through communicative experience and thus can no longer lay claim to the role of the uninvolved observer. (1988: 153)

In the hermeneutic frame, "all understanding," as Bleicher says, "is prejudiced" (1982: 70). That is, all interpretation is assumed to be based on foreknowledge and, therefore, bias. Therefore, in analyzing a text, for example, Gadamer, reminds us that "the important thing is to be aware of one's own bias so that the text may present itself in all its newness and thus be able to assert its own truth against one's own foremeanings" (Bleicher, 1982: 71).

And finally, hermeneutics, unlike ahistorical, objectivity-oriented interpretive sociology, is fundamentally interested in historical consciousness. To once more cite Gadamer: "Historical consciousness is interested in knowing not how men, people, or states develop in general, but, quite on the contrary, how this man, this people, or this state became what it is; how each of these particulars could come to pass and end up specifically *there*" (1979: 116).

IS THERE A THIRD WAY?

From the positivist viewpoint, valid knowledge acquisition—that is, science— is predicated on the necessity of objective measurement of precisely defined phenomena. Precise measurement requires documentation of all referents so that any competent scientist can independently verify the work of another. To the positivist, any concept or theory that has not been objectified (that is, has not been either operationally defined or authenticated by specified procedures and instrumentation) is scientifically meaningless.

From the standpoint of hermeneutics, human behavior and its products (culture and society) are not precisely quantifiable because they are the product of subjective determinants, the nature of which can only be probed and partially understood by even the most sensitive and gifted investigator.

Richard Shweder contends that despite their clear differences, positivists and hermeneuticists both reject the possibility of a science of human subjectivity. In each perspective, there are only two possibilities: "subjectivity devoid of matter (culture) and matter devoid of subjectivity (nature)" (1986: 177). In his view, the objective-subjective distinction upon which the dichotomous views positivism and hermeneutics is based is outmoded, and that it is time to consider the possibility of a science of subjectivity.

Shweder thinks that such a science requires a broadened conception of rationality and meaning. A broadened conception of rationality would include analysis of the influence of rational, nonrational and irrational processes on subjective experiences. As he sees it,

> A rational process is a self-regulating process controlled by, or at least guided by, impersonal criteria, reason, and evidence. It can be distinguished, on the other hand, from nonrational processes, where reason and evidence are irrelevant to subjective experience. . . . On the other hand, rational processes can be distinguished from irrational processes, where there is a breakdown or degradation of the capacities that support rationality. (180)

Furthermore, the study of the meaning of something in the broadest sense includes not only notions of objective and subjective meaning (meanings that are general and empirically verifiable and those that are personal and idiosyncratic), but also that (1) subjective meanings are not always random or individually unique, and (2) seemingly subjective words and terms may be "orderly, reliable, impersonal, and shared."

Essentially, then, Shweder calls for a blurred distinction between the so-called objective and subjective, an analytical perspective based on the possibility of "divergent rationalities" and a science of subjectivity. From his vantage point,

> The object world . . . is subject dependent. Subjectivity is objectlike. Rationality is compatible with diversity. The emergence of schools of thought, cults, and cultures is to be expected—perhaps even encouraged. Reality is not independent of our version of it. Within any version there is a distinction to be made between what's real and what's unreal, but not necessarily the same distinction. (191)

• • • • • SUMMARY AND CONCLUSION

Social scientists have become increasingly critical of the positivistic philosophy that has long dominated their several disciplines. The positivistic assumption of the unity of science, particularly as related to the goal of identifying nature's invariant natural laws, has been questioned to the point where many are willing to either reject it or adopt a hermeneutic viewpoint. If isolation of natural laws comes to be regarded by sociologists as no longer feasible, the original basis for separating pure and applied sociology, the theoretical from the practical, no longer attains. Lacking an alternative rationale, separation of the subjects by time and function becomes unjustified and unnecessary. This must be regarded as only a distant possibility as separation of the theoretical and the practical has become an entrenched convention. Even more remote, however, is the possible "withering away" of established ways of differentiating between positivistic and interpretive social science.

The positivistic and hermeneutic perspectives are an outgrowth of the ancient Western philosophical tradition of distinguishing between the physical and natural sciences on the one hand and the historical-behavioral-socio-cultural sciences on the other. The distinction has given rise to a series of opposing positions and concepts—objectivity versus subjectivity, quantity versus quality, materialism versus idealism, and naturalism versus animism. On one hand are those who would emphasize scientific study of human behavior and society toward the end of acquiring solid evidence upon which to improve the lot of all humankind; on the other are those who stress the need to acknowledge the unique and creative potential of every individual and the need and value of promoting human emancipation from all non-self-imposed constraint. Although both points of view have much to offer, there is a tendency among sociologists to commit to one or the other.

To the positivistically inclined, all phenomena, animate and inanimate, are governed by natural laws whose identification by means of objective and value-free methods is the goal of all science. To the hermeneutically inclined, phenomena do not have a reality independent of the mind that interprets them. In this frame, science, as any other shared interpretive skill, is based on symbolic and linguistic conventions, and, therefore, inherently value biased. To the critically predisposed hermeneuticist, the positivistic effort to objectify the study of human behavior leads to the collection of information useful for authoritative manipulation of people. They aim to "deconstruct" the pervasive influence of positivism and replace it with a critical philosophy aimed at freeing people from all efforts to structure their lives independently of their will.

Among those sympathetic to the hermeneutic critique of positivism are those equally critical of certain implications of adoption of the hermeneutic perspective. With hermeneutics uppermost in mind, Alan Wolf, writes,

> A new approach has emerged, unlike that of the 1950s, when scholars believed in value neutrality even while rarely practicing value neutrality; if there is no reality out there upon which we can all agree, it is a short step to the conclusion that all knowledge is a political weapon in the hands of one group or another. Power, and only power, is therefore understood to determine which ideas receive a hearing and which do not. Sociology thus becomes part of the struggle for ideological hegemony in advanced capitalist societies. . . . As political lines harden, intellectual curiosity may give way to sectarianism, self-censorship, name calling, and other signs of battle fatigue. What out to be an opening would become, in a politicized atmosphere, instead a closing. (1990: 141, 143)

To some, however, the presence of competing perspectives encourages intellectual freedom by providing a check on the possibility of domination by any one viewpoint. And, as suggested above, the competing claims of the positivistic and hermeneutic perspectives suggests to others the need to seek a middle ground, one that incorporates selected elements of each. Those of this view are few, and the identification of a synthesis seems, at best, only a remote possibility.

The existence of entrenched positivistic views and a growing hermeneutic opposition has certain implications for those concerned with reconciling the often conflicting aims of pure and applied sociology. When doing applied work, for example, one is often confronted with having to decide whether commitment to scientific aims is more important than infringement on subjects' individual rights. The problems and issues involved in such a situation are diverse and complex. They are the central concern of the next chapter.

• REFERENCES

Adorno, T.W. 1976. "Sociology and Empirical Research." In T.W. Adorno, et al., *The Positivist Dispute in German Sociology*. London: Heinemann Educational Books Ltd.

Adorno, T.W., H. Albert, R. Dahrendorf, J. Habermas, H. Pilot, and K.R. Popper. 1976. *The Positivist Dispute in German Sociology*. London: Heinemann Educational Books Ltd.

Bhaskar, R. 1986. *Scientific Realism & Human Emancipation*. London: Verso.

Bleicher, J. 1982. *The Hermeneutic Imagination*. London: Routledge & Kegan Paul.

Catton, W.R., Jr. 1966. *From Animistic to Naturalistic Sociology*. New York: McGraw-Hill.

Cicourel, A.V. 1964. *Method and Measurement in Sociology*. New York: Free Press.

D'Andrade, R. 1986. "Three Scientific World Views and the Covering Law Model." In D.W. Fiske and R.A. Shweder, eds. *Metatheory in Social Science*. Chicago: University of Chicago Press, 19–41

Dilthey, W. 1976. "The Development of Hermeneutics." In H.P. Rickman, *W. Dilthey: Selected Writings*. Cambridge, MA: Cambridge University Press, 247–263.

Ermarth, M. 1978. *Wilhelm Dilthey: The Critique of Historical Reason*. Chicago: University of Chicago Press.

Freund, J. 1969. *The Sociology of Max Weber*. New York: Vintage.

Gadamer, H.G. 1979. "The Problem of Historical Consciousness." In P. Rabinow and W. M. Sullivan, eds. *Interpretive Social Science*. Berkeley: University of California Press, 103–160.

_____. 1981. *Reason in the Age of Science*. Cambridge, MA: M.I.T. Press.

Gellner, E. 1986. *Relativism and the Social Sciences*. London: Cambridge University Press.

Habermas, J. 1971. *Knowledge and Human Interests*. Boston: Beacon Press.

_____. 1988. *On The Logic of the Social Sciences*. Cambridge, MA: M.I.T. Press.

Harre, R. 1985. *The Philosophies of Science*. New York: Oxford University Press.

Hempel, C.G. 1942. "The Function of General Laws in History." *The Journal of Philosophy* 38: 35–48.

Kolakowski, L. 1969. *The Alienation of Reason: A History of Positivist Thought*. New York: Anchor Books.

Lundberg, G.A. 1939. "Contemporary Positivism in Sociology." *American Sociological Review* 4: 42-55.

————. 1964. *Foundations of Sociology.* New York: David McKay Company, Inc.

MacIver, R.M. 1942. *Social Causation.* Boston: Ginn and Co.

Martindale, D. 1981. *The Nature and Types of Sociological Theory,* 2d ed. Prospect Heights, IL: Waveland Press, Inc.

Mill, J.S. 1870. *System of Logic: Ratiocinative and Inductive.* New York: Harper & Brothers.

Miller, R.W. 1987. *Fact and Method.* Princeton, NJ: Princeton University Press.

Plantinga, T. 1980. *Historical Understanding in the Thought of Wilhelm Dilthey.* Toronto: University of Toronto Press.

Polanyi, M. 1958. *Personal Knowledge.* Chicago: University of Chicago Press.

Rickman, H.P., ed. 1976. *W. Dilthey: Selected Writings*: Cambridge, MA: Cambridge University Press.

Shweder, R.A., 1986. "Divergent Rationalities." In D.W. Fiske and R.A. Shweder, eds., *Metatheory in Social Science.* Chicago: The University of Chicago Press, 163-196.

Shweder, R.A., and D.W. Fiske. 1986. *Metatheory in Social Science.* Chicago: University of Chicago Press.

Weber, M. 1947. *The Theory of Social and Economic Organization.* New York: Free Press.

————. 1949. *The Methodology of the Social Sciences.* Glencoe, IL: Free Press.

————. 1975. *Roscher and Knies.* New York: Free Press.

Whewell, W. 1843. *The Philosophy of the Inductive Sciences.* London: John W. Parker.

Wolf, A. 1990. "Sociology as a Vocation." *The American Sociologist* 21: 136-149.

CHAPTER 5

● ● ●

Ethics, Morals, and Values in Sociological Theory

Ethics, morals, and values are integral parts of social science. They influence all phases and elements of social research. Theoretical slant, strategy and interpretation, research topic selection, data types and sources, interview schedule and questionnaire construction, data analysis and reporting of findings are structured by values and constrained by ethical and moral prescriptions and proscriptions emanating from society, the general scientific community, a particular discipline and, of course, investigators' individual backgrounds. The purpose of this chapter is to examine the role and impact of these three factors in the development of pure and applied sociological theory.

Of initial concern are common definitions and prevailing interpretations of the three basic concepts. The aim here is to not only differentiate the three, but also to show how they are interrelated. This is followed by a discussion of such topics as value neutrality and value-free science, and ethical problems and issues that they have provoked. Of particular interest is the role of philosophical outlook in the conduct of social science, especially as expressed in the difference between the utilitarian and the deontological positions. Further, a range of well-known cases is considered—from Project Trinity (the effort to construct the first atomic bomb) to Project Camelot (an aborted behavioral and social science effort initiated by the U.S. Department of Defense). Later sections examine the bearing of morality in social science generally and pure and applied sociological theory in particular. The essential point is the need to consider and examine the bearing of normative phenomena on not only societal members and research participants, but also behavioral and social scientists and the kind of knowledge they collect and disseminate.

THE CONCEPTS DEFINED

Ethics and morals are frequently juxtaposed because they are often defined in relation to each other. A common dictionary definition of ethics, for example, is "the science of morals." Despite their close relationship, the two may be differentiated. Ethics refers primarily to a body of principles or rules, such as the codes of ethics adopted by professional bodies. An example is the code of ethics adopted by the American Sociological Association (ASA), which contains some 56 rules subsumed under the following five headings:

I   **The Practice of Sociology,** for example, "Sociologists should adhere to the highest possible technical standards in their research, teaching and practice."

II **Publications and Review Process,** for example, "Sociologists must acknowledge all persons who contribute to their research and to their copyrighted publications."

III **Teaching and Supervision,** for example, "Sociologists should provide students with a fair and honest statement of the scope and perspective of their courses, clear expectations for student performance, and fair, timely, and easily accessible evaluations of their work."

IV **Ethical Obligations of Employers, Employees, and Sponsors,** for example, "When acting as employers, sociologists should specify the requirements for hiring, promotion, and tenure and communicate these requirements thoroughly to employees and prospective employees."

V   **Policies and Procedures,** for example, "The Committee on Professional Ethics appointed by the Council of the American Sociological Association, shall have responsibility for: interpreting and publicizing this Code, promoting ethical conduct among sociologists, receiving inquiries about violations of the Code, investigating complaints concerning the ethical conduct of members of the American Sociological Association, mediating disputes to assist the parties in resolving their grievances, holding hearings on formal charges of misconduct, and recommending actions to the Council of the American Sociological Association."[1]

The main difference between ethical and moral concerns is one of degree. Generally, morals refer to a society's most serious normative expectations— for example, those involving the preservation of life or prohibitions such as the incest taboo. Accordingly, morals, whether violated or adhered to, are susceptible to rigid assessment. According to the *Oxford English Dictionary*, morals pertain "to character or disposition, considered as good or bad, virtuous or vicious," or "the distinction between right and wrong, or good and evil, in relation to the actions, volitions, or character of responsible beings." As Gordon Shea states, the key here is "judgment made according to some perceived standard of good or evil" (1988: 17).

Common to conceptions of the ethical and moral is the notion that enduring relationships and societies are bound by ideals, standards that require reaching beyond the timebound toward something timeless. Ethics and morals require people—especially certain societal functionaries—to conduct themselves on the basis of principles that exceed the immediate, obvious, and practical. The more important and serious the responsibilities, the greater the ideal ethical and moral constraints. Thus, those who must deal with matters of life and death—for example, physicians, biomedical researchers, and police officers—are expected to take exceptional care to preserve life. Because they are entrusted with great autonomy, authority, and power, they should be bound by principles which they adhere to even in the face of popular opinion. Ideally, their harshest judge should not be their peers or the general public but their own conscience and sense of integrity.

Put another way, and in Durkheim's words, "the domain of morality is the domain of duty"; that is, "to conduct one's self morally is a matter of abiding by a norm determining what conduct should obtain in a given instance even before one is required to act" (1973: 23). To anticipate a duty is to have a clear sense of values, of what should be done and how it should be done.

Values, according to the OED, are "principles, standards, or qualities considered worthwhile or desirable." In addition to principles (for example, "the Ten Commandments"), standards (for example, norms from informal expectations, such as rules regarding everyday social etiquette to formally enacted laws), qualities (for example, mental and physical health), values also refer to highly regarded entities or quantities (for example, foodstuffs, clothing, jewelry).

Although the concept of values encompasses standards such as normative expectations, values refer to something more general than norms. "The difference between values and norms," points out Ian Robertson, "is that values are abstract, general concepts, whereas norms are behavioral rules or guidelines for people in particular kinds of situations" (1977: 59).

Societal values are shared conceptions of what is desired and meaningful. A common textbook definition refers to values as "those goals and standards of society in which people have great emotional investment."[2] Values structure and orient behavior by directing it toward ends, from the positive and liberating (equality, freedom) to the negative and repressive (bigotry, prejudice). Scientific objectivity is generally presumed to require adherence to the principle of value neutrality.

VALUE NEUTRALITY

Value neutrality requires the scientist to maintain an open mind, a receptive attitude toward factual or empirical information, especially that which is new and unanticipated. To paraphrase Saul Alinsky (1971: xix), one should relate to the world as it is rather than as it might or should be. Conformity to the ethic requires the scientist to do everything possible to avoid contaminating basic scientific procedures (observation, experimentation, and so on) with personal bias, prejudice, or any sort of unacknowledged preconception that might distort data collection or predetermine results. As Stephen Toulmin describes it, the value neutral prescription compels a "passionless objectivity." "Natural science," he says, "is successful (on this view) just because its inquiries are purely cognitive and so undistorted by the affective preoccupations of individual scientists" (1981: 24). The ethic of value neutrality was a subject of intense critical scrutiny during the 1960s, a period of intense political activity and questioning of all manner of prevailing premises, norms, and values in science and society generally.

The social scientist whose ideas on the subject invariably provided the point of departure of the critically disposed was Max Weber. The focal point of Weber's observations was not so much the general conduct of science but the tendency of his colleagues to use the classroom as a means of venting political bias under the guise of scientific authority. The period when he wrote on the subject, the turn of the century years leading to World War I, was marked by heightened political consciousness in Germany and throughout Europe. Weber did not argue that value judgments either could or should be always avoided. When employed by the teacher, he called for their clear identification and separation from "statements of logically deduced or empirically observed facts." According to Weber,

> What is really at issue is the intrinsically simple demand that the investigator and teacher should keep unconditionally separate the establishment of empirical facts (including the "value-oriented" conduct of the empirical individual whom he is investigating) and his own practical evaluations, i.e., his evaluation of these facts as satisfactory or unsatisfactory (including among these facts evaluations made by the empirical persons who are the object of investigation). (1949: 2)

Among the more aggressive advocates of the principle of scientific objectivity and value neutrality was George Lundberg. He acknowledges the fact that value judgments are involved whenever scientific knowledge is implemented. He insists, however, that scientists are not particularly obligated to determine the ends to which their knowledge may be put. Writing in 1939, Lundberg argued that scientists are obligated only to make public "the immediate and remote costs and consequences of alternative possible courses of action." They may then "in their capacity as citizens join with others in advocating one alternative rather than another, as they prefer" (1964: 28). As he summarizes the point, science provides the car and the chauffeur, but it does not "tell us where to drive."

Behind Lundberg's position is the premise that science is the servant, not the master of humankind. In democratically constituted society, science is a means to ends all citizens may have an equal right to influence and determine.

In Lundberg's view, scientific knowledge is collected by objective and impersonal means for whatever subjective and personal uses humankind desires.

Neither Lundberg nor Weber contend that value judgments play no role in the conduct of science. Both acknowledge the fact that values influence the problems selected for examination by behavioral and social scientists, as well as theoretical slant, choice of research strategy and method, and data interpretation. The point emphasized by each, however, is that these facts are inescapable problems to analyze and confront rather than natural intrusions to be accepted without question. Anything that might contaminate the objective validity of science must be, in their view, systematically studied and taken into account as in any controlled scientific experiment. Both hold strong views on science as a highly rational and value neutral endeavor for a number of reasons, not the least important of which is its possible use by the charismatic and manipulative for reasons other than human liberation or the attainment of democratically determined goals.

However noble and logical the reasons for its articulation, the doctrine of value neutrality, as in the case of so many idealistic concepts, has both positive and negative attributes. On the positive side, it promotes scientific objectivity and the validity of information obtained by scientific means. On the negative side, it is associated with promoting insensitivity to moral questions and the human consequences of scientific experiment and results. In applied science, an outstanding example of the problem is project "Trinity," the American effort led by theoretical physicist Robert Oppenheimer to develop the first atomic bomb.

Evidence suggests that Oppenheimer and his colleagues were so caught up by the scientific challenge of developing the first atomic weapon that they virtually ignored the moral implications of what they were doing until after their success at Los Alamos, New Mexico, in July 1945. According to Philip Stern,

> Within seventy-two hours, laudatory words from Washington would begin to be heaped on Oppenheimer and his colleagues. General Groves called the achievement "a high-water mark of scientific and engineering performance. . . . Oppenheimer was later to recall that at the time "it was hard for us in Los Alamos not to share that satisfaction, and hard for me not to accept the conclusion that I had managed the enterprise well and played a key part in its success."
>
> In the ensuing days, however, "the whole community [of Los Alamos] experienced a kind of cathartic shock," according to one authoritative account. "Unfaced issues suddenly loomed large. The scientists now talked of little else but the effect of the bomb upon the postwar world." (1969: 81-82)

Apparently, the impact of what they had unleashed on the world was not really felt by the Oppenheimer team until after the dropping of the atomic bomb on Hiroshima. As Stern tells it,

> the efforts of a few to assemble a celebratory party proved at best halfhearted. According to one account: "People either stayed away or beat a hasty retreat.

Oppenheimer found a level-headed young group leader being sick in the bushes and knew that the reaction had begun." (82–83)

In applied social science an example of moral and ethical indifference associated with adherence to value neutrality is the ill-fated Project Camelot. In 1964, the Special Operations Office (SORO) of the Army Department announced the provision of funds for a study "to determine the feasibility of developing a general social systems model which would make it possible to predict and influence politically significant aspects of social change in the developing nations of the world" (Horowitz, 1967: 4–5). That is, the study aimed to develop a system for collecting and using data on the revolutionary potential in developing nations (Latin America first of all) and assisting governments to alleviate the conditions conducive to revolution. The operating period was to be three to four years at an annual budget of about one and one-half million dollars. However, the project was cancelled by the Secretary of Defense less than a year after it was announced.

Project participants included a variety of social scientists (anthropologists, economists, political scientists, psychologists, and sociologists). A sociologist, Rex Hopper, headed the project. When work of the planned research reached the press and politically responsible elements at home and abroad, the reaction was predictably negative. The project was suspected of being a CIA or Defense Department front, an attempt to protect American interests in Third World nations by developing a means for the timely identification and elimination of threatening political movements.

A central concern of those critical of their professional colleagues' involvement in Project Camelot was their apparent embrace of values other than that of non-interference in the lives of citizens of other sovereign nations. The aim was to learn something about people that could be used against them. Those to be studied were not to be accorded respect equal to the paying client. This is not, of course, an uncommon possibility in applied work, and, therefore, its possible antecedents require careful consideration. There is, for one thing, an inclination to wish to provide clients with what they want, even to play the role of servant. In the case of Project Camelot, according to Horowitz, "it became clear, that the social scientist was not so much functioning as an applied social scientist as he was performing the role of supplying information to a powerful client" (37).

To the idealist, principles such as freedom of inquiry—the persistent application of an independent, open, and critical mind—are never to be compromised. To the realist, compromises must be made if the social scientist is to play an active and creative role in human affairs. This is the essential tact pursued by Project Camelot participant and defender Robert Boguslaw. He questioned the "real world" validity of the value neutral doctrine advocated by Lundberg. In his words,

I have no quarrel with Lundberg's desire to predict social weather. . . . I do, however, take issue with his concept of social science as an activity that can be pursued in a value vacuum. The notion of science as a means for providing an exhaustive analysis of all possible alternatives from which the nonscientist can select is simply not viable for the world I know. . . . Lundberg's concept of science is one that postulates only established situations. He implicitly omits consideration of the possibility of an emergent situation science. Such a view permits the social scientist to avoid responsibility for policy guidance. (1967: 117–118)

If Boguslaw rejects the practicality of Lundberg's conception of value neutrality, he appears to embrace the notion that "the end justifies the means" when he suggests that practical goals may take precedence over conventional ethical ideals. If social scientists are to play an active role in practical affairs and the creation of important public policy, he suggests that they must become active in such client-sponsored research as Project Camelot.

On Means and Ends

Boguslaw's position is compatible with *utilitarian* ethical theory. Those who conceive of science as a means to ends and something subject to conventional moral constraint favor a *deontological* ethical position.

Utilitarian ethical theory is also referred to as consequentialism because its basic principle is that "the rightness or wrongness of an act can be judged by its consequences" (Holden, 1979: 537). To the utilitarian, the test of an act's worth is whether or not it effects greater good than harm. Utilitarian thinking, for example, would justify risking the lives of some in order to test the effectiveness of a new and promising cancer cure. It would permit short-term harm for long-range benefits. "Thus," notes Constance Holden, "the introduction of hepatitis virus in a childrens' home might be justified on the grounds that many cases of hepatitis will ultimately be prevented by the research" (537). Fundamentally, utilitarian ethics are based on maximizing benefits to the greatest number. As Jeffrey Reiman states, "utilitarians hold that the purpose of morality is to maximize satisfaction (more precisely, net satisfaction, i.e., the sum of satisfactions minus the sum of dissatisfactions) for everyone, and the ultimate moral rule is: Act always so as to maximize (net) satisfaction for everyone" (1979: 36–37).

A major criticism of consequentialism is that it sacrifices individual and numerical minority rights and interests to those of the whole. So long as the net balance of the effects of a possible action is positive for most, any harm done to individuals and minorities is acceptable—that is, not ethically problematical. Unless minorities are singled out for special consideration, utilitarian ethical thought would justify their maltreatment and abuse if the consequences for the majority are more positive than negative. As John Rawls puts it, from the vantage point of the consequentialist "there is no reason in principle why the greater gains of some should not compensate for the lesser losses of others; or, more importantly, why the violation of the liberty of a few might not be made right by the greater good shared by the many" (1988: 17).

Indifference to minorities is matched by an impersonal attitude toward the individual. To the consequentialist, the individual is simply a piece of "the larger puzzle that the utilitarian is responsible for putting together" (Reiman, 1979: 43). In the utilitarian frame, the interests of the whole take precedence over those of individual parts.

Nonconsequentialists, or deontologists, reverse the analytical frame. Instead of outcomes, they emphasize the actor's ethical responsibilities. The most rigid form of deontological ethics is what Thomas Nagel refers to as absolutism. According to Nagel, while utilitarianism stresses the primacy of "what will happen," absolutism gives primacy to "what one is doing" (1988: 52).

To the absolutist, certain acts are to be avoided whatever the consequences. Thus, while utilitarians accept the necessity of taking one life to save many, absolutists refuse to murder under any circumstances.

As Nagel sees it, however, absolutists aim not to replace but to limit utilitarianism. Absolutists, he says, can be expected to pursue the utilitarian end of maximizing good and minimizing evil, but only so long as they are not required to compromise principles such as the prohibition against murder.

Basically, deontological ethics hold actors responsible for their decisions and actions before rather than after the fact. Responsibility entails choice based on adherence to rules and principles that limit and obligate the actor. According to Nagel, "there are special obligations created by promises and agreements; the restrictions against lying and betrayal; the prohibitions against violating various individual rights, rights not to be killed, injured, imprisoned, threatened, tortured, coerced, robbed; the restrictions against imposing certain sacrifices on someone simply as means to an end" (1988: 157).

Predictably, the dominance of the consequentialist view throughout the 1960s provoked a deontological response. Two consequentialist studies in particular were and continue to be responsible for much of the counterattack—one by a well-known psychologist, Stanley Milgram, and the other by a doctoral student in sociology, Laud Humphreys.

Milgram's study (1963) dealt with obedience to authority. With the Nazi treatment of Jewish people in World War II much in mind, Milgram aimed to determine the extent to which ordinary people would knowingly violate principles such as those prohibiting inflicting unprovoked physical harm on others rather than defy an authoritative directive. Those who participated in the study did so as part of a learning experiment. They had every reason to trust the competency of the experimenter. Participants were ordered to inflict increasingly severe electrical shocks upon others. They were not told that their victims were actors who, in fact, did not receive shocks. Milgram wished to determine how far people would go before they would become disobedient.

There were two major findings. The first was the tendency of "a substantial number" to "go through to the end of the shock board"; that is, to comply rather than become disobedient. The second was that the situation put people in a state of conflict. On the one hand they wished to comply with the experimenter's orders, and on the other they wished not to harm anyone. The result was considerable anxiety. Milgram states,

> I observed a mature and initially poised businessman enter the laboratory smiling and confident. Within 20 minutes he was reduced to a twitching, stuttering wreck, who was rapidly approaching a point of nervous collapse. He constantly pulled on his earlobe, and twisted his hands. At one point he pushed his fist into his forehead and muttered: "Oh, God, let's stop it." And yet he continued to respond to every work of the experimenter, and obeyed to the end. (1963: 377)

Milgram states that "procedures were undertaken" after the experiment "to assure" that participants left the laboratory in a healthy frame of mind. "A friendly reconciliation was arranged between the subject and the victim," according to Milgram, "and an effort was made to reduce any tensions that arose as a result of the experiment" (1963: 374).

Critics of Milgram's research ethics, such as Diana Baumrind, were not convinced of the adequacy of his efforts to protect participants' well-being. In her view,

> It would be interesting to know what sort of procedures could dissipate the type of emotional disturbance . . . described. In view of the effects on subjects, traumatic to a degree which Milgram himself considers nearly unprecedented in sociopsychological experiments, his casual assurance that these tensions were dissipated before the subject left the laboratory is unconvincing. (1964: 422)

As Baumrind sees it, the end did not justify the means. In her words,

> Unlike the Sabin vaccine, for example, the concrete benefit to humanity of [Milgram's] piece of work, no matter how competently handled, cannot justify the risk that real harm will be done to the subject. I am not speaking of physical discomfort, inconvenience, or experimental deception per se, but of permanent harm, however slight. I do regard the emotional disturbance described by Milgram as potentially harmful because it could easily effect an alteration in the subject's self-image or ability to trust adult authorities in the future. (422)

In Baumrind's view, studies such as Milgram's should not be undertaken without subjects being fully informed of the possible dangers of involvement and without convincing evidence of the effectiveness of post-experiment restoration treatment.

Milgram's detailed reply to Baumrind emphasized several important points. To begin with, he found Baumrind to have confused an unanticipated result with the experiment's basic procedure. The tension and stress experienced by participants was, he points out, unanticipated. But the end, in his eyes, justifies the means:

> Baumrind sees the subject as a passive creature, completely controlled by the experimenter. I started from a different viewpoint. A person who comes to the laboratory is an active, choosing adult, capable of accepting or rejecting the pre-

scriptions for action addressed to him. Baumrind sees the effect of the experiment as undermining the subject's trust of authority. I see it as a potentially valuable experience insofar as it makes people aware of the problem of indiscriminate submission to authority. (1964: 852)

The Humphreys case basically follows the same pattern in regard to positions on the matter of experimental means and ends. Humphreys' subject was male homosexual activity in public restrooms, referred to in the homosexual subculture as "tearooms." To observe participants, he practiced covert participant observation. He gained acceptance into the homosexual community and played the role of "watchqueen," the lookout who warns sex act partners that someone other than a "regular" is nearing or entering the restroom.

The sample studied included 100 individuals whose names and addresses were traced by license plate identification. Humphreys was able to interview them as part of a survey sponsored by a local agency to assess the social health of males in the general community. To protect respondents, the master list of names was safely kept under lock and key. Humphreys found no indication that respondents recognized him when interviewed. He altered his appearance, drove a different car, and allowed a year to pass between sample identification and interview date.

As Joan Sieber (1982: 2) points out, Humphreys' findings contradicted prevailing popular impressions. Most of those studied, for example, were married (54 percent) rather than single, and the majority, who might be presumed to be essentially confirmed homosexuals, were as inclined to be bisexual as homosexual. Of the total studied, only some 14 percent were confirmed members of the gay community.

Interestingly, while the gay community praised Humphreys' study, many fellow sociologists were quick to challenge his ethics. He anticipated a good deal of what might concern his critics. In the postscript of his book, Humphreys acknowledged the questionable nature of his research ethics. His defense stressed that (1) "any conceivable method" used in human research contains at least some potential for harm, (2) "there are no 'good' or 'bad' methods—only 'better' or 'worse' ones," and (3) students of deviant behavior "must become accustomed to the process of weighing possible social benefits against possible cost in human discomfort" (1970: 169–170).

Humphreys' position is reminiscent of that of Saul Alinksy, whose relevant ideas were published a year after Humphreys'. According to Alinsky, "the real and only question regarding the ethics of means and ends is, and always has been, 'Does this *particular* end justify this *particular* means?'" (1971: 24) In the final analysis, opined Alinksy, "the means-and-end moralists or non-doers always wind up on their ends without any means" (25).

The consequentialist position favored by Humphreys and Alinsky was compatible with the activist climate of the times. The conservative reaction to the left leaning 1960s and early 1970s has boosted the status of deontological ethics. Instead of praising its boldness or the significance of its findings, contemporary social scientists most often refer to Humphreys' work as an example of questionable research ethics, particularly infringement of respondent rights.[3]

To summarize, utilitarianism and deontology identify two different philosophical orientations. Although they may be applied without conflict, their fundamental aims and principles are so antithetical as to make them polar opposites. The moral base of the utilitarian side is the presumed overriding good of, in Reiman's terminology, "the maximization of net satisfactions"; that of the deontological side is maximization of respect for individual rights and freedom. Doubtless, one's position with respect to these two attitudes may have a decisive bearing on the conduct of pure and applied social science and investigators' theoretical orientation.

It would appear that comparatively impersonal and group–oriented utilitarian ethics are most compatible with structuralist theoretical perspectives and quantitative research methods. Correlatively, deontological ethics seem most compatible with social-psychological theory and qualitative research methods. And while the two ethical positions may be practiced in either pure or applied contexts, utilitarian ethics seem particularly suited to applied sociology and deontological ethics to pure sociology. Nonetheless, the utilitarian point of view has been and continues to be the most prevalent in both pure and applied theory and research.

Utilitarian philosophy is compatible with the notion of value-free science, a conception of the scientist as one seeking objective truth. To the objectivist, scientifically relevant phenomena can and should be studied dispassionately— that is, with emotional detachment and without predisposed contaminating bias of any sort. In good measure, Lester Ward separated pure and applied sociology in the interests of scientific objectivity. By making applied sociology dependent on pure sociology, Ward would inhibit if not prevent such factors as vested interest, personal bias, and ideological conviction from determining the type and quality of data to be implemented. Nonetheless, as noted in Chapter 2, knowledge is obtained and interpreted from certain rather than all possible perspectives. Objectivity, in other words, is always relative and a matter of degree. As Max Weber pointed out: "There is no absolutely 'objective' scientific analysis of culture—or . . . of 'social phenomena' independent of special and 'one-sided' viewpoints according to which—expressly or tacitly, consciously or unconsciously—they are selected, analyzed and organized for expository purposes" (1949: 72). The theoretical orientations of early American sociologists were influenced by certain tacit assumptions and viewpoints inherited from Enlightenment and post-Enlightenment thought.

VALUES, MORALITY, AND SOCIAL THEORY

Rousseau's premise that "Man is born free, and yet is everywhere in chains" informs a great deal of early as well as contemporary sociology. But, as Ellsworth Fuhrman has noted, it gave rise to two conflicting and unreconciled viewpoints. It was assumed by Rousseau and other eighteenth-century philosophers that people were born with the capacity to practice "the golden rule," that is, to behave in an orderly and altruistic manner. If they did not, the assumption was that society was to blame. But whence came human society? Was or was it not an expression of "human nature"? If it was not, what were its origins? What factors other than human nature could be the causal source of human society? Such questions, later pursued by Durkheim and Marx in particular, were generally avoided by nineteenth Century American sociologists. In Fuhrman's words, "human nature was thought to be biologically and/or physiologically endowed with fixed qualities, which in turn shaped the organization of society" (1986: 70). To improve the human condition, one had only to reform social institutions, not seriously question one's basic premises about human nature. The idea that people are "victimized" by arbitrary societal conventions, extrasomatic rather than intrasomatic factors, is a moral theme that unites sociologists past and present.

It was reaction to Enlightenment assumptions such as Rousseau's that stimulated the development of positivism. To the positivist, scientific statements are of a different order than ethical or moral statements. "The positivist," says Jacob Bronowski, "holds that only those statements have meaning which can in principle be verified. . . . Statements which contain the word *is* can be of this kind; statements which contain the word *ought* cannot" (1972: 58).

As sociology became more positivistic, its reformist zeal yielded to a more scientifically neutral outlook. As Fuhrman sees it,

> prior to the First World War, the sociological heirs to the Enlightenment expressed an underlying optimism about what a science of society could accomplish. Generally, however, sociologists believed that 'good' and 'progressive' social reform could be achieved only if the methods and procedures of science were followed. . . . As sociology grew, the link between sociological discourse and reform became less obvious for those interested in reform, who increasingly saw sociology as irrelevant, and was broken by sociologists adamantly opposed to the link in the first place. (1986: 74)

However amoral the scientific constraints, Fuhrman contends that sociological discourse is inherently moral. That is, the discipline's units of analysis (social facts) and its general frame of reference (that human thought and action are a product of social being) are rooted in the premise that moral imperatives are causally relevant phenomena. Thus, "in spite of attempts to rid moral and political concerns from sociological theory, a moral discourse remains buried within the project because it: expresses an ethical telos, has underlying value interests, possesses a discourse impossible to separate from everyday moral discourse; and has moral effects in terms of social reform" (1986: 75).

Unfortunately, because his concerns were of a different sort, Fuhrman did not examine the implications of his reasoning for pure and applied sociological theory, particularly whether or not only one or both should be morally committed to social reform. And if the latter, what, if any, division of labor there should be between the two. Others, however, have commented on the desired place of morality in contemporary sociological theory generally.

Ted Vaughan and Gideon Sjoberg, for example, agree with Fuhrman that modern sociological theory has strayed from the classical concern with achieving the good and just society by means of social reform. In their view, sociologists have become preoccupied with the administration of a society whose ends appear to be tacitly, if not uncritically accepted. "Sociological theory and practice have become," they say, "part of the administrative apparatus and more and more instrumentally and technically oriented" (1988: 127).

Like Fuhrman, Vaughan and Sjoberg argue in favor of bringing morality back into sociological theory. They call for a reassessment of "the nature of social theory." In their view, any social theory contains some sort of moral orientation. Consequently, moral concerns have been suppressed rather than eliminated. They believe that sociologists "weave" into their analyses certain uncritically accepted moral perspectives.

To Vaughan and Sjoberg, sociological theory has become a means for the attainment of primarily non-disciplinary ends. The goals, in other words, emanate from extant societal interests and concerns rather than the moral center of the science of society. Vaughan and Sjoberg do not say how much of the problem is due to sociologists "buying into" the status quo or being "bought off" by clients, whether public agencies or private firms. Economic realities and the conservative political mood of the day are obvious intrusive factors. But they are not the factors that Vaughan and Sjoberg suggest are behind the situation.

In their view, the chief culprit is the prevailing positivistic view of science, which favors logico-deductive theory. To Vaughan and Sjoberg, theory is not the impersonal, "objective" and mechanical device that positivists envision. All science, they feel, rests on knowledge claims based on interpretation and criteria which arise from a social context, for example, a community of scholars. As far as they are concerned, "the production of theoretic knowledge can thus be viewed as a social process characterized by features found in other social contexts" (1988: 130).

Essentially, although no mention is made of it, Vaughan and Sjoberg invoke the equivalent of the hermeneutic alternative to positivistic theory. That is, as a human product, social theory is presumed to involve more than uncontaminated reflection of "natural" social phenomena. It adds a particular interpretive slant to perception, one that is presumed to be inherently influenced by moral criteria such as anticipated normative expectations regarding expected, patterned, even obligatory behavior. They emphasize what hermeneuticists would be expected to, namely, the notion that theory is a "social process" and as such must acknowledge its essential moral underpinnings or predispositions. As they put it: "Like the classical theorists, we must analyze major empirical issues in the modern world within a broad theoretical framework—one that makes explicit our moral presuppositions as social scientists and as human beings" (1986: 137).

In addition to making moral premises explicit, Vaughan and Sjoberg would have sociologists take a moral stand. That is, in the manner of Lester Ward they believe that the sociological goal is not simply to illuminate the nature of human society but to do something to improve it. They advocate commitment to the cause of human rights. Because they presume the fundamental human quality to be reflectivity, the ability to "simultaneously shape and be shaped by social reality," they urge sociologists to support the right of people everywhere to decide for themselves how best to balance the ideals of individual freedom and social responsibility. As they summarize their message,

> The strategy we have suggested would clearly transform the essential nature of empirical and theoretical activity in sociology. . . . If sociologists are to address the great issues of our age, they must not passively accept and reinforce "what is"—a moral stance in and of itself—but they must actively engage in the construction of new and more human social arrangements. This would permit sociologists to re-engage themselves in a noble calling that is in keeping with their heritage. (1986: 140)

MORALLY RESPONSIBLE SOCIAL SCIENCE

Problems involving the moral commitments and emotional needs of social scientists have long been of concern to positivists and all those concerned with research objectivity. Moral commitment may be at the heart of unified, meaningful and effective social theory but it also may promote the zeal that leads to subjectivism and dogmatism. To counteract the intrusion of the personal biases of the observer, Lundberg, it will be recalled, requires the operational definition of terms—the identification of concepts so as to permit empirical and independent verification and corroboration. And to protect the citizenry as well as locate social science within democratically constituted society, Lundberg separates the sociologist's right to collect knowledge from the obligation to determine its implementation. As he sees it, the skill of sociologists may generate potentially useful knowledge and theoretical insights, but the ends to which it may be put are no better decided by them than anyone else. Put another way, Lundberg may be interpreted as striving to separate pure and applied sociology to check elitistic ambition and promote a tempered and cautious rather than an unrestrained and dogmatic outlook. Sociologists may commit themselves to morally important matters such as the promotion of human rights, but the citizenry has the right to expect sociologists to act in a morally responsible manner and to decide for itself what use to make of the products of any science. Consequently, certain rules and procedures have been devised to promote morally and ethically responsible social and behavioral science and reconcile potential areas of conflict between citizens and those who study them and their society. General topics of particular concern include the invasion of privacy, the practice of deception, and research participant harm.

The Right to Privacy

Social scientists identify those they study by terms such as "subjects" and "participants." "Subjects" is often the referent because it connotes objectivity—that is, distance between investigators and the objects of their attention. "Participants" is preferred by those mindful of the rights of citizens in democratic society and the moral requirement of voluntarism. As Margaret Mead states, the two terms suggest quite different images:

> Research on human subjects calls up images of repugnance and terror: The subject is seen as a victim, the experimenter as brutalized, the results compromised by the methods through which they were obtained; and the public view of the scientist is one of suspicion and rejection. Participation in research by human beings who are enthusiastically related to the explorations of new knowledge not only for the benefit of mankind, but for the sheer enjoyment of being a part of great intellectual adventures calls up exactly the opposite set of images. (1969: 374)

To obtain voluntary research participants, social scientists must exercise considerable tact and sensitivity. People must be told study aims and purposes and why they have been selected for inclusion. And because the information obtained may be variously perceived, interpreted, disseminated and used, investigators must be prepared to take every precaution to ensure respondent anonymity and confidentiality in response reporting. Hence, section I(B) of the ASA's Code of Ethics contains the following provisions:

> Subjects of research are entitled to rights of biographical anonymity.

> To the extent possible in a given study sociologists should anticipate potential threats to confidentiality. Such means as the removal of identifiers, the use of randomized responses and other statistical solutions to problems of privacy should be used where appropriate.

> Confidential information provided by research participants must be treated as such by sociologists, even when this information enjoys no legal protection or privilege and legal force is applied. The obligation to respect confidentiality also applies to members of research organizations (interviewers, coders, clerical staff, etc.) who have access to the information. It is the responsibility of administrators and chief investigators to instruct staff members on this point and to make every effort to ensure that access to confidential information is restricted.

Deceptive Practices

As apparent in the above discussion of the Milgram and Humphreys studies, deception in behavioral and social science research is rejected out of hand by some and defended by others. Item No. 1 in Section I(B) of the ASA's Code of Ethics contains the following statement: "Sociologists should not mislead respondents involved in a research project as to the purpose for which that research is being conducted." Acquisition of important and otherwise unobtainable information is among the most often cited reasons for deception.

Albert Reiss (1968; 1971), for example, was able to study police brutality first-hand (in high crime areas in Boston, Chicago, and Washington, D.C. in 1966) by obtaining permission to ride in patrol cars for another stated purpose. "So far as the men in the line were concerned," he states, "our chief interest was in how citizens behave toward the police, a main object of our study" (1968: 16). According to Edward Diener and Rick Crandall, Reiss rationalized the deception on the basis of "the public's right to know about the behavior of public employees" (1978: 74). If so, this line of reasoning was meant to be taken in a more abstract than concrete sense.

When Reiss' study results became public, the police administrators involved wished to know the names of officers responsible for recorded abusive behavior in order to take punitive action. Reiss refused to divulge names on the basis of confidentiality: "we were bound to protect our sources of information" (1968: 15). No mention is made of the alternative need of the public to be protected from continued abuse at the hands of known abusers.

By invoking the ethic of respondent confidentiality, Reiss and his colleagues did not, of course, absolve themselves of having knowingly practiced a deception conducive to respondent distrust. The study accomplished its goals but perhaps at the expense of comparable future studies. Having reason to suspect social scientists' motives and aims, police officers were, if anything, encouraged to deny others future access to direct study of their work habits. Section I(B) of the ASA's Code of Ethics warns that "irresponsible actions by a single researcher or research team can eliminate or reduce future access to a category of respondents by the entire profession and its allied fields." Needless to say, what may be "irresponsible" to one may not be to another. However, the purity of one's motives may have little or nothing to do with the consequences of one's actions. Thus, in making the above statement the ASA would, if anything, encourage one to err on the side of caution by rejecting the practice of respondent deception.

Diener and Crandall claim that deception in social-psychological research has become "commonplace." A review of the available evidence suggested to them that "direct lying to subjects" was evident in 19 to 40 percent of "recent personality and social psychological research" (74). Notwithstanding the possible negative effects of lying to respondents on future research, one wonders how much the practice has harmed respondents, psychologically and physically. Those concerned with the subject advocate researcher compliance with ethical principles and rules to minimize harm to research participants.

The Right to Protection from Harmful Effects

Of course, in pursuing their quest for knowledge, investigators must make every effort to protect research participants from any possible involuntary physical or emotional harm. Depending on the nature of the study and the context, the goal may be easier to state than comply with. Some believe that harmful effects cannot always be anticipated, and that the best the researcher can do is strive to prevent "unnecessary harm to subjects." In Norman Denzin's view, for example,

> The goal of any science is not willful harm to subjects, but the advancement of knowledge and explanation. Any method that moves us toward the goal without unnecessary harm to subjects, is justifiable. (1968: 502)

The ASA's Code of Ethics is more restrictive. The slightest degree of anticipated risk beyond that encountered in daily life requires informed consent. Item No. 4 in Section I(B) states,

> The process of conducting sociological research must not expose respondents to substantial risk of personal harm. Informed consent must be obtained when the risks of research are greater than the risks of everyday life. Where modest risk or harm is anticipated, informed consent must be obtained.

"Informed consent," state Diener and Crandall, "is the procedure in which individuals choose whether to participate in an investigation after being informed of facts that would be likely to influence their decision" (1978: 34). The principle of informed consent evolved from the use of human subjects in medical research. The most notorious example in recent history is the experiments conducted during the Nazi era on concentration camp prisoners. Nazi research included "horrific experiments on healthy prisoners' reactions to various diseases (such as malaria, epidemic jaundice, and spotted fever), poisons, and simulated high altitudes; studies on the effectiveness of treatments for different types of experimentally induced wounds; and the measurement, execution, and defleshing of more than 100 persons for the purpose of completing a university skeleton collection" (Kimmel, 1988: 52).

At the Nuremberg trials, Nazi doctors endeavored to defend their actions by pointing to the long-standing world tradition of experiments involving prison inmates. They identified three American cases. The first involved a Harvard medical professor, Colonel Strong, who, with the approval of the Philippine authorities, infected a group of condemned offenders with plague. In another experiment on Philippine inmates, he caused subjects to develop beriberi.

The second involved an experiment conducted on twelve white prisoners in Mississippi to determine a cure for pellagra. In return for promised parole or release, the prisoners were infected with the disease. All became seriously ill.

The third case involved prison inmates in Chicago and New Jersey. Volunteers were infected with malaria in search for a cure. Inevitably, the results were serious illness for many and no cure. In his 1967 work, M.H. Pappworth, the source of this material, cites a 1960 reference indicating that some 20,000 federal inmates were voluntarily participating in medical research (1967: 61).

Prisoners are only one of several low status segments of society that have been exploited for experimental purposes. As Reynolds points out, "prisoners, slaves, the poor, charity patients, peasants, and others considered less worthy by the investigators, who tended to belong to the privileged classes in society, were utilized as research subjects, often carelessly and with little regard to the consequences for them" (1979: 86). Today, he says, all social categories are regarded as being of equal worth.

Reynolds identifies four basic components of informed consent: competence, voluntarism, full information, and comprehension. As in the case of the general concept of informed consent, these four were a product of the Nuremberg trials. Item No. 5 in Section I(B) of the ASA's Code of Ethics captures the basic spirit of the four in the following statement:

> Sociologists should take culturally appropriate steps to secure informed consent. . . . Special actions may be necessary where the individuals studied are illiterate, have very low social status, or are unfamiliar with social research.

ETHICAL PRINCIPLES, RESEARCH, AND THEORY

However ethically correct and justified, the principle of informed consent is somewhat controversial. While it may foster respondent cooperation and further research aims, it may, if taken literally, adversely influence if not invalidate experiments that depend on varying degrees of respondent ignorance of research means and ends. Psychological studies of verbal conditioning are a case in point. According to Jerome Resnick and Thomas Schwartz, several hundred studies of the topic have been published, "the subjects usually being kept ignorant in varying degrees of many critical aspects of the experiment and their participation in it" (1973: 134).

Resnick and Schwartz examined the impact of different degrees of informed consent in a study involving two groups of undergraduate psychology students at Temple University. One (the "nonethical group") was asked to volunteer for a study to determine "the ways in which college students form sentences and express themselves in verbal communication." The other (the "ethical group") was given all the essential details of the experiment, including all hypotheses regarding the effect of partial versus fully informed consent and verbal conditioning by the experimenter on the way participants construct sentences. As those in the nonethical group manifested "significant positive conditioning" and those in the ethical group "significant negative conditioning," the authors concluded that the ethical standards under which an experiment is conducted are powerful independent variables, having potentially strong determining effects on the way subjects will behave in an experiment" (136–137). As Kimmel indicates, studies by others (Gardner, 1978; Dill, Gilden, Hill, and Hanselka, 1982; Robinson and Greenberg, 1980) have shown that all manner of informed consent procedures can compromise the validity of research findings.

Survey research appears to be less negatively influenced by fully informed consent than the manner in which the subjects of respondent anonymity and confidentiality are handled. Eleanor Singer, for example, designed a study to "measure the effects of variations in (1) the amount of information provided to respondents about the content of a survey ahead of time, (2) the assurance of confidentiality given to respondents, and (3) the request for and timing of a signature to document consent" (1978: 144). The survey was conducted on a national sample and involved questions in sensitive areas, such as drug use and sexual behavior. None of the three factors was found to have an appreciable impact on response rate. However, Singer notes, "there are suggestions in the data that asking for a signature before the interview has a sensitization effect, so that better data are obtained if the respondent is asked to sign a consent form afterwards" (144).

As Kimmel (1988: 74) points out, other studies (Singer and Frankel, 1982; Loo, 1982) indicate improved respondent involvement in surveys when they are made fully aware of study aims and allowed to express their concerns with sympathetic and open interviewers. Nonetheless, some studies (for example, Lueptow, Mueller, Hammes, and Master, 1977) indicate that fully informed consent can reduce both overall response rate and response to certain questions.

Unfortunately, systematic studies of the impact of ethical factors on theory testing are unavailable. Some idea of their influence can be gleaned from those whose work touches on the subject. The Resneck and Schwartz (1973) study cited above, for example, showed that different degrees of informed consent generated such polar responses as to preclude either confirmation or rejection of hypothesized expectations. But the relationship between theory and ethics is not all one way. Ethical matters may cause problems for theory testing and formulation, and the application of theory may provoke ethical problems.

After conducting a study designed to evaluate a program to reduce male gang related delinquency, Richard Brymer and Buford Farris (1967: 299) discussed points at which the application of their theoretical orientation violated ethical precepts. Because they employed a symbolic interactionist perspective, one based on viewing delinquency "as the result of the cumulative consequences of a person's interaction with various sets of other persons," they were required to interview a number of people. The interviewing process entailed invading the privacy of acquaintances, friends, and relatives without the prior consent of the delinquents. It also involved deception because certain information obtained from delinquents could not be revealed to parents without risking interview termination or the loss of invaluable information. But the authors do not wish to suggest that the "symbolic interactionist framework" employed by them is the "only theory that creates problems of ethics." According to them, "Ethical issues seem to be inevitable, and perhaps a byproduct of all research studies. However, the form and content of these issues may well be a function of the particular theoretical framework which one carries into research" (1967: 300–301).

It does appear, however, that symbolic interactionist approaches using participant observation may create ethical problems that structural theoretical orientations employing survey methods do not. For example, even though deception may occur in both (for example, by concealment of identity in the one and by less than full disclosure of research aims in the other), participant observation studies offer the potential for more open-ended interaction with people and, therefore, pose a more unpredictable ethical challenge.

Perhaps the major lesson to be learned here is that the social scientist must be prepared to deal with any number of anticipated and unanticipated ethical problems and issues. Taking a cue from Diener and Crandall, it is probably wise to assume that the more pure and theoretical one's work, the more difficult it is to anticipate how and by whom its results might be interpreted and applied. Diener and Crandall suggest that the

> way to prevent abuses is to be alert to destructive applications of theoretical knowledge and work against them. . . . Often a scientist must also be involved in translating theoretical work into practical applications, and at this stage he may also exert control and help prevent misuses. (201)

•••• *SUMMARY AND CONCLUSION*

In summary, ethical and moral problems in pure and applied behavioral and social science arise for a number of reasons and from different sources. The complexity of the situation is due generally to the fact that science is both a particular social institution with its own norms and values and a component of larger societies within which it is practiced. Hence, the aims and values of science—for example, the implementation of objective experimentation toward the end of knowledge advancement—may conflict with societal values concerning general citizen rights and responsibilities and generally prevailing moral prescriptions and laws concerning "fair play" and the protection of life, human and otherwise. However pure the scientific motive, to fail to fully inform those questioned or studied of one's purposes, true identity, or known risks is to violate the ethical standards of the social and behavioral sciences, if not societal laws regarding the crime of fraud. Sometimes, however, it is not opposing but complementary societal and scientific attitudes and values that generates ethical problems. The drive to success, susceptibility to the notion that the "end justifies the means" is as evident in science as any other profession. Risk taking, for example, is as common to those who seek scientific breakthroughs as it is to those who seek great wealth. But the ethical and moral problems of scientific research are not confined to instances of risk taking in the manner of violating scientific conventions or societal standards. Formally sanctioned and approved scientific achievements, such as the harnessing of atomic energy and identification of the structure of the DNA molecule, have evoked profound ethical dilemmas.

These examples from the physical and natural sciences have provoked the ethical and moral concerns of people worldwide because of their profound potential consequences for human health and survival. The ethical and moral problems generated by the behavioral and social sciences are much less likely to have such an effect. In fact, they are apt to be contained within the scholarly community. The controversy surrounding the Milgram and Humphreys studies, for example, stemmed primarily from the reactions of behavioral and social scientists.

The ethical and moral dilemmas that sociologists encounter or arouse in pure or applied endeavors are more likely to be due to perceived conflicts between their own research aims and humanistic principles (including sensitivity to the ethics of research involving human "subjects") than to value conflicts between their professional aims and the public interest. This is in good measure because sociology, as Vaughan and Sjoberg point out, is a moral science. Its causal phenomena are social facts—norms, rules, laws, and institutions whose influence is presumed to derive from group morality.

But in the history of sociology, morality has been more than something sociologists study. It has been integral to the aim of ameliorating the human condition by compiling the scientific evidence deemed necessary for the construction of effective policies designed to cure major social ills and promote liberation from the yokes of tyranny and ignorance. Moral commitment to societal improvement is variously expressed. Some, for example, seek to actively implement the means (conflict) and ideals (a communal society) of Marxist theory. They aim to blend theory and practice toward the end of human emancipation from all forms of oppression. Others, devotees of positivism, for example, would temper reformist and revolutionary zeal by separating theory and measurement, knowledge collection and knowledge implementation. To the one, the end justifies the means. To the other, adherence to the canons of scientific objectivity and the principles of democratic decision making are the necessary means of effecting the common good. In Popper's terms, some express their moral commitment by advocating and practicing "utopian" and others "piecemeal" social engineering. Most have taken the less controversial piecemeal approach, and the next chapter examines their concerns about and role in public policy formation and implementation.

- **NOTES**

1. *Code of Ethics. American Sociological Association:* Washington, D.C.: January 28, 1989.

2. R. Perrucci, D.D. Knudsen, and R.R. Hamby, *Sociology* (Dubuque, Iowa: Wm. C. Brown Company Publishers, 1977), 24.

3. See, for example, Edward Diener and Rick Crandall, *Ethics in Social and Behavioral Research* (Chicago: The University of Chicago Press, 1978), 123.

- **REFERENCES**

Alinsky. S. 1971. *Rules for Radicals.* New York: Random House.

Baumrind, D. 1964. "Some Thoughts on Ethics of Research: After Reading Milgram's 'Behavioral Study of Disobedience.'" *American Psychologist* 19: 421–423.

Boguslaw, R. 1967. "Ethics and the Social Scientist." In I.L. Horowitz, ed. *The Rise and Fall of Project Camelot.* Cambridge, MA: M.I.T. Press.

Bronowski, J. 1965. *Science and Human Values.* New York: Harper & Row.

Brymer, R.A., and B. Farris. 1967. "Ethical and Political Dilemmas in the Investigation of Deviance: A Study of Juvenile Delinquency." In G. Sjoberg, ed., *Ethics, Politics, and Social Research.* Cambridge, MA.: Schenkman.

Denzin, N. 1968. "On the Ethics of Disguised Observation." *Social Problems* 15: 502–506.

Diener, E., and R. Crandall. 1978. *Ethics in Social and Behavioral Research.* Chicago: University of Chicago Press.

Dill, C.A., E.R. Gilden, P.C. Hill, and L.L. Hanselka. 1982. "Federal Human Subjects Regulations: A Methodological Artifact?" *Personality and Social Psychological Bulletin* 8: 417–425.

Durkheim, E. 1973. *Moral Education.* New York: Free Press.

Fuhrman, E.R. 1986. "Morality, Self and Society: The Loss and Recapture of the Moral Self." In M.L. Wardell and S.P. Turner, eds., *Sociological Theory in Transition.* Boston: Allen & Unwin.

Gardner, G.T. 1978. "Effects of Federal Human Subjects Regulations on Data Obtained in Environmental Stressor Research." *Journal of Personality and Social Psychology* 36: 628–634.

Holden, C. 1979. "Ethics in Social Science Research." *Science* 206: 537–540.

Horowitz, I.L. 1967. *The Rise and Fall of Project Camelot.* Cambridge, MA: M.I.T. Press.

Humphreys, L. 1970. *Tearoom Trade.* Chicago: Aldine Publishing Company.

Kimmel, A.J. 1988. *Ethics and Values in Applied Social Research.* Beverly Hills: SAGE Publications.

Loo, C.M. 1982. "Vulnerable Populations: Case Studies in Crowding Research." In J.E. Sieber, ed., *The Ethics of Social Research: Surveys & Experiments.* New York: Springer-Verlag.

Lueptow, L., S.A. Mueller, R.R. Hammes, and L.S. Master. 1977. "The Impact of Informed Consent Regulations on Response Rate and Response Bias." *Sociological Methods & Research* 6: 183–204.

Lundberg, G.A. 1964. *Foundations of Sociology.* New York: David McKay Company, Inc.

Mead, M. 1969. "Research with Human Beings: A Model Derived from Anthropological Field Practice." *Daedalus* 98: 361–379.

Milgram, S. 1963. "Behavioral Study of Obedience." *Journal of Abnormal and Social Psychology* 67: 371–378.

————. 1964. "Issues in The Study of Obedience: A Reply to Baumrind." *American Psychologist* 19: 848–852.

Nagel, T. 1988. "War and Massacre." In S. Scheffler, ed., *Consequentialism and Its Critics.* New York: Oxford University Press.

Pappworth, M.H. 1967. *Human Guinea Pigs: Experimentation on Man.* Boston: Beacon Press.

Rawls, J. 1988. "Classical Utilitarianism." In S. Scheffler, ed., *Consequentialism and Its Critics.* New York: Oxford University Press.

Reiman, J.H. 1979. "Research Subjects, Political Subjects, and Human Subjects." In C.B. Klockars and F.W. O'Connor, eds., *Deviance and Decency*. Beverly Hills: SAGE Publications.

Reiss, A.J. Jr. 1968. "Police Brutality—Answers to Key Questions." *Trans-Action* 5: 10–19.

————. 1971. *The Police and The Public*. New Haven, CT: Yale University Press.

Resnick, J.H., and T. Schwartz. 1973. "Ethical Standards as an Independent Variable in Psychological Research." *American Psychologist* 28: 134–139.

Reynolds, P.D. 1979. *Ethical Dilemmas and Social Science Research*. San Francisco: Jossey-Bass Publishers.

Robertson, I. 1977. *Sociology*. New York: Worth Publishers, Inc.

Robinson, R., and C.I. Greenberg. 1980. "Informed Consent: An Artifact in Human Crowding." In J.R. Aiello (Chair), *Crowding in High Population Density*, symposium presented at the annual meeting of the American Psychological Association.

Shea, G.F. 1988. *Practical Ethics*. New York: American Management Association.

Sieber, J.E., ed. 1982. *The Ethics of Social Research: Surveys and Experiments*. New York: Springer-Verlag.

Singer, E. 1978. "Informed Consent." *American Sociological Review* 43: 144–162.

Singer, E., and M.R. Frankel. 1982. "Informed Consent Procedures in Telephone Interviews." *American Sociological Review* 47: 416–427.

Stern, P.M. 1969. *The Oppenheimer Case: Security on Trial*. New York: Harper & Row.

Toulmin, S. 1981. "Evolution, Adaptation, and Human Understanding." In M.B. Brewer and B.E. Collins, eds., *Scientific Inquiry and the Social Sciences*. San Francisco: Jossey-Bass Publishers.

Vaughan, T.R., and G. Sjoberg. 1988. "Human Rights Theory and the Classical Sociological Tradition." In Wardell and Turner, eds., *Sociological Theory in Transition*.

Weber, M. 1949. *The Methodology of the Social Sciences*. New York: Free Press.

CHAPTER 6

● ● ●

Social Theory and Social Policy

Influencing public policy dealing with major societal issues has been an integral part of sociology from its inception. The initiators of American sociology, for example, were keenly involved in major policy issues of the day. Lester Ward championed the cause of free public education for all, from the lowest to the highest levels. To accomplish his aim, Ward, a progressive social Darwinist, advocated social policy based on the premise that equal educational opportunity was prerequisite to true freedom, effective democratic participation and decision making, and the development of the scientific knowledge essential for guided progressive social change and the survival of humankind. Ward's ideological arch rival, William Sumner, a conservative social Darwinist, maintained a decidedly anti–reformist and laissez faire approach to social policy. He viewed progressives such as Ward as mischief makers likely to cause more harm than good. In his view society is governed by natural forces that will produce the best possible social results if allowed to operate with minimal interference by humankind. Sumner was among the few prominent first generation American sociologists who did not accept the premise of progressive social change via melioristic intervention in the evolutionary process. Most early American sociologists, however, "combined the belief in progress with an acceptance of melioristic interventionism, using the former as a sanction for the latter" (Hinkle and Hinkle, 1954: 11).

An ideological predilection for a politically liberal approach to social reform comes closest to describing the majority viewpoint among contemporary sociologists. However, in the aftermath of the War on Poverty programs of the

121

1960s and the ascendancy of conservative ideological thinking and policies in recent years, the participation of sociologists in national governmental social policy has been severely attenuated. This chapter examines the recent historical record, charting the involvement of sociologists in shaping recent social policy primarily in the areas of education and poverty. Of central concern are the theoretical premises and orientations of those who have participated in social policy initiation and development at the national level. To put the discussion in context, the initial subject of concern is social scientists' conceptions of the proper relationship between the conduct of science and involvement in social policy oriented activity. As will become evident, the subject is fraught with problems and issues more conducive to opinion diversity than opinion unity.

SOCIAL SCIENCE AND SOCIAL POLICY

Generally social scientists have emphasized two major positions regarding the proper connection between their scientific and policy interests and obligations. The position taken by Lundberg, the idea that social scientists must separate their professional obligation to amass empirically verifiable information from efforts to influence its implementation, has been the most widely considered. The second position, which came to the fore in the 1960s and is based on the Marxist premise of the essential unity of theory and practice, blends the roles of social scientist and social activist. In the Marxist view, social theory is prerequisite to effective social action and involvement in social action is prerequisite to the building of scientifically accurate and practically effective social theory. In essence, the one separates science and politics and the other does not. Preference for one or the other position is influenced by a variety of factors, particularly the degree of confidence one has in the ability of available social scientific theory and knowledge to effect more social good than harm. Most appear to be inclined toward the view that the quality of social science knowledge is not sufficient to justify a concerted effort to ensure its timely implementation to solve or treat a major social problem. To those who feel this way, more basic research is needed to isolate the causal antecedents of specified phenomena. Those in the opposite camp believe this view to be a rationalization, an expression of fear of the consequences of public involvement and lack of commitment to humanity and practical problem solving.

Between the "purists" and the "activists" are the pragmatists, those willing to involve themselves in practical problem solving (with or without a client) by means of "piecemeal" reform if nothing else. To those who take this approach (probably most social scientists), individuals and groups routinely require assistance from those who possess less than total knowledge of their subject. Pragmatic reformers are generally careful to avoid exaggerating an ability to effect cures or definitive solutions in favor of promising to do the best they can with available means. In the absence of a well developed social policy theory, they have had to rely on their own sense of the relevance of a given theoretical element (concept, perspective, ideology) in a given case. This is not to suggest, however, that those who have applied their social science training to practical problem solution and policy formation have been all that theoretically inclined. As Mishra reminds us,

> the reformist tradition is pragmatic and practical rather than theoretical and speculative. Its interest lies not so much in building a knowledge base about social . . . institutions as in understanding the nature and dimensions of a particular social problem—poverty, child abuse, homelessness—with a view to its solution. (1981: 3-4)

The question is, what theoretical elements have been employed in social policy work with what results, and what knowledge has been acquired from practical policy experience that may be useful in developing policy relevant social theory? Unfortunately, and certainly not too surprisingly, policy involved pragmatists have been more inclined to bemoan the absence of applied social policy theory than to apply their skills and experiences to its construction.

THE SOCIAL POLICY EXPERIENCES OF SOCIAL SCIENTISTS

Social scientists have directly and indirectly influenced social policy in a variety of areas. A primary vehicle of policy relevant social science has been sponsored research (by both private and public agencies and foundations). Gunnar Myrdal's *An American Dilemma: The Negro Problem & Modern Democracy,* whose theoretical orientation and findings have influenced Supreme Court decisions (for example, *Brown v. Board of Education*) and race related public policy for decades, was sponsored by the Carnegie Foundation with a broad and general charge, to undertake "a comprehensive study of the Negro in America" (Keppel, 1972: xlvi). Myrdal clearly led the project with practically relevant intentions. In a letter submitted to the Carnegie Foundation, he wrote:

> The study, thus conceived, should aim at determining the social, political, educational, and economic status of the Negro in the United States as well as defining opinions held by different groups of Negroes and whites as to his "right" status. It must, further, be concerned with both recent changes and current trends with respect to the Negro's position in American society. Attention must also be given to the total American picture with particular emphasis on relations between the two races, Finally, it must consider what changes are being or can be induced by education, legislation, interracial efforts, concerned action by Negro groups, etc. (1972: l-li)

Since World War II, federally sponsored programs and research have been a primary source of policy oriented social science. National policies dealing with social problems that involve the country's black population most of all—crime, equal educational opportunity, insufficient low income housing, poverty, and urban riots—have been shaped by the involvement of sociologists and other social scientists in a variety of federally sponsored activities. In chronological order, some of the more important of these in terms of policy implications and lessons learned are the following: President Lyndon Johnson's War on Poverty, the *Equality of Educational Opportunity* survey (the so-called Coleman report), and Presidential Commissions such as The Commission on Law Enforcement & The Administration of Justice; The National Advisory Commission on Civil Disorders (the Kerner report); The Commission on Obscenity & Pornography; The National Commission on the Causes & Prevention of Violence; and The Commission on Population Growth & The American Future. The first in historical sequence, the War on Poverty, will be discussed last because its subject has attracted the most enduring general attention.

The Coleman Report

The Equality of Educational Opportunity survey was requested by Congress and mandated by Section 402 of the Civil Rights Act of 1964. Section 402 states that the Commissioner of Education "shall conduct a survey and make a report to the President and Congress, within two years of the enactment of this title, concerning the lack of availability of educational opportunities for individuals by reason of race, color, religion, or national origin in public educational institutions at all levels in the United States, its territories and possessions, and the District of Columbia." The study, completed in 1966, was led by two sociologists, James S. Coleman and Ernest Q. Campbell. Their co-authors were five members of the Office of Education.

Questionnaires were administered to public school teachers, principals, district school superintendents, and students in some 4000 schools (30 percent of the schools selected did not participate). In addition to 645,000 students, all administrators in the sample and some 60,000 teachers participated in the study.

As journalist Godfrey Hodgson (1975: 25) notes, Coleman was not told exactly why Congress ordered the study. In an article that appeared in *The Public Interest,* Coleman wrote that he thought it probable that "if the survey was initially intended as a means of finding areas of continued intentional discrimination, the intent later became less punitive-oriented and more future-oriented: i.e., to provide a basis for public policy, at the local, state, and national levels, which might overcome inequalities of educational opportunity" (1966b: 70). Hodgson surmised that Congress wished "to document the obvious" in order to provide the administration with the evidence necessary to successfully challenge those opposed to implementing policy aimed at equalizing minority educational opportunities. As it turns out, Coleman, along with most, assumed that the study would confirm the premise of extreme quality differences in the public schools attended by blacks and whites. Well into the survey, Coleman states in an interview: "the study will show the difference in the quality of schools that the average Negro child and the average white child are exposed to" (Hodgson, 1975: 26). Differences between the two were found, but they were not nearly as great as was assumed.

Among the major findings were the following:

1. The fact of school segregations (both blacks and whites were more likely than not to attend schools in which they were in the majority, but whites were much more likely to attend schools disproportionately white than blacks attend schools disproportionately black);
2. There was little difference between the quality of physical facilities in schools attended by whites versus minorities ("Observing the nationwide averages . . . it appears that school children of all groups differ relatively little in the physical school facilities available") Coleman et al., (1966a: 67);
3. High school curriculum range comparability (only "small differences were found between schools attended by white minority students as to the availability of the following curriculum choices: college preparatory, commercial, general, vocational, agriculture, and industrial arts" (1966a: 96);
4. Extracurricular activities were just as available to minority groups as whites ("This is particularly true in secondary schools where we find that the average of the availability of . . . activities is 67 percent for Negroes . . . and 69 percent for whites;") (1966a: 117);
5. There was no relationship between the race of pupil and amount of teacher training ("Compared to teachers of the average white student, teachers of the average Negro . . . are neither more nor less likely to have advanced degrees . . . are neither more nor less likely to have majored in an academic subject") (1966a: 148); and
6. Significant differences between black and white students on standard achievement tests which increase from grade 1 to grade 12 (" . . . by far the largest part of the variation in student achievement lies within the same school, and not between schools; comparison of school-to-school variations in achievement at the beginning of grade 1 with later years indicates that only a small part of it is the result of school factors, in contrast to family background differences between communities; there is indirect evidence that school factors are more important in affecting the achievement of minority group students. . . .") (1966a: 297).

As can be imagined the results provoked equal measures of shock, outrage and disbelief. As Daniel Moynihan tells it, this reaction was first expressed within the Office of Education. As he states:

within the Office of Education . . . Coleman's conclusions caused not consternation but something near to alarm. Clearly this was not information that was going to be well received; the correct bureaucratic instinct was to turn to the political executives of the Department of Health, Education, and Welfare for guidance. Consultations were held, reaching all the way to the office of the Secretary, resulting ultimately in a summary report which was political rather than a professional document. The political instinct was towards obscurity. (1968: 24)

Predictably, the findings were variously received by the ideologically committed. Black militants saw the data as supportive of the failure of the reformist effort to effect integration and justification for black separatism. Among political conservatives, the evidence was indicative of the futility of compensatory education due to basic genetic differences between the races. According to Moynihan, liberal reformers "correctly interpreted" the report as "the most powerful social science case for school integration that has ever been made" (1968: 28).

In the academic community, methodological limitations were the center of attention. Robert Nichols (1966), for example, found the study wanting because it relied on a cross-sectional rather than a longitudinal design and failed to include measures of students' initial ability. Due to these shortcomings and the view that it is not customary in the United States for educational practice to be guided by research, Nichols inferred that the study "will likely have little influence on educational policy" (1966: 1314).

The report focused on data collection procedures and the presentation and description of evidence. It did not examine the policy implications of the findings. Coleman addressed the subject in articles that appeared after publication of the study.

Coleman's policy concerns reflect his assessment of the study's significant findings. To begin with, because of the strong relationship between achievement scores and family economic and educational status and the fact that achievement differences were more pronounced within than between schools, he concluded that "family background differences account for much more variation in achievement than do school differences" (1966: 73). Further, interschool variations were attributed to a school's social environment (for example, students' aspirations and educational background and teachers' educational background and achievements). When the social environment indicated by these measures was held constant, the relationship between achievement measures and facility and curriculum factors (per public expenditures, library holdings, and so on) disappeared. Overall, Coleman traces the source of inequality to the home and its cultural environment, the inability of schools to overcome the home's impact on the student, and, lastly, the cultural homogeneity of schools which serves to perpetuate the values of the home and its social milieu (1966b: 73-74).

Coleman's implicit theoretical orientation can be traced to the sociological or Durkheimian practice of seeking the cause of social facts in antecedent social facts as well as the contributions of symbolic interactionists such as Cooley and Mead, who emphasized the primacy of the family in socialization and learning by imitation. Accordingly, Coleman recommended working toward equalizing educational opportunity by (1) replacing the family environment of the disadvantaged with an educational environment (for example, by earlier school enrollment and by attending schools which begin early and close late), (2) reducing the racial and social homogeneity of the schools, and (3) improving the effectiveness of educational programs. In his view, neither pouring money into the schools of the disadvantaged nor "pro forma integration" via forced bussing would be sufficient to accomplish these aims. Furthermore, in Coleman's estimation the only viable policy for goal attainment was one that did not entail improving the educational status of the disadvantaged at the expense of the educationally advantaged. A massive increase in educational expenditures was needed to create new kinds of schools for all children. As he saw it,

> The solutions might be in the form of educational parks, or in the form of private schools paid by tuition grants (with Federal regulations to ensure racial heterogeneity), public (or publicly subsidized) boarding schools . . . , or still other innovations. This approach also implies reorganization of the curriculum within schools. . . . Methods which greatly widen the [student's skill] range are necessary to make possible racial and cultural integration within a school—and thus to make possible the informal learning that other students of higher educational levels can provide. (1966b: 74-75)

In a later paper, Coleman elaborated on the kind of new school needed. He called for "open schools," institutions whose main function is not to instruct but "to coordinate" pupils' activities by facilitating their development via guidance and testing. Ways to open the schools included (1) privatizing instruction by allowing contracts with private firms to teach elementary subjects such as reading and arithmetic, and (2) granting parents the right to (a) select the most appropriate school in which to enroll their children, and (b) decide whether or not to enter them in reading and arithmetic programs offered by private agencies outside the public schools.

By these means, Coleman sought to challenge what he perceived to be generally change resistant educational bureaucracies. By requiring public educational systems to compete with the private sector to provide basic schooling, local school authorities would have to learn better ways to satisfy the public or suffer the consequences. Because parents would be able to decide which alternative curriculum best met the needs of their children, they could, Coleman said, "for the first time in education, have the full privileges of consumer's choice" (1967: 25).

Other ways of opening the schools included encouraging local community organizations to develop cultural enrichment and action programs involving students from different schools and of different races and social class backgrounds. Coleman believed the time had passed "when society as a whole [is] willing to leave the task of education wholly to the public education system, to watch children vanish into the school in the morning and emerge from it in the afternoon, without being able to affect what goes on behind the school doors" (1967: 27).

Whatever the validity of Coleman's recommendations, most judged the policy implications of his study to be ambiguous. At the heart of the problem was the absence of a specified theoretical structure beginning with conceptual clarity. Coleman acknowledged the problem of conceptual ambiguity in an often reprinted paper published in 1968.

As Coleman stressed, any programmatic response to his and other research was dependent upon the meaning attached to the dependent variable, the concept of equality of educational opportunity. Coleman found the current meaning of the term to differ from what it meant in the past and what it may most likely mean in the future. The concept, said Coleman, originated in the nineteenth century. Prior to the industrial revolution the concept was meaningless because children were expected to follow in their parents' footsteps. Occupational choice and skill training were determined by family of orientation in a highly institutionalized social class structure. In America, virtually from the beginning, said Coleman, educational opportunity stressed equality, as indicated by the provision of free education at the local level, a common curriculum and same school attendance by children of all social classes.

The first stage in the evolution of the concept, then, was "the notion that all children must be exposed to the same curriculum in the same school" (Coleman, 1968: 14). The second stage appeared when it was decided that as future occupational positions varied different curricula had to be provided. The third stage accepted and allowed institutionalization of the notion of "separate but equal" educational facilities for blacks and whites. The fourth stage began in 1954 when the Supreme Court ruled that the "separate but equal" doctrine promoted inequality and was, therefore, no longer legally acceptable. With the decision, Coleman noted, an "unarticulated feeling began to take more precise form," namely, "a concept of equality of opportunity which focused on *effects* of schooling" (1968: 15). The latest stage in the evolution of the concept was represented by the survey ordered by Congress and conducted by Coleman and his associates. According to Coleman, "in planning the survey it was obvious that no single concept of equality of educational opportunity existed and that the survey must give information relevant to a variety of concepts" (1968: 16). In other words, the ambiguous nature of the findings was to a considerable extent a consequence of the absence of a commonly agreed upon definition of the concept of equality of opportunity.

Glen Cain and Harold Watts judged the Coleman study wanting on more general theoretical grounds. In the absence of an explicit theoretical design, they could find no way to accurately interpret the study's statistical analyses and findings: "Without a theoretical framework to provide order and a rationale for the large number of variables [included in the survey], we have no way of interpreting the statistical results" (1970: 229).

In Cain and Watts's view the analytical focus of the Coleman study should be on how new and modified public policies influence directly and indirectly the joint distribution (for example, the relationship between pupils' self concept and their achievement test scores) of the several variables examined. Such a task, they point out, requires identifying those elements in a joint distribution that are constant and those subject to direct change by the implementation of certain policies. Specifications of this sort are, as they say, generally referred to as a theory or a model. The problem is that they could find "no explicit discussion" of such a theoretical orientation in the Coleman Report. In their view, however, any prescribed policy contains at least some underlying theoretical orientation or premise: "It is not that one can choose to draw conclusions from the objective facts alone without the aid of any theory, but that if one leaves the theory implicit, ambiguous self-contradicting premises go unnoticed" (1970: 237).

Coleman's reply to Cain and Watts includes several major points. First, Coleman contends that it was inappropriate to specify a theoretical model, because all the variables related to achievement are unknown. Indeed, he says, if the precise relationship between known variables was known, policy questions would be non-problematical. Second, in situations where knowledge is limited, it is more valuable, according to Coleman, to apply "a set of relatively simple and straightforward models" than a single highly specified model. It was for this reason that Coleman and associates opted for use of linear regression analysis. As Coleman explained it,

> When the number of potential causal variables is quite large, both the alternative models and statistical results may be used not only to estimate parameters—as implied by Cain and Watts—but also to sense the relative importance of these variables under alternative causal structures. This is what we did, and this is what I believe important in an area where the theoretical structure of causation is as poorly known as in education. (1970: 243)

Lastly, theoretical models are not as well developed in sociology as economics. As Coleman sees it, economists such as Cain and Watts are used to working in areas with well developed theoretical models. But sociologists, he notes, "ordinarily work in areas without such theoretical models, and the task of their empirical analysis is to gain more information about possibly relevant variables and about plausible causal structures" (1970: 243).

Coleman's position is representative of a general tendency in contemporary sociology. Theory modeling and testing is generally avoided for a number of reasons, chief among which is insufficient or inexact information and knowledge of a subject or a process. The pre-study absence of an explicit theoretical orientation (a specified frame of reference, well-defined concepts, and clearly stated and defended hypotheses) is not thought to be detrimental to the conduct of research and the application of advanced means of statistical analysis. Methods and measurement are typically regarded as either independent or the determinant of theory, presumably on the basis of the tacit assumption that induction must precede deduction. But how much knowledge must one have of a subject before theorizing is allowed? Must theorizing be limited only to advanced knowledge of a subject? What constitutes advanced knowledge in sociology and the other social sciences? Isn't an important element of any scientific endeavor the construct of theories that move from the known to the unknown? How is one to obtain useful applied knowledge, knowledge useful in the development and implementation of social policy, that is not theoretically generalizable on the basis of the best evidence available? Data relevant for so-called pure or applied purposes must be interpretable. If explicit theorizing is not the vehicle, then implicit theorizing is. But what is the difference between implicit theory and unexamined bias or preconceived opinion or ideological conviction? As the discussion below on the experiences of social scientists who participated in several Presidential Commissions shows, failure to confront and adequately answer such questions has contributed heavily to the frustration and disappointment of those who have participated in important applied endeavors and all too often generated a negative impression of the validity of sociological knowledge among its potential consumers.

Presidential Commissions

Presidential Commissions are established for a number of reasons. One of the more important is the need for time to develop an effective and politically judicious response (policy, program) to an insistent complex social problem (crime), a sensitive public issue (pornography), or event (riot). Policy roles played by commissions include fact-finding, policy evaluation, policy recommendation, policy advising, and public education (Lipsky and Olson, 1977: 93). Presidential Commissions also have important non–policy functions—for example, to permit "an executive to defer action while appearing to act" and to be responsive to constituent needs "without taking substantive action" (Lipsky & Olson: 94). Lipsky and Olson found that 66 Presidential Commissions were created between 1945 and 1968.

In 1973, Mirra Komarovsky, President of the American Sociological Association, led the organization of plenary sessions at the annual meeting to examine the experiences of sociologists who had participated in four recent Presidential Commissions. Certain patterns emerged in the commentary of the four. Most apparent was common disappointment in the general reception and policy impact of their labors. For example, Otto Larsen, a member of the Commission on Obscenity and Pornography (1967), stated that the Commission "was conceived in the Congress, born in the White House, and after twenty-seven months of life, was buried without honor by both parent institutions" (Komarovsky, 1975: 9). And Charles Westoff, a participant in the Commission on Population Growth and The American Future (1970), observed that "President Nixon's response to the Commission's report was a disappointment at every turn. . . . [T]he response was narrowly political and greatly at variance with the concerns about population that the President had expressed less than three years earlier" (Komarovsky: 58).

To one degree or another, all four participants encountered the problem of reconciling scientific ideals (the pursuit and acquisition of objectively valid knowledge) and political realities (the tendency of Presidents and Congress to reject and publicly disassociate themselves from controversial Commission findings and recommendations). Political naivete was a generally admitted problem. For example, James Short, a member of the the National Commission on the Causes and Prevention of Violence (1969), summarized his experience by saying, "I am frank to admit that I was naive and unprepared for many aspects of the Violence Commission experience. I learned a great deal, but service on a national commission is not a very good setting for on-the-job training, if one is interested in results" (Komarovsky: 91).

Rather than political naivete, another commission participant attributed failure to the absence of practically and policy relevant sociological theory. In accounting for the failures of The Commission on Obscenity and Pornography, Larsen said that the social sciences were prepared to apply adequately developed research methods but not a theory of social policy. "In short," he said, "we did not have a policy research theory to guide our strategy" (Komarovsky: 23).

Lloyd Ohlin, a member of the President's Commission on Law Enforcement and Administration of Justice (1965), stressed both the strengths and weaknesses of theory in guiding the Commission's work. On the positive side, he found social science theory (concepts, perspectives) to be more useful than new research findings in developing commission recommendations. On the other,

> Explanations concerning the sources of crime and the functioning of the criminal justice system, though informative, lacked specific action implications. In addition, the sociologists serving as consultants to the Commission were reluctant to specify the logical implications of their analyses in the form of action recommendations for the Commission. *When they did try to do this, the recommendations were often more influenced by personal ideological conviction than by appropriately organized facts and theories as arguments* [emphasis added]. (Komarovsky: 109–110)

Participation in the above Presidential Commissions, then, dramatized a problem commonly encountered by sociologists engaged in applied work: the difficulty of reconciling the aims and concerns of clients with the canons of social science. Clients seldom have the same degree of open-mindedness toward data that social scientists do. In this case, the clients were presidents, politicians with ideological convictions and political commitments to defend. Predictably, they could not be expected to be favorably disposed toward evidence supporting policies and programs incompatible with their political interests but quite compatible with those of their opposition. The most common reaction to awareness of clients' sensitivities and limitations has been to apply the most objective methods possible with the aim of collecting information compelling acknowledgment by even the most biased or defensively predisposed. But even the most objective data must be interpreted, and in the absence of a clearly specified and interpretable pre-study theoretical design, investigators' ideological conviction has filled the void.

Obviously, once even the best of social science data can be perceived to require ideological interpretation, its compelling possibilities are rendered invalid by the easy charge of being hopelessly tainted and arbitrary. Reversion to ideological interpretation of data by sociologists engaged in important applied social policy work such as Presidential Commissions is most certainly a consequence of the failure of pure sociology to confront the need to control for the intrusion of ideological factors by effectively integrating theory and research.

The ideological shortcomings of the dominant theoretical orientation in sociology at the time of the Johnson and Nixon Presidential Commissions (the structural-functional perspective) was well documented (see, for example, Demerath and Peterson, 1967). As noted earlier, a common reaction has been to elevate the importance of measurement and depress the role of theory. Theory is to be carefully restricted to grounded knowledge. Commenting on the tendency of some to blame the discipline's theoretical limitations for their failure to be more effective participants in the above four Presidential Commissions, Raymond Mack's reaction was to point out that sociologists should be able to provide Presidential Commissions with both methodological skill and theoretical insight. "But when we are asked for generalizations about behavior as central to the interests of our discipline as crime, violence, or population growth," he notes, "our initial response is to retreat from the hazards of theoretical generalization and to seek security in the field, designing research and gathering data" (Komarovsky: 148).

Yet even the results of competently prepared theoretical analysis may not be sufficient to overcome clients' predisposed aims and political sensitivities. An outstanding example is the fate of the work of a team of social scientists employed by the Kerner Commission (the National Advisory Commission on Civil Disorders created in 1967 by President Johnson).

A primary Commission assignment was to determine the causes of the several riots that erupted in inner city neighborhoods across the country in 1967. Accordingly, Robert Shellow, a social psychologist and a member of the Commission's executive staff, assembled a group of social scientists whose task it was to develop a theoretical explanation of the riots from data collected on individual riots. Developed under extreme time constraints, the group's final report, "The Harvest of American Racism," greatly displeased the Commission's executive staff. "Shortly after it was presented to staff executives, the commission rejected the document, downgraded or dismissed the social scientists, dismissed almost 100 people and changed its schedule" (Lipsky and Olson: 183).

Behind the document's rejection was its contradiction of certain preconceptions and its emphasis on white racism as an overriding causal factor. Thus, contrary to the assumption that the riots were basically politically motivated rebellions, the social scientists found indication of political content in only six of the twenty cities analyzed. Lipsky and Olson note that the document "urged recognition of the fact that behavior may range from a "spree" at one pole to a politically oriented crowd at the other" (184). The document's conclusion was a warning:

> There is still time for our nation to make a concerted attack on the racism that persists in its midst. If not, then Negro youths will continue to attack white racism on their own. The Harvest of Racism in America will be the end of the American dream. (Lipsky and Olson: 185)

According to Lipsky and Olson, the executive staff's criticisms of the document focused on its structure rather than its content. It was said to be "unsuitable," "too long," "diffuse," and "poorly organized" (1972: 186). More damning was the claim that the authors conveyed a more authoritative tone than the data justified.

As Lipsky and Olson point out, even though "The Harvest of American Racism" was never published many of its basic themes were integral to the Kerner Commission's final report. In the summary on the first page of the report one finds the following:

> This is our basic conclusion: Our Nation is moving toward two societies, one black, one white—separate and unequal. . . . What white Americans have never fully understood—but what the Negro can never forget—is that white society is deeply implicated in the ghetto. White institutions created it, white institutions maintain it, and white society condones it.

The general reaction to the involvement of sociologists in Presidential Commissions is that it is an important endeavor to encourage. However, the major lesson learned is that the policy impact of sociological input in such politically sensitive contexts is likely to be minimal unless new and more practically relevant approaches, theories, and methods are devised. As Robert Scott and Arnold Shore state, "sociological theory and research have sometimes led to policy recommendations, but most of these recommendations have been ignored or rejected by national political leaders as unrealistic or implausible" (1979: 27). At the heart of the contemporary critique of the policy relevance of social science theory is the view that structural perspectives are practically unrealistic. This is particularly evident in the conservative critique of the consequences of the programs of the War on Poverty.

The War on Poverty

On March 16, 1964, President Lyndon Johnson advanced proposed legislation to Congress calling for a "War on Poverty." As he explained it,

> We are citizens of the richest and most fortunate nation in the history of the world. One hundred and eighty years ago we were a small country struggling for survival on the margin of a hostile land. . . . The path forward has not been an easy one. But we have never lost sight of our goal: an America in which every citizen shares all the opportunities of his society, in which every man has a chance to advance his welfare to the limit of his capacities. We have gone a long way toward this goal. . . . To finish that work I have called for a national war on poverty. Our objective: total victory. (Will and Vatter, 1970: 9)

On August 20, President Johnson signed into law the Economic Opportunity Act of 1964.

The Act and the War on Poverty represent a unique point in American history, an acceptance of long developing liberal ideological views and the involvement of social scientists in both the creation and implementation of national social policy as never before. In itemizing reasons for the passage of the Economic Opportunity Act, Robert Haveman emphasizes "faith in the efficacy of social planning held by social scientists and other academics whose influence in government was at its zenith" (1987: 14).

The concept of equality of opportunity has deep roots in American history and social science. The notion of America as a land of opportunity is surely as old as the European founding of the country. In social science, the concept of opportunity was central to Lester Ward's advocacy of a sociocratically administered society.

Ward believed that humankind's special asset was the mind. Its cultivation, he thought, should be given the highest national priority. Accordingly, he advocated free public education for all, from the lowest to the highest levels. With the development of reason and intellect would come the next stage in the evolution of democratic society, sociocracy. As noted in Chapter 1, one of Ward's major points in differentiating sociocracy from socialism and individualism is the following: "sociocracy would confer benefits in strict proportion to merit, but insists upon *equality of opportunity* [emphasis added] as the only means of determining the degree of merit" (1899: 292–293).

That Ward's ideas and theoretical premises deeply influenced the aims and policies of key historical figures in the Democratic Party is without question. According to Henry Commager, Lester Ward "provided the intellectual foundations on which men such as La Follette and Wilson and Franklin Roosevelt were later to build" (1967: xxviii). Lyndon Johnson was a protege of Franklin Roosevelt's.

Johnson's aim of eradicating poverty by equalizing the competitive opportunities of the deprived encouraged progressive legislation and the creation of a variety of social programs. Some of the better known include Head Start, Upward Bound, Follow Through, and the Teacher Corps, products of the Elementary and Secondary Education Act of 1965. The most controversial, the one that proved to be the Achilles' heel of the War on Poverty, was the Community Action Program.

Community Action Programs (CAPS) were an integral part of the Economic Opportunity Act of 1964. Their ostensible purpose was to provide locally targeted populations with a formal means of participating in the administration of the federal programs created on their behalf. In the phrasing of the day, the poor were to be allowed "maximum feasible participation" in federal programs by means of Community Action Programs. As it turned out, according to insiders such as Daniel P. Moynihan (1969), participation came to be interpreted as domination, or a "maximum feasible misunderstanding." In brief, instead of harmony and integration, CAPS promoted a level of militancy and divisiveness that provoked intense opposition and diminished support for the War on Poverty.

Interestingly, Moynihan traces the failure of the War on Poverty not to its applied aspects—the manner in which its various programs were implemented—but to the sociological theory upon which it was based. The theory was developed by Richard Cloward and Lloyd Ohlin and first applied in Mobilization for Youth, a program to combat delinquency in New York City.

Cloward and Ohlin acknowledge indebtedness to Robert Merton's deviance theory. Merton (1957), following Durkheim's lead, viewed deviance as a reaction to a disjunction between acceptance of culturally prescribed goals and access to the legitimate means for their attainment. In the words of Richard Cloward and Lloyd Ohlin, "pressures toward the formation of delinquent subcultures originate in marked discrepancies between culturally induced aspirations among lower-class youth and the possibilities of achieving them by legitimate means" (1960: 78). As they see it, then, delinquency is a predictable response to blocked opportunities for legitimate goal attainment. As Moynihan states, to Ohlin and Cloward delinquent acts are not done willingly out of "callousness but normlessness, an anomic condition induced by society" (1969: 50). He finds "a striking quality about" Cloward and Ohlin's Mobilization for Youth proposal, namely, "the degree to which its Program for Action corresponds in structure and detail to the Economic Opportunity Act that was presented to Congress two and a quarter years later" (1969: 58).

Moynihan views the conceptual orientation common to Mobilization for Youth and the War on Poverty as a product of the intellectual climate of the times. In his words,

> the idea of expanding opportunities had suffused the Washington atmosphere, just as it had suffused that of New York in which the MFY program had been conceived. Similarly, the two programs not only corresponded in detail, but in the priorities assigned to the various proposed activities. The first issue to be joined, both in combatting delinquency and warring on poverty, was that of jobs for young people. The second was education for young people. Only then came community action, and thereafter services to special groups. . . . These were ideas that made sense to people in the 1950's and early 1960's. (1969: 58)

According to Moynihan, both Mobilization for Youth and the War on Poverty failed to realize their aims because they were based on the assumption of more radical social change than was either likely or possible. The evidence indicates, he points out, that the Cloward and Ohlin theory was based on a minority viewpoint in the field. Because most criminologists stressed the importance of early childhood socialization patterns, they were inclined to be much less optimistic than Cloward and Ohlin concerning the prospects for rapid social change. Moynihan thinks political partisanship and ideological conviction played a significant role in the theory's popularity and application. He contends that American social scientists have a dual nature. On the one hand they are "objective seekers after truth." On the other, they are inclined to be "passionate partisan[s] of social justice and social change" (1969: 177). During the 1960s, says Moynihan, social scientists had "quite extraordinary access to power," an advantage they used to promote the kind of changes they thought best and most useful.

Vulnerability to charges of ideological predisposition is a major weakness of sociological research, pure and applied. Because there is some tendency among social scientists (particularly the positivistically inclined) to view basic sociological theory as inherently ideologically contaminated, a common response has been to emphasize measurement of detail to the virtual abandonment of explicit pre-study theorizing. But this has not meant the abandonment of implicit reliance on a particular theoretical slant, a structural point of view. Failure to make explicit the strengths and weaknesses of the structural frame of reference has led to charges of ideological bias by those favoring an individualistic ideological position.

STRUCTURALISM VERSUS INDIVIDUALISM

A subject of basic concern to sociologists is the interaction of individual and society, the influence of intra-individual factors (psycho-biological elements such as motives and drives) on extra-individual factors (socio-cultural or structural elements such as norms, values and institutions) and vice versa. Unfortunately, the history of social policy creation, development and change reveals a tendency to emphasize one side of the equation rather than the other. Mostly, policy has been created from a blame-the-victim-rather-than-the-system point of view. The aim has been to provide some general assistance (private or public support, financial and otherwise) for individuals viewed as temporarily inconvenienced or in need because of their own inability to adequately anticipate and respond to life's challenges. Much less often social structure (something beyond individual victims' ability to control) has been identified as the object of treatment to solve a human predicament (for example, the policies enacted and programs developed under Franklin Roosevelt's administration to counter the severe social and economic effects of the Great Depression). It has been difficult to synthesize and simultaneously apply the individual and structural viewpoints because each is deeply embedded in an opposing ideological position.

The individual perspective reflects an American cultural tendency to emphasize citizens' freedom and rights independently of their obligations and responsibilities. The structural perspective, based on philosophical positions developed by Europeans (for example, French social contract theory) and favored by sociologists, is one that conceives of individual freedom as a product of an overriding social bond. From the sociological or structural point of view, there is a definite difference between an individual problem and a social problem. C. Wright Mills, for example, distinguished between "the personal troubles of milieu" and "the public issues of social structure." As he explained it,

> When, in a city of 100,000, only one man is unemployed, that is his personal trouble, and for its relief we properly look to the character of the man, his skills, and his immediate opportunities. But when in a nation of 50 million employees,

15 million men are unemployed, that is an issue, and we may not hope to find its solution within the range of opportunities open to any one individual. The very structure of opportunities has collapsed. Both the correct statement of the problem and the range of possible solutions require us to consider the economic and political institutions of the society, and not merely the personal situation and character of a scatter of individuals. (1959: 9)

The point here is not that there is a precise dividing line between individual and social problems—the two are invariably interrelated—but that the origin of some problems experienced by individuals is external to them. Unemployment during the Great Depression was generally acknowledged to lie in the complexities of the economic institution rather than worker attributes. From the structural viewpoint, the cause of a problem is to be sought in social institutions, factors presumed to have a reality apart from individual consciousness.

But blaming social institutions for individuals' problems does not come easy in a society in which the individual is regarded as the ultimate reality. Individualists acknowledge the influence of social institutions but insist on individual accountability. If freedom is to be meaningful, individuals must be required to anticipate and take full responsibility for whatever effect their intentional and unintentional actions and inactions may have on others. To the individualist, blaming society for a problem is akin to rationalizing a way of evading responsibility.

Without doubt, society may be inaccurately blamed for a given problem; it may indeed be used as a convenient scapegoat by those seeking to avoid culpability. Nonetheless, structuralists insist that it is perfectly logical to blame a social institution (for example, a prevailing practice such as ethnic or racial discrimination, or a formal organizational structure such as the bureaucratic method of decision making) for a problem. From their vantage point, failure to enact policies and implement programs to change harmful social structures is to waste time, energy, and resources. The question is, just how much and in precisely which ways is a given problem causally determined by structural as opposed to individual factors and vice versa? In the absence of generally accepted objectively discriminating criteria, ideological predisposition has been relied upon to answer the question. This is particularly apparent in the ideological disputes between structuralists and individualists over the complex and sensitive area of poverty.

An important spur to the War on Poverty programs of the 1960s was supplied by Michael Harrington's *The Other America*. As he tells it,

The Other America was published in 1962 and was struck by lightning in 1963. In January of that year, Dwight MacDonald wrote a long review of the book in *The New Yorker*, which made poverty a topic of conversation in the socially conscious intellectual world of the Northeast. John Kennedy heard of those discussions and, as two members of his administration later told me . . . , read *The Other America* and was moved by it. It was, they said, one of many factors in his decision to make poverty a central issue in the forthcoming campaign against

Barry Goldwater. Kennedy was assassinated before he could act on that conviction, but Lyndon Johnson followed up on it. When I returned from a year in Europe just before Christmas 1963, I discovered to my amazement that I had played a minor role in a major government shift. (1984: 4-5)

Harrington, a political activist and socialist, convincingly dramatized the plight of the estimated one-fourth of the then population (some 40 to 50 million people) living in poverty in the United States. In portraying their condition, he made it clear that he viewed poverty as a structurally induced problem whose treatment required federal policies and programs.

Harrington distinguished between the old and the new poverty. The old poverty included significant numbers of highly able and motivated individuals needing only an economic upswing to provide them an opportunity to elevate themselves. The new poverty included sizable numbers of individuals left behind in a social and economic progress that they are unable to keep up with. To Harrington, "the other America" was no longer populated by foreigners seeking opportunity in a new land, but "by the failures, by those driven from the land and bewildered by the city, by old people suddenly confronted with the torments of loneliness and poverty, and by minorities facing a wall of prejudice" (1962: 10-11). In contrast to the poor of the country's immigrant past, the contemporary poor are not in a position to help themselves without vast government support. The problem is, however, that those in authoritative positions with the ability to do something about the problem do little or nothing because "they view the effects of poverty—above all, the warping of the will and spirit that is a consequence of being poor—as choices" (1962: 16-17).

Harrington was convinced that poverty in America had become a culture, a total way of life whose change required a new approach and a national social policy. His view and structural approach matched the mood of the moment and gained the support of the liberal intellectual community. As Charles Murray states,

> What emerged in the mid-1960s was an almost unbroken intellectual consensus that the individualist explanation of poverty was altogether outmoded and reactionary. Poverty was not a consequence of indolence or vice. It was not the just desserts of people who didn't try hard enough. It was produced by conditions that had nothing to do with individual virtue or effort. Poverty was not the fault of the individual but of the system. (1984: 29)

In a 1984 publication, Harrington re-examined poverty in America. He spoke of new "structures of misery," in particular, unemployment and social dislocation due to the growth of a corporate economy inclined to abandon American labor for cheaper labor in other lands. Countering the tendency of the concerned to blame President Reagan for the problem, Harrington contended that the current "structures of misery" are the consequence "of massive economic and social transformations and they cannot be understood apart from an analysis of them" (1984: 7-8).

But Harrington's structuralist viewpoint was no longer in vogue. By 1984 conservatism had routed liberalism. Conservative critics such as George Gilder and Charles Murray called for a return to individualistically oriented social policy. Conservatives believe structurally based social policy exacerbates poverty by making people more rather than less dependent. By providing support without work, welfare, in this view, deprives its recipients of the incentive necessary to adapt and fend for themselves. As Gilder puts it, welfare "breaks the psychological link between effort and reward, which is crucial to long-run upward mobility" (1981: 69). In his view, the route out of poverty lies in work, family, and faith.

The first principle is work. According to Gilder, the poor always have had to work harder than those of higher social status. The problem is that the current poor, white people most of all, "are refusing to work hard" (1981: 68).

After work, an essential prerequisite to upward mobility is "maintenance of monogamous marriage and family." According to Gilder, marriage compels a husband and father "to channel his otherwise disruptive male aggressions" into his role as family provider. Thus, strengthening the male role is deemed "the first priority" of any serious program to eliminate poverty in poor families.

After work and family in Gilder's scheme comes faith. "Faith in man, faith in the future, faith in the rising returns of giving, faith in the mutual benefit of trade, faith in the providence of God are all essential to successful capitalism" (1981: 73).

Practice of what Gilder preaches requires rejection of basic liberal premises regarding the causes of poverty and its treatment. Thus, in liberal thinking, he says, a disproportionate number of black people have low incomes due to racism and discrimination. In his opinion, this assumption is incorrect. It slanders whites and "deceives and demoralizes blacks." In obstructing the truth, it suggests that blacks can't make it in the United States without government aid, or by means of "the very programs that in fact account for the worst aspects of black poverty and promise to perpetuate it" (1981: 66).

A second alleged incorrect liberal assumption is poverty reduction by decreasing inequality via income redistribution. As he explains it, increasing the income of poor people requires increasing the general rate of investment. Increasing the rate of investment increases the wealth of the rich. The poor, attracted to the work force by expanding opportunities, will experience a greater proportionate increase in income than the rich. Nonetheless, "the upper classes will gain by greater absolute amounts, and the gap between the rich and the poor may grow" (1981: 67).

At bottom, liberal premises and programs are fraught with "moral hazards," according to Gilder. These include the fact that (1) unemployment is increased rather than decreased by unemployment compensation, (2) (AFDC) Aid for Families with Dependent Children increases rather than decreases dependency, (3) disability insurance encourages the conversion of "small ills into temporary disabilities" and "partial ills" into "permanent disabilities," and

(4) social security encourages neglect of the aged and discourages intergenerational ties (1981: 111).

In a widely read work, Charles Murray expressed much the same viewpoint. He refers to the liberal thinking behind the War on Poverty as the "elite wisdom" of the structurally inclined. Under the "elite wisdom" of the structuralists, welfare, says Murray, is dispensed to people presumed incapable of helping themselves. The cure for the problem, in his view, is the replacement of "the elite wisdom" with "the popular wisdom." As he describes it, the popular wisdom is that of average working men and women. It is, he says, based on hostility toward welfare because "it makes people lazy" and schools that are so busy busing students that they fail to teach them how to read. Lastly, the popular wisdom is said to disapprove of favoritism toward minorities and government interference in areas that "are none of its business" (1984: 146). "Stripped of [its] bombast and prejudices," says Murray, the popular wisdom contains three premises "that need to be taken into account," namely,

1. People respond to incentives and disincentives. Sticks and carrots work.
2. People are not inherently hard working or moral. In the absence of countervailing influences, people will avoid work and be amoral.
3. People must be held responsible for their actions . . . . (1984: 146)

On these premises, he contends that a program is available that can convert the hard-core unemployed into steady workers, reduce the birth rate of single female teenagers, reverse the breakup of poor families, and increase the socioeconomic mobility of poor families. As Murray describes it, "The proposed program . . . consists of scrapping the entire federal welfare and income-support structure for working-aged persons including AFDC, Medicaid, Food Stamps, Unemployment Insurance, Worker's Compensation, subsidized housing, disability insurance, and the rest" (1984: 228). Working age people would be forced to rely on the job market, friends and relatives, and locally available services. "It is the Alexandrian solution: cut the knot, for there is no way to untie it" (1984: 228).

Of the two works, Murray's is generally regarded as the more serious because of its reliance on data. As Sheldon Danziger and Peter Gottschalk differentiate the two, "Murray has been dubbed the 'thinking man's George Gilder' because he provides tables and references where Gilder relies primarily on assertions" (1985: 33). Nonetheless, as Wilson notes, despite Murray's statistical compilations, liberals have little difficulty countering his arguments and conclusions (1987: 17).

At the heart of differences between Murray and his critics is variable interpretation of the impact on poverty of income transfer programs and general economic trends. Murray views the evidence as suggesting that poverty declines have been the result of improved economic conditions rather than increased welfare benefits. His critics see the opposite. To Robert Greenstein, for example, economic decline from 1968 to 1980 "dropped people into poverty" as broadened welfare benefits "lifted them out" (1985: 15). And where Murray argues that increased income transfers to the unemployed account for higher rates of unemployment because they decrease work incentive, the critics find no such evidence. Murray's "explanation—that increased transfers induced declines in work effort, thereby increasing pre-transfer poverty—does not fit the facts" (Danziger and Gottschalk: 33).

Murray's liberal critics have been variously inclined to acknowledge the validity of his and other conservative's individualistic critique of the structuralist interpretation of poverty, or the view that individuals in poverty are not hopeless system victims but ultimately responsible for their own condition and its alleviation. To Christopher Jencks, Murray's work puts the social policy debate in proper context for three basic reasons: (1) it does not dwell on the costs of social policies but whether or not they work, (2) it emphasizes helping people as it discourages those who would cheat the system, and (3) it reminds us that effective social policy includes both rewards and punishments (1985: 49).

From a decidedly tempered ideological vantage point, Nathan Glazer has recently recounted his conception of lessons learned from the War on Poverty. As a professed liberal at the time and a member of the Housing and Home Finance Agency during 1962-63, Glazer describes the early 1960s as a time when people were convinced that the country had the resources to wage a war overseas and eradicate poverty at home. But toward the end of the 1960s, he sensed that something had gone wrong, namely, that the bureaucratic structures and programs devised to combat poverty were creating as many problems as they were solving. The predicament is traced to the liberal view of social problems. "The typical stance [in the liberal] view of social policy is blame—not of course of the unfortunates suffering from the social problem the social policy is designed to remove, but blame rather of our society and our political system" (1988: 3). In working on social policy in housing, health, and social welfare, Glazer became impressed with two salient facts: (1) that social policy is aimed at alleviating human misery by creating new structures to replace those that have broken down in the wake of industrialization and urbanization (the family, ethnic group, neighborhood, and church), and (2) that actions taken contributed to the further weakening of traditional institutions and in important ways exacerbated the general problem.

In addition to contributing to further attenuation of the supportive influence of traditional institutions, liberal social policy, says Glazer, contributed to a rising level of unhappiness and frustration among its beneficiaries because it increased their expectations and heightened their sensitivity to inequality. The more that was promised and provided, the more that was hoped for and demanded; and the greater the effort to equalize opportunities and outcomes in particular areas (jobs, housing, schooling), the greater the awareness of inequities in other and more general areas (status, privilege, power, influence).

In terms of lessons learned, Glazer identifies three factors that limit the effectiveness of social policy. The first refers to the dialectical nature of policy implementation. "It was illusory," he says, "to see our social policies as only reducing a problem; any policy has dynamic aspects such that it also expands the problem, changes the problem, generates further problems. . . . [S]ocial policy is then challenged to deal adequately with these new demands that follow the implementation of the original measures" (1988: 5).

The second is the professionalization of services. That is, in the early stages of program development, experts are few and interest widespread. But once initiated, programs tend to become the specialized province of professionals who form interest groups with independent needs. Glazer writes: "So, in the poverty program we encouraged the rise of community-action agencies as a way of overcoming the bad effects of professionalism, and we soon found that the community organizers had become another professional group, another interest group with claims of their own which had no necessary relation to the needs of the clients they served" (1988: 66).

Lastly, there is always the problem of limited knowledge. With complex subjects such as poverty, one is unlikely to be able ever to devise a policy and implement programs that anticipate all important repercussions. In fact, says Glazer, a lesson of the War on Poverty experience is that the greater the knowledge, the less confident one becomes in terms of exactly what is to be done. As he puts it, "it . . . appears that whatever great actions we undertake today involve such an increase in complexity that we act generally with less knowledge than we would like to have, even if with more than we once had" (1988: 7).

As to what can be done to devise effective social policy to treat major social problems, Glazer is convinced that a focal point must be traditional social practices and restraints. As to the guidance this idea provides, he suggests two lines of thought: "first, it counsels hesitation in the development of social policies that sanction the abandonment of traditional practices, and second, and perhaps more helpful, it suggests that the creation and building of new traditions, or new versions of old traditions, must be taken more seriously as a requirement of social policy itself" (1988: 8).

To briefly summarize, national social policy is heavily if not decisively shaped by the ideological commitments of advocates and critics. The basic lesson learned by sociologists who have participated in important policy concerned efforts such as Presidential Commissions is that the effectiveness of their recommendations lies in integration of theory and research methods and the development of a practical theoretical orientation that interrelates structural and individual factors. Structures and individuals can be both causal determinants and effects. Individuals may in fact be the victims of social structures, but they are also responsible agents capable of taking control of their own lives. The challenge, then, is to develop practical solutions to the problem of interrelating structural conditions and individual choices not from some ideological commitment to an ideal society but in terms that help living actors better adapt to their life situations.

• • • • • *SUMMARY AND CONCLUSION*

From the beginning, sociologists have been concerned about creating a science capable of shaping social policy to solve insistent social problems. However, the premise of those who initiated sociology in America was that participation in applied work awaited identification of societal laws. The separation of pure and applied sociology and the primacy accorded the former have encouraged separation of theoretical and practical ends and limited practical experience in subjects such as social policy creation and implementation. It is not surprising, therefore, that the recent experiences of those who have participated in important policy related efforts such as Presidential Commissions have been less than gratifying.

The strengths that sociologists perceive themselves to bring to applied work are largely methodological—for example, an ability to design survey research instruments and analyze data statistically. But data must be interpreted, and in the absence of theoretical specification sociologists have been inclined to rely on their general structural perspective and generally ideologically left leaning world view. In consequence, any claims to scientific objectivity have been vulnerable to claims of theoretical one-sidedness and ideological bias. Ways to combat the situation include integration of theory and method, a combined structural and individual theoretical approach, the identification of all theoretical assumptions, and the construction of testable hypotheses. Success in all these will not, of course, eliminate the ideological factor. They may, however, serve to focus greater attention on problems and their solution and less on the hidden agendas of policymakers and their consultants.

• REFERENCES

Cain, G.G., and H.W. Watts. 1970. "Problems in Making Policy Inferences from the Coleman Report." *American Sociological Review* 35: 228-242.

Cloward, R.A., and Ohlin, L.E. 1960. *Delinquency and Opportunity*. Illinois: The Free Press of Glencoe.

Coleman, J.S., E.Q. Campbell, C.J. Hobson, J. McPartland, A.M. Mood, F.D. Weinfeld, and R.L. York. 1966a. *Equality of Educational Opportunity*. Washington, D.C.: U.S. Government Printing Office.

Coleman, J.S. 1966b. "Equal Schools or Equal Students?" *The Public Interest* 4: 70-75.

_____. 1967. "Toward Open Schools." *The Public Interest* 9: 20-27.

_____. 1968. "The Concept of Equality of Educational Opportunity." *Harvard Educational Review* 38: 7-22.

_____. 1970. "Reply to Cain and Watts." *American Sociological Review* 35: 242-249.

Commager, H.S. 1967. *Lester Ward and the Welfare State*. New York: Bobbs-Merrill.

Danziger, S., and P. Gottschalk. 1985. "The Poverty of Losing Ground." *Challenge* 28: 32-38.

Demerath, N.J. III, and R. Peterson. 1967. *System, Change, and Conflict.* NY: Free Press.

Gilder, G. 1981. *Wealth and Poverty.* New York: Basic Books, Inc.

Glazer, N. 1988. *The Limits of Social Policy.* Cambridge, MA: Harvard University Press.

Greenstein, R. 1985. "Losing Faith in 'Losing Ground.'" *The New Republic* (March 25): 12–17.

Harrington, M. 1962. *The Other America.* New York: Macmillan.

————. 1984. *The New American Poverty.* New York: Holt, Rinehart and Winston.

Haveman, R.H. 1987. *Poverty Policy and Poverty Research: The Great Society and the Social Sciences.* Madison: University of Wisconsin Press.

Hinkle, R.C., and G.J. Hinkle. 1954. *The Development of Modern Sociology.* New York: Random House.

Hodgson, G. 1975. "Do Schools Make a Difference?" In D.M. Levine and M.J. Bane, eds., *The "Inequality" Controversy: Schooling and Distributive Justice.* New York: Basic Books, Inc.

Jencks, C. 1985. "How Poor Are The Poor?" *The New York Review of Books* (May 9): 41–49.

Keppel, F. 1972. Foreword in G. Myrdal, *An American Dilemma: The Negro Problem in Modern Democracy.* New York: Pantheon Books.

Kerner, O. (Chairman). 1968. *Report of The National Advisory Commission on Civil Disorders.* Washington, D.C.: U.S. Government Printing Office.

Komarovsky, M. 1975. *Sociology and Public Policy.* New York: Elsevier.

Lipsky, M., and D.J. Olson. 1977. *Commission Politics: The Processing of Racial Crisis in America.* New Brunswick, NJ: Transaction Books.

Merton, R.K. 1957. *Social Theory and Social Structure.* Glencoe, IL: Free Press.

Mills, C.W. 1959. *The Sociological Imagination.* New York: Oxford University Press.

Mishra, R. 1981. *Society and Social Policy: Theories and Practice of Welfare.* Atlantic Heights, NJ: Humanities Press.

Moynihan, D.P. 1968. "Sources of Resistance to the Coleman Report." *Harvard Educational Review* 38: 23–35.

————. 1969. *Maximum Feasible Misunderstanding.* New York: Free Press.

Murray, C. 1984. *Losing Ground: American Social Policy, 1950–1980.* New York: Basic Books, Inc.

Myrdal, G. 1972. *An American Dilemma: The Negro Problem and Modern Democracy.* New York: Pantheon Books.

Nichols, R.C. 1966. "Schools and the Disadvantaged." *Science* 154: 1312–1314.

Scott, R.A., and A.R. Shore. 1979. *Why Sociology Does Not Apply: A Study of the Use of Sociology in Public Policy.* New York: Elsevier.

Ward, L.F. 1899. *Outlines of Sociology.* New York: Macmillan.

Will, R.E., and H.G. Vatter, eds. 1970. *Poverty in Affluence.* New York: Harcourt, Brace and World.

Wilson, W.J. 1987. *The Truly Disadvantaged: The Inner City, the Underclass, and Public Policy.* Chicago: University of Chicago Press.

CHAPTER 7

• • •

Summary,
Discussion, and
Conclusion

The aim of the previous chapters has been to chart basic problems and issues involving the relationship between pure and applied sociological theory. The purpose here is to review the nature of the analysis, identify important points and patterns, and draw appropriate inferences.

A working theme of this text has been the value of systematically interrelated pure and applied theory. The problem is that those who initiated the distinction between pure and applied sociology (Comte and Ward) envisioned them as historically separable branches rather than continuously operating, mutually influencing parts of a larger whole. Pure sociology was assigned the task of collecting the basic knowledge prerequisite to the goal of any science, that is, the identification of laws. Once identified, societal laws were to be implemented by applied sociology toward the end of ameliorating the human condition. Behind the strategy was Comte's fear, born of the lessons of the French Revolution, of the negative consequences of social change undertaken prior to the acquisition of precise knowledge of society—its basic elements and their interrelationship. Presumably, scientifically acquired knowledge would provide some assurance that proposed changes would accomplish more good than harm.

Comte and Ward said very little about applied sociology and its practitioners. Comte spoke of the emergence of a governing priesthood, but said little about its relationship to past and future governing contexts. Ward believed that democracy would inevitably evolve into a sociocracy, a social order governed on the basis of scientific knowledge. Mind, the rational intellectual component, was humankind's unique adaptive strength. It seemed to Ward that the direction of societal development was toward increasing rationality in all spheres, particularly the management and organization of human affairs. Therefore, he foresaw a time when society would emphasize identification of the most intellectually able among its ranks, whose task it would be to create social policies and programs based on syntheses of all relevant scientific knowledge. Exactly how the intellectual elite and electorate were to interact was not specified. Like Comte, Ward indicated no particular concern about the authoritarian and totalitarian possibilities of his vision. More importantly in the present context, neither he nor Comte identified developmental stages intermediate to the establishment of pure sociology and the emergence of applied sociology. Most certainly, the high responsibility envisioned for applied sociologists would not occur without lengthy preparation and the occurrence of considerable social change. In brief, the Comte-Ward conception of the roles and aims of pure and applied sociology provides little concrete guidance to one wishing to comprehend the interrelationship of pure and applied sociological work in contemporary society.

Nonetheless—and not surprisingly—some contemporary authoritative attempts to clarify the connection between pure and applied work manifest the influence of outmoded elements of the Comte-Ward viewpoint. It is commonly held, for example, that pure and applied sociology share common means (theories and methods) but have different goals. One is said to seek knowledge accumulation quite independently of its possible relevance for solving social problems. The other is said to be no more and no less than immediate problem-solving oriented. In other words, just as Comte and Ward would have it, the two are basically distinct entities. That each might centrally share the tools, aims, and experiences of the other in a close symbiotic sense seems little appreciated. The closest one comes to a unified concept is the idea of a continuum—that is, pure and applied sociology are thought of as opposites, with certain, sometimes indeterminable, kinds of work seen as belonging more to one than the other. That the two might best be regarded as natural complements rather than opposites is still problematical.

The major link between pure and applied sociology has been research methods. Research skill is as critical to the success of basic scholarly work as practical employment. The research methods of the detached scholar may have great significance for the practically engaged, and vice versa. The problem is that this connection has not provided the bridge to the problem of basic knowledge accumulation that one might hope would be the common goal of both pure and applied sociologists. It has not done so largely because theory is a neglected element. In fact, methods of research have replaced theory as the central tool of social and behavioral scientists in general. The importance of theory as a tool—a means—and a goal has diminished for several reasons, among the most important of which are the difficulty of disentangling objective and heuristic scientific theory from ideological conviction and the growing conviction that the isolation of laws in the physical science sense is untenable in the behavioral and social sciences.

The entanglement of theoretical orientation and ideological predisposition is a consequence of such factors as the difficulty of separating personal and emotional aims from impersonal and objective means (including disagreement concerning the proper connection between induction and deduction), and different philosophies of science (hermeneutics versus positivism).

PERSONAL MOTIVES VERSUS SCIENTIFIC COMMITMENT

While most behavioral and social scientists generally have little difficulty reconciling their personal and emotional goals with the canons of valid scientific procedure, many experience great difficulty. During the 1960s, ideologically committed radical sociologists challenged and sought to differentiate themselves from their mainstream colleagues. At annual meetings of the American Sociological Association it was routine for radical sociologists to hold their own alternative sessions. The Marxist-oriented radicals saw themselves as on the side of the exploited and their counterparts as on the side of the exploiters, the managers of the capitalistic mode of production and their lackeys. At the 1968 American Sociological Association convention, Martin Nicolaus observed that the convention

> is not a coming together of those who study and know, or promote study and knowledge of, social reality. It is a conclave of high and low priests, scribes, intellectual valets, and their innocent victims, engaged in the mutual affirmation of a falsehood, in common consecration of a myth.
>
> Sociology is now and never has been any kind of objective seeking out of truth or reality. Historically, the profession is an outgrowth of 19th-century European traditionalism and conservativism, wedded to 20th-century American corporation liberalism.
>
> This is to say that the eyes of sociologists, with few but honorable (or: honorable but few) exceptions, have been turned downwards, and their palms upwards. (1970: 275)

If there was no such thing as scientific objectivity or value-free science, the only question worth asking was: "Whose side are we on?" Was one a warm blooded humanist on the side of the downtrodden or a cold-blooded scientist on the side of the downtrodders? To speak of the two as not necessarily incompatible was to be accused of being a "wishy-washy" liberal. As Gouldner described the situation, "I fear that the myth of a value-free social science is about to be supplanted by still another myth, and that the once glib acceptance of the value-free doctrine is about to be superseded by a new but no less glib rejection of it" (1970: 218).

With the ebbing of the intense activism of the 1960s and the ascension of ideological conservatism, concern with the "subjective versus objective" dilemma has predictably declined. But it must be considered to be an ongoing problem, and one likely to assume added importance in the wake of the continuing growth of applied social science. The issues are of no less relevance to pure as applied sociologists. Should basic scholars never consider serving interests other than their own? Are there not practical social problems of basic scholarly relevance? Who should be the clients of the applied sociologist? Must clients always be those with an ability to pay? Such questions require more overt attention if some of the major issues involved in the effort to reconcile the personal and humanistic concerns of social scientists with their objective and scientific principles. Any adequate synthesis of the two sides must inevitably hinge on a better understanding and specification of the differences between theory and ideology.

Both theory and ideology are frames of reference, or preconceived ways of viewing and interpreting subjects of importance. Essentially, however, theory is something tentative, a hypothesis to be tested and either supported or rejected by objectively obtained evidence. Ideology is something more rigid, a term closer in meaning to dogma than theory. A standard dictionary definition of ideology refers to a "body of ideas reflecting the social needs and aspirations of an individual, group, class, or culture." Dogma generally refers to beliefs or principles regarded as absolute truths. Ideologies and dogmas are givens to those who hold them. The ideologue and the dogmatist aim not to test their beliefs but to apply them. In sociological terms, theory is a tool for the study of social phenomena and ideology a way of structuring them.

Of course, theory may become ideology and dogma. The 1960s critiques of structural-functional theory, for example, emphasize its one-sided emphasis on the study of social order and compatibility with a politically conservative ideological orientation. And the dominance of the structural-functional perspective provoked references to it as an ism, an accepted set of beliefs or doctrine. The natural opposite to social order and consensus oriented structural-functionalism was social change and dissensus-oriented Marxism. As to whether or not a synthesis of the two was possible, probably the best authoritative answer of the day was that some social problems are best studied from the "integration" and others from the "coercion" point of view (see Dahrendorf, 1959: 157-165).

To positivists, the call for ideological diversification or pluralism was hardly a satisfactory way of dealing with the problem of scientific objectivity. It appeared to suggest that research method, not theory, was the proper route to the end. With the ascension of methodological criteria as the measure of research validity, the role of theory in data acquisition and interpretation became of secondary importance. It became accepted truth that employment of logico-deductive theory was inappropriate until sociological phenomena could be acceptably quantified and their effects isolated. Application of deductive schemes, no matter how tentative or qualified, prior to solution of "the measurement problem" encouraged a more restrictive and biased view of social phenomena than was warranted. Induction, in other words, must precede deduction. The problem is, however, that as one cannot study anything systematically from all possible angles at once, and without having certain assumptions of what is to be studied and why, theory, implicitly if not explicitly, is an integral component of measurement. And even precisely measured phenomena must be interpreted. In the absence of available tested theory within the methodological limitations of the discipline, sociologists engaged in applied work such as Presidential Commissions have admittedly had to rely on personal means such as ideological conviction to interpret evidence and make practical social policy recommendations. Concern with immediate social problems requiring less than perfect understanding of relevant phenomena has spurred interest in hermeneutics, a philosophical viewpoint that challenges the appropriateness of the dominant positive philosophy for the study of human behavior and society.

HERMENEUTICS VERSUS POSITIVISM

Positivism has long been the leading philosophy of science. Comte, the acknowledged initiator of the positivistic movement in sociology, assumed that societal facts are subject to the same scientific mode of scrutiny as all other natural phenomena. The unity of science continues to be a prevailing postulate. Carl Hempel has been among the more influential advocates of the concept. He rejects the logic of those who would distinguish between the descriptive and the theoretical, between historical and exact sciences. He writes,

> The remarks made in this section are but special illustrations of two broader principles of the theory of science: first, the separation of "pure description" and "hypothetical generalization and theory-construction" in empirical science is unwarranted; in the building of scientific knowledge the two are inseparably linked. And, second, it is similarly unwarranted and futile to attempt the demarcation of sharp boundary lines between the different fields of scientific research, and an autonomous development of each of the fields. The necessity, in historical inquiry, to make extensive use of universal hypotheses of which at least the overwhelming majority come from fields of research traditionally distinguished from history is just one of the aspects of what may be called the methodological unity of empirical science. (1942: 48)

The common goal of the positive sciences is identification of laws, or the isolation of invariant relationships among measured quantities under empirically specified conditions. Early advocates of positivism in the behavioral and social sciences had the difficult task of convincing their colleagues that human behavior and society are capable of objective analysis and quantification by the same methods available to the physical sciences—observation, measurement, and experimentation. Their opponents were inspired by a variety of philosophical positions including creationism.[1]

Some objected not so much to the emphasis placed by positivists on the postulate of scientific unity and the search for laws, but to the neglect of the study of human phenomena, individual and group, for its uniqueness, especially its "subjective variability" (see, for example, Bisbee, 1937). They were and continue to be variously guided by hermeneutic philosophy.

Hermeneuticists emphasize the symbolic nature of human interaction and the creativity and adaptability of human behavior. As stated in Chapter 4, to the hermeneuticist human behavior may be subject to causal analysis, but it is the expression of an entity capable of change and variable responsiveness to the same stimuli. The type and range of behavior possible under constant, different, and changing conditions and circumstances are of particular interest.

Methodologically, the hermeneuticist is especially concerned not only with observing behavior first hand, but also with obtaining the actor's viewpoint. Fundamentally, hermeneuticists view human behavior as something subject to interpretation rather than precise and definitive measurement. The more consistent the interpretations of behavioral events from different viewpoints, the greater the assurance of observational accuracy.

The "relativity" of hermeneutics, its interest in studying human behavior as something unique in nature, coincides with the growing interest in the ancient idea of viewing nature as consisting of different orders of phenomena requiring analysis from different phenomenological perspectives with different aims. Across the social sciences, there is, as indicated in Chapter 4, increasing questioning of the validity of the search for societal laws.[2] Seeking regularities of limited generalizability and historical relevance rather than invariant patterns of timeless validity seems the more realistic aim to many. But this is a minority viewpoint because the ideals of positivism continue to hold sway. While ideals may not be realizable, attempts to approximate them may well have more positive than negative consequences.

Whether the aim is the isolation of laws or regularities, the role of theory in the process remains to be clarified. Frustration over the apparent inability to identify societal laws is primarily a concession to the limitations of inductive or methodological procedures rather than the art of deduction or theoretical interpretation. For a variety of reasons, sociologists are much less tolerant of the application of imperfect deductive theory than imperfect research methods. The two would seem to be equally dangerous. Unexamined are the consequences for disciplinary goal attainment of the underdeveloped state of theory and the art of theorizing. Without enhancement of ability to synthesize the findings of diverse studies of comparable subjects and to anticipate the unknown from the known, it is difficult to envision success in the isolation of "regularities" or "laws." Both are interpretations, and all scientific interpretation is theoretical as nothing can be assumed to be known "once and for all."

The recent expansion of applied sociology has heightened interest in methodological training, the discipline's most marketable skill and, if anything, was contributed to ever greater neglect of theory. It is the immediate data and research needs of the client rather than disciplinary goals that command the primary attention of the contemporary applied sociologist.[3] The positive possibilities in practical work for theory building and skill training have emerged historically in policy-related work. Effective involvement in policy formation and evaluation requires theoretical skill, an ability to draw inferences from available evidence concerning the likely consequences of adopting and implementing different courses of action. A common explanation given by sociologists for their ineffectiveness in policy work is the absence of practical policy-relevant theory. Lacking theoretical guidance, sociologists have relied on their quantitative skills and value biases. "Commonly what sociologists do," says Albert Reiss, is "to assemble facts that relate to changes proposed by others who espouse their values" (1970: 289). In his view, the lack of a generally relevant policy theory severely restricts sociology's usefulness for social engineering. Only quite recently has there been indication of serious interest in the importance of developing theory-guided efforts in social engineering.

THEORY-GUIDED APPLIED RESEARCH

Over the past decade, Huey-Tsyh Chen and Peter Rossi have co-authored a series of articles concerned with what they refer to as "theory driven" evaluation research. Program evaluation is a major source of employment for applied sociologists. Among the major reasons for the demand for program evaluation is the traditional stop-gap atheoretical approach to social problem treatment in the United States. It should come as no surprise, therefore, that the general finding of evaluation studies is that few programs have the intended effects. "We now know," state Chen and Rossi, "that rehabilitation efforts fail to reform prisoners; that more money and curriculum changes fail to increase the teaching ability of schools; that poverty is scarcely to be alleviated by counseling the poor; that housing, when improved, leads to no corresponding changes in the quality of lives of residents; and manpower training programs scarcely improve the employment chances of graduates; and so on . . . " (1980: 106–107). As they state, such findings have been interpreted to indicate that social science knowledge is not yet adequate to the task of effective social engineering. The fault, they say, lies not in inadequate development and implementation of research methods or program construction but in the failure to design theoretically structured program evaluations. In their view, "a priori knowledge and social science theory can adequately anticipate the effects that a given social program can be expected to have" (1980: 108). Hence, to remedy the situation they call for a "multi-goal, theory-driven approach" to program evaluation.

The emphasis placed on multiple goals reflects an effort to overcome the limitations of conventional evaluations, which tend to be confined to appraising effects of only formally specified program goals and outcomes. Chen and Rossi properly argue that programs have intended and unintended consequences, each of which may be either positive or negative. The aim is to use available knowledge and theory to anticipate the variety of possible effects. In federally sponsored income maintenance studies, for example, prevailing evidence and theory suggested that work is not only a source of money, or a means to maintain life, but also identity and status. Hence, providing the needy with direct income payments could be expected to have no necessary deleterious impact on either work incentive or continued employment. Of course, the two dependent variables may be quite independent of each other and require separate theoretical interpretations. However useful it may be for anticipating and pursuing such particular lines of inquiry, theory is envisioned by Rossi and Chen to have a larger, more general role to play in program evaluation.

Programs aimed at treating social problems are designed primarily by non-social scientists. Program evaluation by social scientists within their theoretical perspectives and basic interests can serve both disciplinary aims of knowledge accumulation and clients' aims by providing them with alternative interpretations and insights they are likely to be unaware of. The overall consequence may be a closer working relationship between clients and evaluators. As Chen and Rossi state, a possible outcome of their multi-goal, theory driven approach "is a closer link between program designers and evaluators at the point of program formulation and design" (1980: 112).

Unfortunately, later articles by Chen and Rossi (1987, 1989) indicate little change in the status of theory in evaluation research. It continues to be underutilized to the point of disuse for a variety of traditional reasons—financial cost, time limitations, client and researcher disinterest, and so on. The one branch of applied sociology that has most integrated theory in its work is clinical sociology.

THEORY AND CLINICAL SOCIOLOGY

In some ways clinical sociology is to sociology what clinical psychology is to psychology. Like its psychological counterpart, clinical sociology is an essentially practical treatment-oriented branch of the larger discipline. However, it uses a much more eclectic approach to problem solving than clinical psychology. It employs any available sociological theory that may be useful to treat a problem, it may utilize any available research methods and measurement techniques, and its clients may be individuals or groups (and groups may range from dyads to entire communities).

An individual's problem is approached strictly from the sociological perspective. That is, a person's problem is viewed as a product of social interaction and membership in certain groups. Of specific interest are the clients' "significant others," those instrumental in influencing their self-concept, values, and normative expectations (parents, siblings, and so on). Thus, all members of the client's family circle might be included in the treatment process. Also of fundamental importance are the various positions or statuses clients may occupy in society (corporate executive, PTO president, church deacon, and so on) and the diverse roles associated with them. The clinician may use such information to diagnose a problem such as role conflict, and in other ways sensitize clients to the bearing of social factors in their predicament.

They may operate on a one-to-one basis with a client or as a member of a treatment team.[4]

As a consultant to a local community (a municipal agency, a regional council, a neighborhood association, a group of concerned citizens, and so on), the clinical sociologist may perform a variety of functions—conflict mediation, organizer, project facilitator, researcher, and much more.[5]

Regardless of its diverse activities, clinical sociology makes wider use of basic sociological theory than other types of applied sociology (some idea of its theoretical range was conveyed in Chapter 3). A good portion of the reason for this fact is the aim of its practitioners to implement sociological theory and knowledge in accordance with the classical disciplinary goal of active intervention in social life to improve the human condition. Clinical sociology is defined by its devotees as "a historical tradition within the larger discipline based on the premise that sociological knowledge, perspective, and method can and should be used to guide and facilitate interventions for positive change at any or all levels of social life" (Straus, 1985: 183).

Despite its theoretical strengths, clinical sociology shares with other types of applied sociology—perhaps even more so—a neglect of service to pure sociology. It aims to use pure sociology, not contribute to its further development by theoretical synthesis of diverse facts in regard to important issues, problems, and subjects toward the general goal of basic knowledge accumulation. It also shares with other applied endeavors the tendency to ignore careful weighing of the influence of ethical and moral factors in what it can and cannot do. Clearly, applied clinical endeavors must confront a variety of ethical and moral concerns (when does the possibly neutral aim of "intervention" become biased behavioral manipulation, a human rights violation, invasion of privacy, and so on?). Responses to actual and potential ethical and moral dilemmas must be carefully considered both because of their bearing on the welfare of human "subjects" and because they may have important repercussions on the possible expansion and constriction of avenues of practice and research.

ETHICAL AND MORAL CONSIDERATIONS

Ethics and morals are closely related terms. Ethics refers to standards or principles of proper conduct. Commonly this relates to the moral choices individuals must make in relating to others. Morals involve appraising human conduct for its goodness or badness. Sociologists regard the two as norms, or established notions of correct conduct in given situations. Of the two, morals are regarded as the more serious norms. When violated, as by an act of premeditated murder, they evoke the most severe negative sanctions. When upheld to the extreme, as, for example, by upholding the norm of altruism on the battlefield by risking one's life to protect comrades, they evoke the highest forms of group approval. However, unless otherwise stated, reference to the one generally includes reference to the other.

Professional organizations such as the American Sociological Association and American Psychological Association have codes of ethics rather than codes of morals. Their creation took time because their reason for existence was and is debatable.

A primary argument against professional codes of ethics is the unnecessary duplication of generally prevailing principles and laws, or the idea that established customs and legal codes are sufficient protection for service providers and their clients. Those who disagree believe professionals must be held more accountable than usual—by themselves as well as others—because of the potential to inflict great harm upon those they work with in their trade. Ethical codes, then, remind practitioners of their high responsibilities, and encourage them to exercise caution and be extremely mindful of the rights and well-being of their "subjects."

Of course, one can't always be perfect, and chances must be taken. In the treatment professions, medicine in particular, practitioners strive to inform patients of the risks involved in prescribing different courses of action, the odds of recovery based on the best evidence available, and so on. But warnings and providing information are only a part of professional competency. Even the most competent err at the point of application, as the rise in medically related malpractice suits partially indicates.

In any science, basic research must be undertaken to acquire advanced knowledge, and goal attainment often entails new, different and radical forms of experimentation. Milgram's study of obedience to authority and Humphreys' investigation of homosexual activity in public restrooms are illustrations from behavioral and social science. In both cases, the experimenters knowingly took ethical chances to obtain desired knowledge. Milgram hoped his experiment would test subjects' sensitivities and took measures to treat possible negative effects. Humphreys, too, knowingly risked the well-being of those he studied and took certain precautions to protect them. After the fact, both thought their efforts necessary, and believed the benefits of knowledge gained outweighed any harm to subjects that may have been caused. As reported in Chapter 5, many of their colleagues disagreed.

As indicated in Chapter 5, there are two basic philosophical positions in regard to the means and ends of science. Those such as Humphreys and Milgram, who basically contend that the end justifies the means, fit the utilitarian point of view. Those who argue that the means of science are always primary fit the deontological position. To the deontologically inclined, it is ethically intolerable to sacrifice the well-being of anyone in the name of a larger good. Put another way, no harm of any sort is ethically excusable. Investigators and practitioners must always be held accountable for their actions. As extreme as this may seem, it must be remembered that a major impetus for renewed interest in deontological philosophy is the medical experiments conducted by Nazi doctors during World War II. The life and death powers of the medical profession are no less present in democratic than authoritarian regimes. Essentially, the utilitarian position defends the cause of science and the deontological position the interests of individual citizens. The struggle between the two delimits the boundary line, however vague and imprecise, between acceptable science and violation of human rights. In so many words, professional codes of ethics generally remind those to whom they apply of the two sides and the responsibilities and risks of possible violations.

The ethics of research involving human subjects, in pure and applied settings, then, serve to inhibit risky ventures because they encourage the conventional and the safe. It is to be expected, therefore, that knowledge growth is and must be somewhat retarded by the importance placed on the ethics of basic research and ethical factors involved in applied work, particularly when involuntary behavioral modification and social change may be involved.

Ethical considerations restrict knowledge growth by blocking the social scientist's quest for the power requisite to effective control of experimental conditions and findings. To become a science in the ideal sense, sociology requires the same freedom to manipulate relevant phenomena as physics or biology. But comparable freedom in this sense would seem to require dictatorship, something abhorrent both to non-Marxist social scientists and all defenders of democratically constituted society. A consequence of limited experimental control is efforts to test the boundaries of the ethically tolerable (as in the case of the Milgram experiment and the Humphreys study) and ideal type theorizing in the manner of Parsonsian so-called "grand theory." The problems of power and control are as evident in applied work as basic research. They pose a two-sided predicament for applied sociologists.

On the one hand is the matter of conscience. Being well paid by a client may be quite pleasing, but it all too frequently entails relinquishing any formal control over the uses to which data and study results may be put. For many this is an ethically unacceptable and socially irresponsible situation. On the other hand, relinquishing any involvement in practical affairs seems equally ethically intolerable. Howard Waitzkin provides the following example of the ethical dilemma facing the social scientist concerned with influencing political decision making:

> for the social scientist there is a tension between the optimistic assumption that scientific rationality can solve social problems and the realistic observation that he himself lacks power. He may search for power, and for ways to bring his work to the attention of decision-makers. Yet . . . he hesitates to consort too freely with those in power, fearing that the quality of his work and even his personal integrity might be compromised through involvement in politics. (1970: 170)

Participation in applied work invariably tests one's ethical ideals. The question is, is it more important to uphold one's personal and scientific ideals by involvement or non-involvement in practical work under less than ideal circumstances? Unfortunately, the question does not admit itself to a neat and generally satisfactory answer. It depends on any number of personal and other considerations. However, few wise people claim that learning does not entail risk, the risk of learning something uncomfortable about oneself and others and the risk of learning by the often practical necessity of having to acquire and implement knowledge under less than perfect conditions. Risk of the latter sort is particularly evident in social policy related work. The subject is of special importance because social policy formation and implementation entails not only the necessity of confronting and reconciling ethical challenges but also the interrelationship of basic and applied knowledge. A creative leap must be made from the known to the unknown, from the factual to the theoretical, involving the well-being of a target population. Not to be overlooked is that successful participation in the creation and application of important social policy is an important gauge of the progress and importance of sociology.

ETHICS, THEORY, AND SOCIAL POLICY

Social policy work involves employment by those in decision-making positions whether in the private or public sector. As policy implementation may have important behavioral consequences, the ethics of behavioral modification and control are to be carefully considered. Prior to involvement in policy related work—as a consultant, investigator, analyst, or whatever—the ethically responsible sociologist would want to have answers to certain questions, including employers' aims and intended means of goal attainment. Is the effort a response to management or employee, political official or political constituency initiative? Will representatives of the targeted population be involved in any or all phases of the project? Is the aim to generate voluntary and involuntary behavioral effects? Is the implicit or explicit aim to achieve greater behavioral control over employees or constituents? Will one be able to formally influence the uses to be made of his or her contributions? To be sure, one may be confronted with such ethically loaded questions in any type of applied employment, but most assuredly in policy-related matters.

On the issue of the ethical responsibilities of sociologists for the uses made of their work, some believe the solution lies in political activism and the acquisition of political power. Marxist sociologists are the prime example. Probably most contemporary sociologists favor a more passive or less ambitious approach. An example is the following position taken by Peter Rossi and James Wright:

> Although it is undoubtedly irritating to know that it is difficult for a social scientist to play a major role in the making of policy, this is, in fact, as it should be. A society in which social scientists play crucial policy roles through their research is a society in which human values have been subordinated to technocratic considerations, a world in which social scientists have become philosopher kings. In a truly democratic society, social science must be content with an advisory but not dominating role. Only the autocratic are confident enough in their righteousness of their own values to impose them on others. When policymakers ask of the social scientists, "Will it work?" we often have the skills, and therefore the obligation, to respond with the best research and analysis we can muster. But when they ask, "Is it just?" it is best if we leave the answers to others. (1985: 331)

In a decentralized, highly pluralistic political system—an ideal situation in which there are competing interest groups with equal power—there would be little to quibble with in this position. However, in the real world, in both private and public sectors, not all effected parties typically have equal access to and influence on authoritative decision makers. Hence, when employed by authorities, applied sociologists may provide input supportive of the interests of some at the expense of others. In the private sector, this has sometimes meant providing information to management interested in more efficient ways of manipulating employees with or without either their participation or prior consent. Is it not ethically irresponsible to ignore such possibilities in democratically constituted society? Isn't it a basic principle of democratic society that all citizens are responsible for the consequences of their actions as they relate to the rights of others? Because their skills and data may be used to manipulate social structure and people, shouldn't sociologists hold themselves particularly accountable to the democratic ideal? In a complex world increasingly dominated by the technologically proficient, isn't it essential for the survival of democracy and humankind that all professions and sciences require their members to not only anticipate but to assume responsibility for the uses of their work? However difficult it may be to live up to the ideal, anything less than the attempt encourages the naivete and indifference that leads to such examples as Project Camelot.

To summarize the point, the cause of justice is always the responsibility of everyone, not of someone else. The higher the authority or ability to affect the rights and well-being of others, the greater the responsibility.

A good portion of the tendency to relegate responsibility for upholding ethical ideals to others is related to certain positivistic assumptions—namely, that science is amoral and that methodological precision (accurate identification and measurement of social facts)—is primary and theorizing secondary. A major theme in George Lundberg's work was that "science, as such, is nonmoral" (1964: 28). By this he meant that there was nothing in science dictating the ends to which its products may be used, and that the obligation of scientists is to pursue knowledge wherever it may take them. In Lundberg's view, only in their role as citizens are scientists free to exercise their ethical and moral concerns. This position is well ingrained in contemporary sociology, as indicated by the above statement of Rossi and Wright. So too is the view that methodological considerations are primary and theoretical work secondary.

METHODS AND THEORY

Research methods replaced theory as the primary orienting force in sociology due to a variety of factors, two of the more important of which are the importance attached to making the discipline scientific and the limitations and failures of general theory. As indicated in Chapter 1, sociology was initiated by those wishing to establish a practically useful science of society. The necessary route to the end was presumed to lie in adoption and implementation of a scientific method rooted in the philosophy of positivism. The discipline was divided into pure and applied branches, and it was contended that basic, accurately measured knowledge of society was prerequisite to effective amelioration of the human condition via social planning. From its initiation, in other words, sociology was predicated on the ability to successfully quantify social phenomena and their precise interrelationship, that is, their lawlike patterns. Once assured of having obtained objectively verified knowledge of social facts, sociologists would be able to prescribe policies to cure social problems, to become applied practitioners. As historical circumstances would have it, however, "the measurement problem" did not become immediately the center of attention because of the emergence and overwhelming impact of Darwinian evolutionary theory. "Almost everywhere in western civilization," says Richard Hofstadter, "though in varying degrees according to intellectual traditions and personal temperaments, thinkers of the Darwinian era seized upon the new theory and attempted to sound its meaning for the several social disciplines" (1955: 4). Early American sociologists such as Ward and Sumner may have had their ideological differences, but both were social Darwinists.[6] It was generally assumed that society was subject to progressive evolutionary change. The issue of the era was whether the evolutionary process was subject to acceleration or retardation by human intervention.

Increased interest in the fundamentals of scientific procedure arose as a consequence of the failure of prevailing progressive evolutionary theory to account for such "aberrations" as World War I. The advent of the First World War led to a reassessment of first principles and rejection of premises concerning essential human nature,—for example, the notion that people are born with the moral sentiment to practice "the golden rule." The rational, civilized human adult became something to account for, not presume. Soon after, behaviorism, operationalism and statistical applications became major movements to be reckoned with.

But theory did not sink to its current lowly status until the fall of structural-functional theory in the 1960s. As in the case of the evolutionary theory preceding it, it too proved to have some fatal flaws (in particular, and despite claims to the contrary, a one-sided emphasis on the study of social order and high compatibility with ideological conservatism). By the 1960s, theory and methods had gone their separate ways. By the 1970s, both pure and applied sociology had become highly methodologically oriented, relatively atheoretical endeavors. Increasingly there is call for a more balanced orientation. Some advocate the reinstitution of theory as the primary component. To R.P. Cuzzort, for example,

> Theory can in no way be replaced by methods. Since the beginning of the twentieth century, there has been a disturbing tendency to give methods the prominence that rightfully belongs to theory. Methods, of course, are a necessity in any discipline. . . . But when method takes up more time and energy than theory, something is amiss. And this is what has happened in sociology. . . . The priorities are wrong; theory should always be behind the steering wheel. (1989: xiii)

Cuzzort reasons that because "methods are not the source of creativity in any field," their ascension has led a "drying up of the sociological imagination." Methods, in his view, serve as a brake to the extravagances of theorizing. When too rigorously applied, however, they stifle creativity. According to Cuzzort,

> A truly rigorous scientific epistemology, if applied to the problems social philosophers think about, would produce complete mental paralysis. There must be a proper balance of method and theory. (1989: xiii–xiv)

The inhibiting influence of methods on theory is as apparent in applied as pure sociology. As noted above, for example, a frequent reason given by sociologists for their inability to effectively influence social policy formation and implementation is the absence of a general social policy theory. Despite having been made several years ago, the claim has not led to a concerted effort to rectify the situation. But social policy research continues, and predictably measurement problems are often associated with theoretical limitations. The problem of construct validity is a prime example.

Constructs are terms based on interpretations of relations among observables. Suicide, for example, is a potentially, if not actually observable fact. Durkheim's concept of anomie is a construct used to account for a certain type of suicide—namely, that associated with abrupt loss of important social bonding or anchoring such as the death of a spouse or job termination. It is, of course, one thing to test the validity of a relatively systematically developed theoretical construct such as anomie; it is quite another, as is frequently the case in applied social science, to attempt to measure and evaluate the nature and role of unsystematically defined but commonly used constructs such as those associated with human social development. A review of the papers included in their recently edited work on social policy led R. Lance Shotland and Melvin Mark to a number of important conclusions including the following:

> Our contention is that policy-relevant research can in general be improved by increased attention to construct validity: Construct validity is generally essential for interpretability. One example is the research Belsky cites concerning the effects of day care on social development. As Belsky notes, measures of "social development" might reasonably be interpreted as representing any of several seemingly distinct constructs: Social skills, assertiveness, independence, or the frequency of interaction. Without greater construct validity, it is not possible to be confident about which construct the measures best represent, so interpretation of the research is difficult. (1985: 338–339)

In short, the most advanced measurement techniques are of little use when the units of analysis are not clearly specified.

Units of analysis, the "things" studied, are theoretical concepts, or symbolic interpretations of perceptions. The basic concepts of a science identify the phenomena or items of causal importance. In sociology, norms, or learned rules of appropriate behavior in given situations, are the basic social facts. The identification and causal impact of norms in social life are of fundamental concern to "pure" sociology and, therefore, are integral components of "the" sociological perspective. The problem is that sociologists are seldom hired to simply apply their theoretical orientation or methodological skills as they see fit or for their own disciplinary purposes. Clients' "definitions of the situation," their terms and conceptualizations of problems and subjects to be studied, must be heeded if relevant work is to be undertaken. In many, if not most, cases this is easier said than done for a number of reasons, including the fact that clients' aims tend to be immediate and situationally specific and of no necessary importance to general disciplinary concerns and long-run interests. It is because of this fact that many contend that a scientific discipline is likely to progress most rapidly if problems, theories, and methods develop from interests within than without its confines. But this interpretation may be less relevant to the social than the physical sciences. Major social problems such as those associated with rapid industrialization and urbanization (alcoholism, crime, prostitution, social class conflict, and so on) are generally acknowledged to have supplied the impetus behind the creation of the modern social sciences. The search for practical solutions to contemporary social problems has been and continues to be a central preoccupation of all social science disciplines. Therefore, it is important to consider both what a social science may gain and lose by the involvement of its practitioners in practical affairs and applied work generally. But, considering the historical primacy accorded pure sociology, it is equally important to question the relevance of basic to applied work.

THE INTERRELATION OF PURE AND APPLIED SOCIOLOGY

Because sociology has traditionally been interested in worldly affairs and practical social problem solving, some have assumed that there is no essential difference between pure and applied sociology. They assume that the aims of the two are compatible, and that the theories and methods applicable to the one are applicable to the other. Doubtless, Comte and Ward are largely to blame for this simplistic and questionable interpretation. As stated throughout this work, Ward, following Comte, postulated that the necessary prerequisite to effective social planning and guided social change was the scientific study of society and the identification of its basic laws. Pure sociology was assigned the task of identifying societal laws and applied sociology their implementation.

Comte and Ward suggested that applied sociology would evolve from pure sociology. At some distant point—they did not specify a timetable—applied sociology would simply become the natural extension of pure sociology and the two would for the first time exist simultaneously. No mention was made of the possible impact of applied sociology on pure sociology, how the experience of its practitioners might generate conflicts with and even deflect the course of pure sociology. No consideration was given to the possibility of essential areas of compatibility and incompatibility between the discipline's two branches. It was suggested by Comte, in the wake of the lessons learned from the French Revolution, that the whole possibility of scientifically directed social planning and decision-making might be lost if undertaken prematurely, that is, before isolation of societal laws. Incremental pure and applied sociology, the simultaneous initiation and practice of the two as interrelated endeavors, and learning by trial and failure, seemed misguided to both Comte and Ward.

Few contemporary sociologists take seriously the notion of sociological domination of public policy formation and implementation. Most describe and prescribe a modest role for sociologists engaged in social policy related work. According to Robert Scott and Arnold Shore, for example,

> so long as politics and politicians dominate policy decisions in our society, sociology's role in public affairs will inevitably be modest. Grand-scale . . . schemes in which sociologists and politicians are partners must be abandoned for less pretentious approaches that are more closely attuned to political realities and less closely tied to academic and utopian concerns. (1979: 204)

A major theme of Scott's and Shore's treatise is that sociology has failed to be applicable because its practitioners and theories are disciplinary or pure rather than applied or practically oriented. To Scott and Shore, sociologists have been unprepared rather than prepared for applied work by their near exclusive training in basic sociology. By contrasting the aims of the academic and the policy-maker, they show that applied and basic work have quite different frames of reference. Thus, whereas the academic sociologist seeks to understand society, the policy-maker aims to change it. And even when they study the same problem the questions of concern vary: "The academic asks, 'What do we know?'; the policymaker asks, 'What do we do?'" (1979: 224). In their view, "knowledge for understanding" and "knowledge for action" are basically divergent, not complimentary pursuits. Yet the stress placed on basic work has had certain benefits for the applied sociologist.

Basic work allows for greater freedom of thought, greater opportunity to exercise one's imaginative and creative impulses, than applied work. By means of ideal type theorizing, for example, Talcott Parsons (1951) was able to create the outlines of an orderly social system to reflect the real world against. As Weber indicated, differences between actual and ideal types often provide the means necessary to identify the source of a problem and a possible solution. Weber assumed that just as people are generally motivated to approximate certain ideal values (for example, the effort of Christians to emulate the ideal example and teachings of the exemplar), so groups are often organized and structured around ideal assumptions. In the ideal pluralistic democratic situation, for example, all interests in a particular matter are expected to have equal rights of decision-making participation and the complete attention of all. Dramatization of the gap between the real and the ideal, as political activists such as Gandhi and Martin Luther King, Jr. were well aware, is often the necessary means to effect real world change. When so confronted, the opposition has the choice of defending its alleged hypocrisy or changing its ways. Other ideals involved in basic sociology also have important real world application.

Basic methodological training includes alerting students to ideal research conditions and the ethics of social research. The ideal experiment is one in which the investigator has the ability to control for variables known to influence result validity. To conduct a general attitude survey, for example, it may be necessary to control as much as possible for the possible intrusiveness of sexism or racism. In the best of circumstances, one would hope to be able to evoke honest responses to specific questions concerning respondents' views on these subjects. But these are sensitive areas, and the best to be hoped for is a measure of control over the possible research effects of difficult to measure variables. However, once again awareness of the difference between ideal aims and real world possibilities alerts one to problems, questions, and subjects that are useful in both applied and pure contexts.

The ethics of basic research also sensitize one to potentially important real world subjects. As brought out in Chapter 5, an important ethical consideration in research involving human subjects is informed consent. Ideally, the investigator is expected to provide respondents with all essential details of the proposed research both to enlist cooperation and identify any possible negative effects to be aware of. Fear that providing too much information may discourage the participation of subjects may lead some to ignore or understate areas of potential harm. While this inclination may be as prevalent in pure as applied research, its expression in the latter may be encouraged by the aim of pleasing a paying client and the absence of need to promulgate research methods and findings to colleagues. But awareness of the basic ideal, the imagined reaction of one's colleagues should they learn of an ethical transgression, may serve to deter some and, perhaps, enhance the quality of and respect for applied sociology. But the conduct of applied sociology has no less important consequences for pure sociology.

By immersion in a context where the problem or subject of investigation is determined by a client seeking an immediate or time-specific solution, sociologists are often compelled to adapt to circumstances beyond their control. Theoretical orientation, hypotheses formation and testing, sampling design, questionnaire and interview schedule construction—any and all the basic elements of basic research—may have to be compromised. To many, this fact is sufficient to reject the basic knowledge value of applied work. To others, it is a challenge that must be met if the discipline's historical aim of obtaining practically useful knowledge is to be realized. To some, acceptance of the challenge could lead to the construction of new theories and methods and insights into human behavior not otherwise possible. Marxists, for example, have long argued that social theory must be guided by praxis, or the knowledge gained by the attempt to put theory into practice, and vice versa. Regardless of theoretical predilection, it is important to carefully consider the merits of theory testing and revision in applied contexts—not only for immediately necessary practical ends but also for long-run goals such as the identification of general theories of social behavior and structure.

As the TARP study indicates, highly effective theory testing can be an integral part of applied work. Time and cost constraints may militate against routine applied theory testing but its possibility and promise have been demonstrated. Not to be overlooked as well is the fact that applied contexts should be as fertile a field for generating grounded or inductive theory as basic circumstances. The task is not an easy one. Considerable ingenuity, patience and originality is needed to identify patterns and consistencies in seemingly discrete cases undertaken by different investigators with different aims and methods and under diverse circumstances. Innovative procedures (theoretical and methodological) undoubtedly will be necessary as the process may at many points violate prevailing notions of valid research. Nonetheless, the effort has considerable promise of being highly worthwhile for the development of basic and applied sociology.

Before closing this section it is important to indicate that the theoretical possibilities in applied work are not all positive. Data access, for example, may be limited by the terms of one's employment. One may be hired to participate only in a phase of the research process, perhaps the construction of a questionnaire or to advise a client on possible data analysis means and strategies, without being allowed access to all the others. Such work may be highly rewarding monetarily and of invaluable methodological experience but of little worth to one wishing to explore theory in applied research or test the validity of a theory in an applied context.

••••• *CONCLUSION*

For reasons previously explored—for example, predictive failure and ideological contamination—theory occupies a depressed status in contemporary American sociology. Research methods are stressed, including the notion that accurate measurement of social facts must precede the construction of valid scientific theory. However, in the absence of agreed upon examples of measurable theory about important research topics, American sociology lacks the direction that mobilizes meaningful research and stimulates creativity.

In many ways, the current situation resembles what Thomas Kuhn (1970) refers to as a crisis stage, a period between the loss or rejection of one paradigm and its replacement by another. Kuhn defines a scientific paradigm as an achievement or theoretical insight such as Copernicus' conception of planetary motion and Einstein's general theory of relativity that unifies the work of a group of scientists by providing them with a promising lead, example, or model for successfully combining problem, theory and methods.

The recent growth of interest in applied sociology might well provide new avenues of investigation that lead to the identification of something approximating a Kuhnian paradigm breakthrough. For this to occur however, applied sociologists must become much more interested in linking theory and method in problem analysis than is currently the case. The findings and details uncovered in the study of new subjects have a variety of uses, but unless they are synthesized and interpreted to reveal previously unrecognized patterns indicative of something generally important they tend to be rather quickly filed and submerged under the weight of an ever growing mound of neglected data.

Applied sociology emphasizes methodological training because research skills are in demand by a variety of clients in the public and private sectors. There appears to be no particular interest in expanding the applied curricula to equally emphasize or even include theoretical skill enhancement. Two factors, one endogenous to the discipline and the other exogenous to it, have contributed to the problem.

The exogenous factor is the current status of the academic marketplace. As the nation's economic fortunes have declined, so too have available academic positions. Thus, the motivating impulse behind the recent expansion of applied sociology has been much less to pursue a neglected but promising avenue of investigation than to find alternative employment for sociologists.

The endogenous factor is the growing sense across the social sciences that their presumed goal, the identification of societal laws by application of the scientific method, has been and is likely to remain fruitless. Having yet to confront this fact, or find a suitable replacement for the search for laws, many disciplines, including sociology, appear somewhat anomic—nothing appears particularly important or more worthwhile to pursue than anything else. A great deal of work is being done, but for what major reason beyond the social mobility or economic survival of practitioners is often difficult to discern.

The point here is that if a discipline lacks a clear sense of its goals, it is to be expected that its practitioners will pursue a variety of tasks for short-term purposes. In possession of a theoretical goal such as the identification of patterns or regularities in areas of general and practical importance, a discipline is encouraged to achieve paradigmatic coherence via integration of problems examined, theory, and methods. All three elements must be regarded as essential components of an interrelated whole. Just as those who pursue pure or basic research are required to re-conceptualize common everyday problems and subjects in sociologically relevant terms, so too must the applied or practically oriented sociologist re-interpret for sociological purposes clients' and "subjects'" "definitions of the situation."[7] While it is important to relate to public issues and client needs on their terms, it is equally important to interpret both problem sources in ways that enable identification of common and possibly repetitive patterns and connections. Teasing the general out of the particular requires theoretical sensitivity, a sensitivity mindful of the scientific value of developing hypotheses subject to methodological interpretation. One inference to be drawn from this line of reasoning is that however promising a line of investigation, applied sociology is likely to yield knowledge of limited use for either practical or basic purposes unless it is conducted by those theoretically oriented and motivated to serve not only the specific immediate aims of clients but also general disciplinary needs and interests. As the opposite is equally true it is important to be ever mindful of the fact that "applied research often leads to theoretical understanding, and theoretical breakthroughs permit practical applications" (Diener & Crandall, 1978: 19).

- **NOTES**

1. For a review of the so-called "antinaturalistic" philosophies, see William R. Catton, *From Animistic to Naturalistic Sociology* (New York: McGraw-Hill, 1966), 27–35.

2. For a particularly incisive discussion of this subject, see Roy D'Andrade, "Three Scientific World Views and the Covering Law Model," in D.W. Fiske and R.A. Shweder, eds., *Metatheory in Social Science* (Chicago: University of Chicago Press, 1986), 19–41.

3. In their 1979 publication *Why Sociology Does Not Apply* (New York: Elsevier) R.A. Scott and A.R. Shore contend that a major shortcoming of applied sociology is its practitioners' tendency to be disciplinary—rather than problem- or policy-oriented. They state, for example, that "a main source of the present difficulty with applied sociology is that attempts to make sociology relevant to policy are conceived and executed with disciplinary, and not with policy concerns in mind" (34). Due to the declining availability of academic positions in the wake of national economic recession, sociologists have sought alternative sources of employment, such as applied-oriented private firms and public agencies. Of necessity, then, one would expect applied sociology to have become more client- and less disciplinary-oriented. Impressionistic evidence suggests that the recent expansion of applied curricula has been associated with greater interest than ever in preparation for non-academic, client-oriented employment.

4. For a more thorough discussion of the role of clinical sociology in individual treatment, see P. See and R.A. Straus, "The Sociology of the Individual," in R.A. Straus, ed., *Using Sociology* (New York: General Hall, Inc., 1985), 61–80.

5. For a concise review of the work of the clinical sociologist in community affairs, see J. Fritz, "Communities: Making Them Work," in R.A. Straus, ed., *Using Sociology* (New York: General Hall, Inc., 1985), 136–152.

6. The positions of influential progressive and conservative social Darwinists are contained in Bert James Loewenberg, *Darwinism: Reaction or Reform?* (New York: Rinehart & Company, Inc., 1957).

7. In developing their "general theory of crime," Gottfredson and Hirschi stress the need to reconceptualize crime. In their view, criminological theory has been limited by acceptance of the legal definition of crime. Thus, their point of departure is a definition of crime consistent with what they regard as sociologically relevant knowledge. See M.R. Gottfredson and T. Hirshi, *A General Theory of Crime* (Stanford, California: Stanford University Press, 1990), Chapters 1 and 2.

- **REFERENCES**

Bisbee, E. 1937. "Objectivity in the Social Sciences." *Philosophy of Science* 4: 371–382.

Chen, H.T., and P.H. Rossi. 1980. "The Multi-Goal, Theory-Driven Approach to Evaluation: A Model Linking Basic and Applied Social Science." *Social Forces* 59: 106–122.

_____. 1987. "The Theory-Driven Approach to Validity." *Evaluation and Program Planning* 10: 95–103.

_____. 1989. "Issues in The Theory-Driven Perspective." *Evaluation and Program Planning* 12: 299–306.

Cuzzort, R.P. 1989. *Using Social Thought: The Nuclear Issue and Other Concerns.* Mountain View, CA: Mayfield Publishing Company.

Dahrendorf, R. 1959. *Class & Class Conflict in Industrial Society.* Stanford, CA: Stanford University Press.

Diener, E., and R. Crandall. 1978. *Ethics in Social and Behavioral Research.* Chicago: University of Chicago Press.

Gouldner, A.W. 1970. "The Sociologist as Partisan: Sociology and the Welfare State." In L.T and J.M. Reynolds, eds., *The Sociology of Sociology.* New York: David McKay Company, Inc., 218–255.

Hemple, C.G. 1942. "The Function of General Laws in History." *The Journal of Philosophy* XXXIX: 35–48.

Hofstadter, R. 1955. *Social Darwinism in American Thought.* Boston: Beacon Press.

Kuhn, T.S. 1970. *The Structure of Scientific Revolutions,* 2d ed. Chicago: University of Chicago Press.

Lundberg, G.A. 1964. *Foundations of Sociology.* New York: David McKay Company, Inc.

Nicolaus, M. 1970. "Text of a Speech Delivered at the A.S.A. Convention, August 26, 1968." In L.T. and J.M. Reynolds, eds., *The Sociology of Sociology.* New York: David McKay Company, Inc., 274–278.

Parsons, T. 1951. *The Social System.* New York: Free Press.

Reiss, A.J. 1970. "Putting Sociology Into Policy." *Social Problems* 17: 289–294.

Rossi, P.H., and J.D. Wright. 1985. "Social Science Research and the Politics of Gun Control." In R.L. Shotland and M.M. Mark, eds., *Social Science and Social Policy.* Beverly Hills: SAGE Publications, 311–332.

Scott, R.A., and A.R. Shore. 1979. *Why Sociology Does Not Apply.* New York: Elsevier.

Shotland, R.L., and M.M. Mark. 1985. "Toward a More Useful Social Science." In R.L. Shotland and M.M. Mark, eds., *Social Science and Social Policy.* Beverly Hills, SAGE Publications, 335–370.

Straus, R.A., ed. 1985. *Using Sociology.* New York: General Hall, Inc.

Waitzkin, H. 1970. "Truth's Search for Power: The Dilemmas of the Social Sciences." In J.D. Douglas, ed., *The Relevance of Sociology.* New York: Appleton-Century-Crofts, 169–84.

Index

Humphreys, Laud, 104, 106-107, 111, 118, 154, 155
Hunches, 39

Idealism, 75
Idiographic, 74
Individualism, 4, 136
Induction, 24
Informed consent, 113

Janowitz, Morris, 60-61, 70
Jencks, Christopher, 141, 144
Johnson, D.P., 62, 70
Johnson, G., 64, 70
Johnson, Lyndon, 124, 132, 133, 134, 138
Jupp, B.C., 71

Kennedy, John F., 137, 138
Keppel, F., 123, 144
Kerner, Otto, 144
    Kerner report, 124
    Kerner commission, 132
King, Martin L. Jr., 162
Kleymeyer, Charles, 63-64, 70
Kolakowski, Leszek, 82, 95
Kimmel, Allan J., 113, 114, 115, 118
Klockars, Carl B., 119
Knudsen, Dean D., 117
Komarovsky, Mirra, 130, 131, 132, 144
Kuhn, Thomas S., 17-18, 20, 163, 164, 166

La Follette, Robert, 134
Larsen, Otto, 130, 131
Larson, Calvin J., iii, iv, 26, 46
Lazarsfeld, Paul F., 20, 59, 61, 70
Lenihan, Kenneth, 67, 70
Levi-Strauss, Claude, 37, 46
Levine, D.M., 144
Lipsky, M., 130, 132, 133, 144
Loewenberg, Bert J., 19, 20, 57, 70, 71, 165
Loo, C.M., 115, 118

Looking-glass self, 34
Lueptow, L., 115, 118
Lukes, Stephen, 46
Lundberg, George A., 21, 79-81, 88, 95, 100, 101, 102, 103, 109, 110, 118, 122, 157, 166
Lutterman, Kenneth, 10, 21
Lynd, Robert, iv, 10-11, 21
Lypson, T.A., vii, xi

MacDonald, Dwight, 137
MacIver, Robert, 80, 95
Mack, Raymond, 132
Malinowski, Bronislaw, 53
Manning, Peter, 37, 46
Marcuse, Herbert, 33, 45, 46
Mark, Melvin M., 159, 166
Martin, Patricia Y., 64, 70
Martindale, Don, 75, 95
Marx, Karl, 27-29, 30, 38, 41, 42, 57, 108
Master, L.S., 115, 119
McPartland, J., 143
Mead, George H., 34, 35, 38, 46, 90, 126
Mead, Margaret, 111, 118
Meltzer, Bernard M., 46
Menzies, Kenneth, 32, 46
Merton, Robert K., viii, xi, 25, 33, 45, 46, 52, 53, 70, 135
Metatheory, 26
Micklin, Michael, 19
Milgram, Stanley, 104-106, 111, 118, 154, 155
Mill, J.S., 78-79, 83, 96
Miller, Richard, 74
Miller, S.M., xi, 20, 70
Mills, C. Wright, 56, 69, 136
Mishra, R., 123, 144
Mobilization for youth, 135
Mode of production, 27
Mood, A.M., 143
Morals,
    defined, 99
Moreno, Jonathan, 66, 70

171